Tactical Nuclear Weapons

T0324262

Tactical Nuclear Weapons

Emergent Threats in an Evolving Security Environment

Edited by
Brian Alexander and Alistair Millar

With a foreword by
Stansfield Turner

Brassey's, Inc.
Washington, D.C.

Library of Congress Cataloging-in-Publication Data

    Tactical nuclear weapons : emergent threats in an evolving security environment / edited by Brian Alexander and Alistair Millar ; with a foreword by Stansfield Turner.—1st ed.
        p. cm.
    Includes bibliographical references and index.
    ISBN 1-57488-584-7 (hardcover : alk. paper)—ISBN 1-57488-585-5 (pbk. : alk. paper)
    1. Tactical nuclear weapons. 2. World politics—21st century. I. Alexander, Brian. II. Millar, Alistair.
    U264.T32   2003
    355.02'17—dc21   2003001952

Hardcover ISBN 1-57488-584-7
Softcover ISBN 1-57488-585-5
(alk. paper)

Printed in the United States of America on acid-free paper that meets the American National Standards Institute Z39-48 Standard.

Brassey's, Inc.
22841 Quicksilver Drive
Dulles, Virginia 20166

First Edition

10 9 8 7 6 5 4 3 2 1

Contents

Foreword

Stansfield Turner

Almost all discussions of nuclear arms simply ignore tactical nuclear weapons. For instance, only one arms control agreement in the past 30 years has dealt with this variety of nuclear weapon. This book suggests that the United States may well rue such neglect. There are two reasons that strike me as making this particularly likely.

The first is related to this fact: The single greatest threat to our country today is that terrorists will acquire nuclear weapons and will find ways to employ them on our soil. A Hiroshima-size nuclear bomb would wreak destruction that would make the 11 September 2001 attacks look puny. An irony here is that a key reason tactical nuclear weapons have been given so little attention is because they are labeled "small." In fact, no agreed definition exists of what constitutes a tactical nuclear weapon as opposed to a strategic one, but size is the most common criterion.

We need, however, to put the size of any nuclear weapon into perspective. The explosive power of conventional munitions is measured in pounds of TNT. Conventional bombs delivered by aircraft range from 500 to 2,000 pounds, with some, but relatively few, going to 5,000 pounds. It is impractical to write about the explosive effect of any nuclear weapon in pounds, as there simply would be too many zeros. The convention is to employ two short hands: a ton of TNT, that is, 2,200 pounds; and a kilo, or a factor of 1,000. So nuclear weapons are classified by kilotons (KT), or at the larger end of the scale, megatons (MT). For instance:

- 1 kt = 1 × 2,200 lb/ton × 1,000 tons/kt = 2,200,000 pounds of explosive power, or the equivalent of 1,100 conventional 2,000-pound bombs.
- .1 kt, the smallest tactical weapon in our arsenal, equals 220,000 pounds of TNT, or the equivalent of 110 conventional bombs of 2,000 pounds each.

♦ The weapon dropped on Hiroshima in 1945 was about 12 kt, or the equivalent of 13,200 bombs of 2,000 pounds each.

In brief, we talk somewhat cavalierly of the Hiroshima bomb having been a "small" weapon, but as mentioned above, it would have taken 13,200 conventional bombs of 2,000 pounds each to deliver that much explosive power. That, however, is not a full comparison. The nuclear weapon has three other effects: radiation that kills people and makes entire areas uninhabitable; intense heat that ignites fires; and blinding light.

This means even the smallest nuclear weapon could be a catastrophe for us if it should fall into the hands of terrorists or a rogue state. The damage that might be wreaked would be bad enough; add the trauma of something nuclear having been detonated and not knowing what might come next, and our way of life would change. Unfortunately, the risk of tactical weapons falling into the wrong hands is much higher than we would like. We do not know, and perhaps the Russians do not know either, just how many of these weapons the Russians have sequestered around. With no arms control agreements on small weapons there is no transparency. This book estimates there are from 3,500 to 22,000 tactical warheads in Russia, as compared with 1,650 in the U.S. nuclear arsenal. Further, security against theft and inhibitions against unauthorized sale of Russian weapons is each far less than it should be. While we do not want problems with tactical nuclear weapons to overshadow and delay ongoing efforts to dismantle Russia's strategic nuclear arsenal, there is a strong case for diverting some of the effort to the tactical arena.

The second reason we may regret neglecting the tactical scene is that we have not thought through why we need these weapons. The result: today there is considerable talk about designing and building new tactical weapons. The rationale behind such talk is very weak, though. The root cause of this goes back to 1945. After the detonations at Hiroshima and Nagasaki, we instinctively treated nuclear weapons as the next generation of military hardware. Throughout history almost every new weapon that is more powerful than its predecessor has been incorporated into military arsenals. So, too, did we expect to incorporate nuclear weapons, in effect treating them in our military planning as though they were just larger conventional weapons. Under the exigencies of World War II we had done more damage to Tokyo and Dresden with firebombing and carpet bombing than to Hiroshima with nuclear bombing. Thus, we were inured to such destructiveness and assumed it would continue.

One experience I had with tactical nuclear planning in the 1970s reflected the attitude that nuclear weapons could be treated as large conventional ones. I was commander in chief of NATO's southern flank, responsible for, among other things, the defense of Italy. One day I asked for a briefing on how, in the event of a general war in Europe, we would stop a Soviet thrust through the Alps at the Brenner Pass into northern Italy. The briefer displayed a photo of the road descending from the Brenner to the northern plain. A dozen or so concrete columns that were about 100 feet high supported the road, which literally clung to the side of the mountain. The briefer explained that we would detonate an atomic demolition charge, a small tactical nuclear weapon, at the base of one of these columns. I asked why we would not use TNT to bring down such a vulnerable structure? There was no answer. We had nuclear weapons and they were the best way to be absolutely sure the Soviets would be prevented from using the road. The overkill and the collateral effects on Italy of radiation and fires were simply not addressed.

The long-standing impulse to use the more powerful weapon leads to finding uses for powerful weapons. Today armchair strategists have cast about for targets suitable for tactical nuclear weapons. The primary one is deeply buried, hardened bunkers that are used for weapon storage or for command posts. Interestingly, we already have lots of nuclear warheads that would demolish these safe havens, but we are talking of designing new, smaller ones. The idea is not to do too much "collateral" damage, through excessive blast effect, radiation, or fires. In short, the conundrum of nuclear weapons in an age when firebombing and carpet bombing would be unacceptable is that we want these weapons because their size ensures sufficient destructiveness, but we want them downsized enough so that they won't do too much damage. This is walking a very thin tightrope.

The odds are extremely slim that any president would ever authorize the first use of tactical nuclear weapons. The uncertainties associated with both direct and collateral damages would be daunting. And who could predict what might happen next if a 57-year taboo on the use of nuclear weapons were to be broken? Even beyond that, a president would surely ask, "What alternatives do I have?" One is to employ conventional weapons to destroy ingress and egress points for people, supplies, power, water, air, weapons, etc. A second is to develop conventional weapons that could penetrate all the way to the bunker. The United States is working, for instance, on a multiple warhead conventional weapon where the first warhead opens up a hole and a carefully timed second one burrows in and exploits that. Finally, we need to recognize that just because there is a target out there, we do not necessarily have to be able to destroy it. There will always be a calculus as to whether the importance of the target warrants the risks and uncertainties of unleashing a nuclear weapon.

If I am correct that there will be great reluctance on the part of presidents to unleash tactical nuclear weapons, our developing them and inserting them into war plans could be dangerous. That is, we may be counting on a weapon that will not actually be available when the time comes and we may not have developed the conventional ones that would be used.

An irony in this quest for new, smaller tactical nuclear weapons is that the United States, the most militarily powerful nation in the world, is saying there are circumstances of war in which it will need to resort to nuclear weapons. Surely this legitimizes nuclear weapons for weaker nations that might have no other recourse for defending themselves. And it is the United States that is most likely to be deterred from employing military force by the threat of even a small nuclear attack on its soil or its deployed forces.

It must be in the interest of the United States to lead the world away from nuclear catastrophe since it is a more likely target and has more to lose than anyone else. Getting tactical nuclear weapons under control, rather than attesting to their usefulness by building new ones, should be our goal. This excellent book helps us to understand these issues.

Admiral Stansfield Turner, former director of Central Intelligence, is on the faculty of the School of Public Affairs of the University of Maryland.

Acknowledgments

This volume is a collaborative effort that has benefited from the contributions and support of many dedicated colleagues. The work of writing, editing, and compiling this collection would not have been possible without the skilled work of our staff colleagues at the Fourth Freedom Forum, including our president and contributing author, David Cortright; Jennifer Glick; Ruth Miller; Ann Pedler; and Miriam Redsecker. We owe a special debt of gratitude to Lynn Erskine for keeping the project together in the final stages and for her careful editing and helpful suggestions on content.

We thank our coauthors for their skilled and dedicated efforts in contributing to this volume and for their patience in responding to our queries and comments. The quality of the work that we received added to our high estimation of some of the leading experts on nuclear weapons control issues.

We are also thankful to General George Lee Butler for his encouragement and guidance at the inception of this project.

This work would not have been possible without the financial support of the Fourth Freedom Forum. We express our deepest gratitude to the members of the board of directors of the Fourth Freedom Forum. Their loyal and enthusiastic support has provided the foundation for our continuing writing and research on issues that will help to develop sustainable international cooperation, the rule of law, peace, and security. We are particularly grateful to the Forum's founder and chairman, Howard S. Brembeck. His inspiration and vision of a more civilized world governed by the rule of law has made all of the work that we do at the Forum possible. Thank you.

Alistair Millar
Brian Alexander

Part I

The Problem of Tactical Nuclear Weapons

1

Uncovered Nukes

An Introduction to Tactical Nuclear Weapons

Brian Alexander and Alistair Millar

For three decades arms control treaties have provided a legal basis for the limitation and reduction of long-range nuclear weapons. However, thousands of substrategic, or tactical, nuclear weapons (TNWs) are not monitored or controlled by any existing treaties or formal agreements, even though they can pose security risks equal to or exceeding those of strategic nuclear weapons.

Reducing the risks associated with tactical nuclear weapons is particularly relevant in the context of international terrorism. The scale of the terrorist attacks of 11 September 2001 adds a striking new variable in the debate about preventing nuclear weapons and other weapons of mass destruction from proliferating, whether to terrorist groups, nonstate actors, or nuclear-aspiring states.[1]

At the pinnacle of their existence, tactical nuclear weapons numbered in the tens of thousands and spanned many types of such weapons.[2] The only substantive international effort to address tactical nuclear weapons occurred in the early 1990s with a regimen of unilateral, parallel reductions undertaken by Presidents George H. W. Bush and Mikhail Gorbachev in 1991. It was then capitalized upon by President Boris Yeltsin in 1992 in the wake of the dissolution of the Soviet Union. These presidential nuclear initiatives (PNIs) proposed dramatic and unprecedented unilateral cuts in both the U.S. and Soviet/Russian tactical nuclear weapons arsenals. Initiatives such as these, while bold at the time, possess intrinsic shortcomings that weaken tactical nuclear weapons control today. Ultimately, uncertainties surrounding implementation of the 1991–92 PNIs and qualities of the agreements themselves leave this entire class of nuclear weapons still largely unmonitored and uncontrolled.[3]

The United States has an estimated 1,120 tactical nuclear warheads, most of them stored in the United States, with an additional 150 to 200 stored at ten U.S. military bases in seven countries in Europe.[4] The Russian arsenal, however, is a much different story. There are no clear estimates of the Russian tactical nuclear weapons stockpile, the numbers of which recently have been estimated from around 3,500 to as high as 22,000. Joshua Handler estimates in chapter 2 that the current Russian tactical nuclear arsenal is 3,380. However, estimates of the Russian arsenal are based on limited official information, insufficient data regarding the size of the Soviet TNW arsenal at its peak, and ongoing absence of verification mechanisms. As a consequence, while Handler's number is perhaps one of the most substantiated, other estimates ranging from 4,000 to as high as the 10,000 or 20,000 range cannot be fully discounted.[5] The lack of information about the size of the Russian tactical nuclear weapons arsenal raises uncertainties regarding the security of the storage of these weapons as well as about their protections against accidental, unauthorized, or illicit use. The lack of information on Russian tactical nuclear weapons is a cause for particular concern regarding further progress on international nonproliferation efforts and in the context of heightened international terrorism and potential efforts by state and nonstate actors alike to acquire nuclear weapons capability.

The tactical nuclear arsenals of the United States and Russia will be given greatest consideration in this book, because those of other nuclear states possess far and away the largest stockpiles. Both countries have actively engaged in strategic nuclear arms control, and these agreements could serve as a basis for addressing other global tactical nuclear arsenals. Also, some government officials from both the United States and Russia have called for increased reliance on or development of new classes of tactical nuclear weapons, suggesting that new challenges relating to these weapons could arise in the near future.[6]

The nuclear arsenals of other states also warrant close consideration. Countries such as China, India, and Pakistan possess nuclear weapons that are considered to be, or could be developed into, tactical nuclear arsenals or, in their current form, used as tactical nuclear weapons. Meanwhile, the status of tactical nuclear weapons arms control between the United States and Russia, and the composition of both countries' nuclear arsenals, will also influence how other states develop tactical and strategic nuclear weapons. In chapter 6, Timothy Hoyt examines how growing tensions between India and Pakistan have propelled South Asia into a nuclear arms race where nuclear use on the battlefield remains a critical concern. In the following chapter, Charles Ferguson, Evan Medeiros, and Phillip Saunders discuss tactical nuclear weapons in the context of China.

Characteristics Unique
to Tactical Nuclear Weapons

Tactical nuclear weapons, sometimes known interchangeably as "battlefield," "substrategic," or "nonstrategic" nuclear weapons, are typically distinct from strategic nuclear weapons, and thus they warrant different consideration in international security and in nuclear arms control. In addition to a variety of methods for TNW delivery that are often distinct from strategic nuclear weapons delivery vehicles, this category of nuclear weapons includes a broader array of atomic explosive devices. These range from so-called nuclear landmines and nuclear artillery shells to air-dropped or missile-launched nuclear warheads. The yield of such weapon ranges is typically, but not necessarily, lower than that of strategic nuclear weapons. The yield of a tactical nuclear weapon may range from relatively low—0.1 kiloton (KT)—to yields higher than those of the bombs dropped on Hiroshima and Nagasaki—10–15 KT, and upwards to 1 megaton.[7] To help put these yield ranges into perspective, in the kiloton and megaton ranges, a ton is equivalent to the explosive force of 1 ton of TNT. As a matter of comparison, a December 2001 article in the *National Journal* reported that a relatively small 10 KT detonation in downtown Washington, D.C., would destroy virtually everything within a 275-yard radius. Within a half-mile of the explosion, there would be intense shock and heat, mass fires, and some survivors in reinforced concrete buildings. Two-thirds of a mile outside the detonation area there would be severe shock from the blast, and wood and brick homes would be severely damaged. Just over a mile from the blast there would be significant damage to buildings, and only some damage two miles out. The radioactive fallout, according to the article, would vary according to wind direction and other weather variables, but the plume of dispersion would be 18 miles long and 2 miles wide, affecting a population of approximately 150,000. People outdoors would receive "dangerous doses of radiation, but those staying indoors would greatly lessen their risk."[8]

Although tactical nuclear weapons are frequently believed to possess smaller blast yields than strategic nuclear weapons, some higher-yield tactical nuclear weapons (in the 10–25 KT range, or greater) actually are more powerful than some classes of strategic nuclear weapons.[9] Regardless of yield, as nuclear weapons, the effects of tactical nuclear weapons are markedly distinct from conventional weapons. Even a very low–yield atomic blast would generate highly destructive effects, above and beyond what a conventional explosion of the same size could produce.[10]

Issues of Definition

Distinguishing between a tactical nuclear weapon and strategic nuclear weapon is problematic and has implications that complicate theoretic discussions as well as tactical nuclear arms control initiatives. Several criteria may be employed to define a tactical nuclear weapon. These include range, yield, target, national ownership, delivery vehicle, and capability. Employing any of these criterion, either together or independently, to distinguish a nuclear weapon as "tactical" is subject to conceptual challenges and shortcomings, making it difficult to achieve a definition that is both precise and broad enough to apply to various conditions where control of these weapons is needed.[11]

One solution to this definitional problem is to define tactical nuclear weapons by exclusion. That is, any nuclear weapon not covered by existing treaties would be a de facto tactical nuclear weapon.[12] From an arms control point of view, given that nuclear arms treaties have excluded tactical nuclear weapons, this definition appears to hold some value. However, tactical nuclear weapons come in a great array of varieties, some more easily distinguishable from so-called strategic nuclear weapons than others. Furthermore, some tactical nuclear weapons factor in security and arms control considerations in ways distinct from others. Atomic demolition units (ADUs), for example, could affect security or arms control considerations in ways significantly different from air-delivered tactical nuclear weapons. Therefore, in addressing these weapons, the definition by exclusion option (e.g., lumping all weapons together) may make it difficult to recognize the problems unique to individual types of tactical nuclear weapons. Efforts to deal with less-controversial classes of tactical nuclear weapons may be stalled or disrupted should these weapons be grouped with those posing more intractable arms control issues.

Historical evidence suggests that a universal definition of this weapon type is unprecedented and, perhaps, unnecessary. Security implications and considerations may vary from one situation to another and among weapon types. Likewise, formal arms control initiatives have tended to define the subject of their scope on essentially an ad hoc basis. That is, particular warheads and delivery systems were chosen not just for an interest in controlling them but also because of the feasibility of subjecting them to such control. This approach may also apply to tactical nuclear weapons. For example, counting strategic nuclear weapons by warheads rather than by delivery vehicles under START III or a new round of presidential initiatives may circumvent TNW definitional challenges by focusing on pragmatic versus semantic issues. Ivan Safranchuk reviews this definitional conundrum in chapter 3. He notes that arms control treaties contain no definitions of "tactical" or "strategic" weapons and adds, "there are no universal definitions for tactical and strategic nuclear weapons. Under these circumstances, the debate on the classification continues." Based on Safranchuk's analysis, addressing tactical nuclear weapons from the point of view of arms control initiatives would require approaching specific weapons types in an ad hoc fashion. This approach could be determined by the needs and interests of parties involved in arms control discussions and specific security and weapons contexts under discussion.

Adding to such complications is the fact that any definition of tactical nuclear weapons eventually needs to be viewed multilaterally. Depending on what criteria are selected when determining what a tactical nuclear weapon is, or which specific weapons or delivery systems would be subject to control, some weapons may be strategic in one context but tactical in another. For example, the limited range of China's nuclear forces may make them "tactical" by U.S. standards, but proximity to Russia could classify them as strategic according to Russian perceptions.[13] Similar problems arise in other contexts, such as India, Pakistan, and other current or aspiring nuclear states.

Generally speaking, for the purposes of this book a tactical nuclear weapon is defined as any U.S. or Russian nuclear weapon that is not covered by nuclear arms treaties. Typically, these weapons are designed or intended for some "battlefield" usage. For the purposes of the present volume, a tactical nuclear weapon may also include low-yield, limited-range weapons in arsenals of other nuclear states intended for battlefield usage against enemy forces and military targets (as compared to enemy cities or civilians). However, as definitional complications come into play during the discussions contained herein, a particular nuclear weapon classified as "tactical" may not always match the characteristics offered in this definition.

Plans for New Tactical Nuclear Weapons in the United States and Russia

Since the end of the Cold War, reactions to the changing international security environment in both the United States and Russia have included arguments in support of the development of new versions of tactical nuclear weapons. Thus, in addition to existing stockpiles of tactical nuclear weapons, the role of tactical weapons in international security and arms control may change as a result of calls in the United States and Russia for the development, deployment, and even the possible use of newer classes of tactical nuclear weapons.

New Plans: The United States

In the United States, official and nonofficial sources have advocated the usefulness of a new class of tactical nuclear weapons. For the destruction of hardened deeply buried targets (HDBT), there have been calls for the development of a low-yield nuclear warhead for deployment on so-called "bunker-buster" munitions, such as the B61–11, GBU-28, and other such bombs or their variants. According to a recent nuclear posture review conducted by the Pentagon, a nuclear-capable bunker buster would augment the capabilities of conventional munitions designed to destroy underground bunkers, munitions depots, and other hideaways for arms, leadership, and military-industrial infrastructure of an adversary. In chapter 4, Robert Nelson examines the ramifications of U.S. efforts to develop, test, and eventually use bunker buster–type nuclear weapons.

Analysts at U.S. nuclear weapons laboratories have advocated the development of this kind of weapon. Stephen Younger at Los Alamos National Laboratory, for example, has argued in support of the usefulness of so-called mininukes, or bunker busters, and recommends steps toward their development:

> Some targets require the energy of a nuclear weapon for their destruction. However, precision targeting can greatly reduce the nuclear yield required to destroy such targets. Only a relatively few targets require high nuclear yields. Advantages of lower yields include reduced collateral damage, arms control advantages to the United States, and the possibility that such weapons could be maintained with higher confidence and at lower cost than our current nuclear arsenal.[14]

These low-yield nuclear warheads would be deployed on specially configured earth-penetrating bombs or missiles to target deeply buried or hardened and deeply buried underground targets, such as bunkers and bomb shelters.

In October 2001, the Department of Defense (DoD) completed a congressionally mandated study that explores the use of low-yield nuclear weapons for the purpose of destroying hard and deeply buried targets.[15] The DoD report does not ask for immediate development of low-yield nuclear weapons for destroying HDBT, but it proposes "selection criteria for a possible design feasibility and cost study" for new or modified HDBT defeat nuclear weapons. In other words, the report requests further study of the topic.

If programs for development of new classes of tactical nuclear weapons are pursued, this first would require the undoing of a current congressional prohibition initiated by Representatives Elizabeth Furse (D-Oreg.) and John Spratt Jr. (D-S.C.). The Furse-Spratt provision to the fiscal year 1994 Defense Authorization Bill prohibits nuclear laboratories from research and development that could lead to the creation of low-yield nuclear weapons.[16]

The Furse-Spratt amendment, as well as other congressional opposition to the development of new classes of tactical nuclear weapons, is based in part on the possibility of a nuclear backlash against the United States following the use of such weapons. That these plans would add to the problem of nuclear proliferation by contributing to the incentive of other countries to develop their own nuclear weapons, whether tactical or strategic nuclear weapons, has also been raised before Congress. U.S. Representative Mike Thompson (D-Calif.) noted that one problem with possessing such weapons is that it might encourage military and political leaders to "think more readily about using nuclear weapons." Thompson stated:

> In my view, we should not lower this threshold or make nuclear weapons a more acceptable choice in war. In addition, development of such a weapon is contrary to our nation's goals of reducing and eventually eliminating nuclear weapons. To begin development and stockpiling of a new nuclear weapon would reverse the difficult achievements the United States has made to slow the proliferation of nuclear material and weapons.[17]

The 2002 Nuclear Posture Review and the study on hardened deeply buried targets both advise further study on the development of U.S. tactical nuclear capability. The Bush administration is calling for "greater flexibility" in nuclear forces, and the administration's FY2003 budget requests $15.5 million for cost and feasibility studies of a "robust nuclear earth-penetrator" that could destroy HDBT, such as bunkers and bomb shelters.[18] The outcome of these studies and their effect on the decisions of policymakers remains to be seen. However, supporters as well as opponents of new classes of tactical nuclear weapons will closely watch the progress of studies to explore the options of developing new classes of tactical nuclear weapons.

New Plans: Russia

There have been suggestions among Russian analysts and policymakers that Russia should develop new classes of tactical nuclear weapons. As the cost of maintaining conventional military hardware and supporting personnel has become unmanageable in the era of post-Soviet economic adjustment and downturn, Russia has sought to make up for these qualitative and quantitative deficiencies. The security imperative driving Russian considerations derives particularly from the context of an expanding NATO and uncertainties about the future of Russia's security relationship along its southern and southeastern border. Russia has compensated for its conventional military deficiencies by officially abandoning its pledge not to use nuclear weapons first in a conflict and by increasing its reliance on tactical nuclear weapons, viewed as "war-fighting weapons," that could be used in combat operations.[19]

Documenting Russia's new interest in tactical nuclear weapons is Russia's new "Concept of National Security," which took effect on 10 January 2000. It was followed by a formal document that was published in the weekly military supplement *Nezavisimoe Voennoe Obozrenie* on 14 January 2000. The concept document warns that nuclear attack by Russia could be "forthcoming to repel armed aggression if all other means of resolving a crisis have failed."[20]

Three months later the Russian Security Council approved, and President Vladimir Putin signed, a new military doctrine. This updated doctrine replaces the doctrine of no first strike adopted in 1993 and fleshes out the military policy elaborated in Russia's "Concept of National Security" document. The new doctrine appears to lower Russia's threshold for using nuclear weapons when attacked with conventional weapons. It also explicitly states that Russia's nuclear deterrent can be used to respond to all attacks with weapons of mass destruction and reaffirms Russia's negative security assurances to nonnuclear weapons states.

American analysts have made suggestions that Russia could already be embarking on a new tactical nuclear weapons program. Fritz Ermarth, for example, has stated: "The Russians are talking about making truly usable tactical and strategic nuclear weapons. No concept has been more anathema to the arms control thinking of the past. Yet little attention has been paid to this. Nor have the Russians, to my knowledge, ever agreed to consult with anybody about this."[21]

In chapter 3, Ivan Safranchuk discusses Russian interest in pursuing new tactical nuclear weapons. Safranchuk deduces, based on statements made at a Russian Federation Security Council meeting in April 1999, that the government of Boris Yeltsin at least had endorsed "a blueprint for the development and use" of a new generation of tactical nuclear weapons. This statement was made by then-Secretary of the Security Council, Vladimir Putin.

In deliberating the value of augmented tactical nuclear weapons capability, Russian analysts appear to have picked up on NATO's Cold War arguments for using tactical nuclear weapons as a counterbalance to conventionally superior opposing forces. That is, the U.S.-based tactical nuclear weapons were placed in NATO countries because of superior Soviet conventional forces. Now Russia may want to keep tactical nuclear weapons forward deployed because of superior NATO conventional forces. However, the extent to which such proposals have been implemented is not clear, and doubts exist whether doctrine calling for increased reliance on tactical nuclear weapons has resulted in actual planning. Furthermore, given an economically crippled Russian Federation faced with internecine bureaucratic turf wrangling, the notion of increasing reliance on tactical nuclear weapons is risky or, at the very least, questionable. Whether these plans are brought to fruition depends on Russian self-perception and aspirations regarding its role in the international environment, the strength of the Russian economy, and weaknesses in Russian conventional military capabilities.

In sum, there are advocates in both Russia and the United States for new tactical nuclear weapons, but neither country has appeared to move on programs for such weapons. However, it remains plausible that such programs could emerge.

Tactical Nuclear Weapons and Unauthorized or Accidental Use

Because of their small size and portability, tactical nuclear weapons are more vulnerable than strategic nuclear weapons to accidental or illicit use. Characteristics of command unique to some tactical nuclear weapons—such as pre-delegated launch authorization—and often inadequate safeguards (i.e., effective permissive action links, or PALs) add to their potential unauthorized, accidental, or illicit use.

This is particularly a problem with older Russian models, which are troubled by an aging system of safeguards. Such weapons are also often the topic of stories about inadequate storage, where leakage of nuclear materials can pose severe security risks or environmental hazards. Adding to the fear factor regarding such reports are fundamental uncertainties stemming from insufficient transparency of the Russian nuclear arsenal, which make it harder to account for possibly missing tactical nuclear weapons. While Joshua Handler argues in this book that theft of a nuclear weapon from a storage depot could just as likely involve strategic as tactical weapons, there have been other claims that if terrorists were able to steal a complete nuclear warhead, it would more likely be a tactical weapon.[22] The possibility of theft of a strategic or tactical nuclear weapon is exacerbated by Russia's lax or inadequate customs controls along its borders.

Tactical Nuclear Weapons: Potential for Use by Terrorists

As the world has seen, the rise of international terrorism highlights the potential dangers of tactical nuclear weapons. Because they can be relatively small and portable—particulàrly but not exclusively as in the case of so-called "suitcase" bombs or atomic demolition munitions—tactical nuclear weapons are easier to transport and more vulnerable to theft than other nuclear weapons.[23] In the hands of terrorists, they would wreak a havoc far surpassing the devastating outcomes of the 11 September attacks on New York and Washington. According to the Department of Defense, use of a nuclear weapon by terrorists would most likely be against either a military installation or a political target (e.g., a seat of government, large population center, or commercial port city). In such a scenario, citizens outside the immediate lethal area would be exposed to the prompt radiation of the initial explosion as well as to chronic exposures resulting from the residual radioactive fallout.[24] Terrorist use of a nuclear weapon would have an immense psychological impact as well, extending beyond the immediate physical damage.

Although the U.S. tactical arsenal is comparatively secure from theft attempts, the safety of storage and weapons accounting of the existing Russian tactical arsenal is less certain. The potential for theft of nuclear material or the contracting of nuclear expertise to nuclear aspiring states and nonstate actors is exacerbated by the presence of unemployed or underpaid nuclear technicians who may be tempted to illegally sell nuclear matter to terrorist groups or renegade states. U.S. programs such as the Nunn-Lugar initiative, as well as Russian efforts to consolidate its tactical and strategic nuclear arsenals, are efforts to mitigate such dangers. However, uncertainties regarding accurate numbers of the tactical nuclear arsenal, economic difficulties, and lack of verification mechanisms ultimately leave room for doubt regarding the safety of the storage of Russian tactical nuclear weapons. In chapter 6 Alistair Millar looks at the reaction of the United States, NATO, and Russia as they deal with tactical nuclear weapons in the post–September 11 security environment.

Terrorist organizations have attempted to acquire Russian tactical nuclear weapons, and although there appears to be no evidence that such efforts have succeeded, the possibility exists that one day Russian tactical nuclear weapons could fall into terrorist hands. Indeed, former FBI investigator Oliver Revell said in an October 2001 interview with ABC News, "Osama bin Laden has been in contact with various sources, including Russian Mafia groups, in an attempt to obtain radiological materials, perhaps tactical nuclear weapons."[25] President Bush, on 6 November 2001, in reference to Al-Qaeda, stated, "They are seeking chemical, biological and nuclear weapons," and implied their willingness and that of other terrorist groups to use nuclear weapons (whether strategic or tactical). Numerous other news reports and analyses have suggested the interest and the will of terror networks to acquire and use nuclear weapons, particularly against targets in the United States.

This very real possibility raises the stakes in the international effort to control and reduce tactical nuclear weapons. Even before the attacks of 11 September, the April 2000 Hart-Rudman commission report, *Seeking a National Strategy: A Concept for Preserving Security and Promoting Freedom,* made it clear that "verifiable arms control and nonproliferation efforts must remain a top priority. These policies can help persuade states and terrorists to abjure weapons of mass destruction and to prevent the export of fissile materials and dangerous dual-use technologies."[26]

Use of Tactical Nuclear Weapons against Terrorists

The U.S. response to the attacks on New York and Washington has raised questions about the use of tactical nuclear weapons against terrorist bases or the countries that may harbor them. Whether for use in the battlefield or as a means of destroying underground cave networks and hideaways, particularly in the weeks immediately following September 11th, there was speculation about the role for tactical nuclear weapons in the war in Afghanistan.[27] Indeed, even before that, Paul Robinson, director of Sandia National Laboratories, argued "nuclear weapons do have a place and a purpose today." He suggested development of what he called a "To Whom It May Concern" force, for use against nations or subnational entities.[28] Robinson's nuclear force would include nuclear weapons above the subkiloton range (1 KT or higher), blending tactical and strategic weapons.

Although U.S. officials have not come forward to explicitly advocate use of tactical nuclear weapons against terrorist organizations, any consideration to do so would have to weigh numerous factors. First, their use would set a precedent for the use of nuclear weapons in the battlefield and weaken any efforts to regulate these weapons. Such use could also possibly add incentive and provide a pretext for nuclear, chemical, or biological retaliation by state and nonstate actors ("letting the genie out of the bottle," as the saying goes). Additionally, any use of such weapons would immediately challenge the maintenance of a successful international coalition against terrorists. Such use would also threaten nuclear contamination of civilians within the target state and neighboring states. Finally, the international legality of such use would disrupt international legal architecture regarding proliferation and use of force, including, possibly, the Non-Proliferation Treaty, which forbids use of nuclear weapons against nonnuclear states, the Geneva Conventions, and other provisions.

Tactical Nuclear Weapons in International Security: Considering the Issues

Tactical nuclear weapons have been assigned several purposes in post–Cold War policy planning and analytic discourse. Generally speaking, arguments in favor of the development, deployment, or use of tactical nuclear weapons have included that such weapons enable their possessor to:

- deter the use of TNWs by opponents;
- allow "flexible response" to a broad range of military threats;
- provide nuclear military options below the strategic level;
- help to defeat large or overwhelming conventional or chemical/biological attacks;
- have a placeholder of status, commitment, or prestige.

While there may be merit to the logic of these justifications, each is also beset with individual challenges that undermines the overall value of tactical nuclear weapons arsenals.

Tactical Nuclear Weapons and Deterrence

U.S. and NATO doctrine on tactical nuclear weapons in Europe during the Cold War was, in part, based on the controversial notion that these weapons served as a rung on the escalation ladder—lending them, in effect, a deterrent role—and that tactical nuclear weapons were a security guarantee of the U.S. commitment to Europe. Because NATO conventional forces were generally deemed insufficient to defend against a Soviet attack, the presence of tactical nuclear weapons served both as a line of defense and as a deterrent (based on the notion that a conventional Soviet attack would lead necessarily to the use of tactical nuclear weapons, which would then greatly heighten the risks of a general nuclear war).

In the post–Cold War context of greatly improved NATO relations with Russia, NATO and the United States no longer have the same need for tactical nuclear weapons. Whereas before tactical nuclear weapons were used to compensate for a European conventional inferiority, NATO is now in a position of conventional superiority—because of the decline in Russian capabilities and the advances in Western, particularly U.S., technological capability. Further, economic and political ties have supplanted arguments for keeping U.S. tactical nuclear weapons in Europe as a "vital transatlantic link."

Meanwhile, Russia's military posture vis-à-vis Europe is based on homeland defense, not alliance commitments, as was the case with the U.S.-NATO relationship. Therefore, tactical nuclear weapons in the Russian arsenal do not hold the function of reassurance to ally states that they did in the context of the Cold War U.S.-NATO relationship. Also, because use of tactical nuclear weapons between opponents with strategic nuclear capabilities could yield a broader strategic exchange, the deterrent value that tactical nuclear weapons purportedly provide may already exist via the presence of a strategic nuclear weapons threat. Therefore, Russian tactical nuclear weapons serve a diminished deterrent role, given Russian strategic nuclear capabilities.

Flexible Response to Broad Military Threats

Tactical nuclear weapons, as "battlefield" nuclear weapons, imply a sense of greater usability than strategic nuclear weapons. Doctrine relating to existing tactical nuclear weapons, and plans in the United States and Russia for the development of new classes of tactical nuclear weapon, include overt assumptions that these weapons could be useful in battlefield scenarios *below the strategic nuclear level*—or, in other words, tactical nuclear weapons could be used without resulting in an all-out nuclear war or a scenario of mutually assured destruction.

There are several challenges to the argument that tactical nuclear weapons are indeed "usable" nukes. First, decision makers would likely be hesitant to actually call on their use. The previously cited statement by Representative Thompson summarizes the potential international diplomatic fallout from the use of tactical nuclear weapons, and the notion of "letting the nuclear genie out of the bottle" would be a strong mitigating factor for any decision maker pondering the use tactical nuclear weapons in a battlefield situation.

Historic evidence also suggests that tactical nuclear weapons have not been employed even in situations where their use was considered. Most notably, during the Korean War the United States was faced with several conditions that could have potentially called for the use of tactical nuclear weapons, but policymakers opted against using them. Meanwhile, in other military conflicts such as Vietnam and, perhaps to a lesser extent, Chechnya, decision makers have not turned to tactical nuclear weapons when they could have been options.[29] Particularly from the U.S. point of view, the relative utility of tactical nuclear weapons has declined as other technologically advanced conventional combat options have emerged.

The domestic and international political consequences of a U.S. decision to use tactical nuclear weapons would significantly heighten the costs of such a decision. In addition to being a dramatic rejection of international norms, U.S. global moral leadership would be thoroughly undermined and would, according to Greg Mello, director of the Los Alamos Study Group, "provide a potent focus for simmering anti-U.S. resentments around the world," undermining U.S. national security over the long run.[30]

These arguments are not sufficient to rule out the notion that a decision maker would conclude that use of a tactical nuclear weapon would serve a worthwhile use. However, they do provide considerations that potentially could arise during the conditions under which such a decision would likely be made.

Regarding potential plans by the United States to embark on new tactical nuclear weapons programs, particularly for the destruction of hardened deeply buried targets, even the development of such "mininukes" could potentially yield instability and trigger proliferation. For example, although the United States may intend such weapons as "bunker busters" against hardened underground targets, intentions have provided poor assurance in international security, while capabilities have driven military planning. The case of tactical nuclear weapons would not provide exception to this rule. Even though the United States would state an intended use of these new tactical nuclear weapons, such reassurance would provide a weak foundation on which to build a sense of security among other international players, much less to build arms control efforts or international cooperation on this issue.[31] Other states, instead of simply trusting the intentions of the United States, would face a security dilemma based on stepped-up nuclear capabilities of a potential adversary and be compelled to respond to this threat capability by developing an adequate defense. This could include, perhaps, efforts at developing their own nuclear arsenals to serve, if for no other purpose, as a possible deterrent against a U.S. force.

Another problem with "battlefield" nuclear weapons is that the specific conditions under which these weapons would be deployed or used would require specially trained combat units. However, these personnel would be in grave danger if deployed in tandem with such weapons. An analysis by Ivan Safranchuk suggests that the battlefield environment created by deployment or use of tactical nuclear weapons would pose significant challenges for those using them and that it would be very difficult to actually deploy or use tactical nuclear weapons in the very situations in which they are supposed to be useful.[32] According to Safranchuk, the conditions necessary in land combat for tactical nuclear weapons to be effective are "difficult to achieve in tactical nuclear combat . . . tactical nuclear operations should be performed by combat units with certain characteristics, which are hard to achieve if TNWs are used."[33] In naval operations, Safranchuk notes, there may be fewer such problems because of the potential for separation of the theater of war from nonmilitary targets, although deleterious short- and long-term environmental effects of nuclear contamination would remain a necessary consideration.

A document published by the U.S. military also points to operational pitfalls of the use of tactical nuclear weapons. In the 1996 "Doctrine for Joint Theater Nuclear Operations," caution, relegated on premises of international law, is advocated before the use of any nuclear weapon.[34] The report states that "measures must be taken to avoid collateral damage and unnecessary suffering. Since nuclear weapons have greater potential, in many instances they may be inappropriate."[35]

In a later discussion on gravity bombs delivered by dual-capable aircraft (DCA) and long-range bombers (i.e., air-delivered tactical nuclear weapons), the report cites the following disadvantages: "crew at risk in high-threat environment; lead time required for planning and transit; significant combat support and ground support infrastructure may be required, depending on scenario; equipment may have to be released from other operation plan (OPLAN) tasking."[36]

Thus, "battlefield" scenarios under which tactical nuclear weapons could be used also pose inherent limitations to their actual usability, which would have to be addressed before any such use would be considered.

Tactical Nuclear Weapons as Substrategic Nuclear Options

The lower blast yields of tactical nuclear weapons could be proposed as an argument for substituting strategic arsenals with less deadly and less destructive tactical weapons. It could be suggested, for example, that low-yield tactical nuclear weapons are still capable of fulfilling a deterrent role. These lower-yield nuclear weapons could provide a strategic function if they are used for "countervalue" rather than battlefield or "counterforce" purposes.

Following this logic, it would appear possible that by serving as substitutes for strategic nuclear arsenals, tactical nuclear weapons could enable the reduction of strategic nuclear forces. Great Britain has already moved to follow a similar approach, eliminating land- and air-based nuclear weapons capability and moving its remaining 350 tactical warheads onto Trident submarine-launched ballistic missiles (SLBMs), leaving the U.K. with a single-leg nuclear force. According to a Ministry of Defense official: "A sub-strategic strike would be the limited and highly selective use of nuclear weapons in a manner that fell demonstrably short of a strategic strike, but with a sufficient level of violence to convince an aggressor who had already miscalculated our resolve and attacked us that he should halt his aggression and withdraw or face the prospect of a devastating strategic strike."[37]

Following this model, other countries could embark on smaller strategic nuclear programs while enhancing their tactical nuclear arsenals. Indeed, efforts in the United States and Russia to reduce strategic nuclear weapons, along with exploration of new categories of tactical nuclear weapons, essentially echo this argument.

While such programs could potentially reduce the world's strategic nuclear arsenals, it should be noted that the incorporation of tactical nuclear weapons into strategic arsenals is a tacit rejection of the logic that led to the Non-Proliferation Treaty. That is, rather than moving toward zero nuclear weapons, increasing reliance on them undermines efforts to encourage other states not to develop their own nuclear arsenals. Perhaps more important, the development and deployment of tactical nuclear weapons would sidestep one of the primary concerns outlined by this book: tactical nuclear weapons are uncovered nukes. There are no specific international legal mechanisms to regulate the possession, development, or deployment of tactical nuclear weapons. As such, increasing reliance on them is to encourage the use of nuclear weapons without providing legal and ethical guidelines. Unless greater efforts to regulate tactical nuclear weapons are undertaken, any move that increases reliance on them encourages international nuclear anarchy and fundamentally jeopardizes international security based on nonproliferation.

The Use of TNWs against Conventional, Chemical, and Biological Attacks

It has been suggested that tactical nuclear weapons may be useful against chemical or biological weapons. One such use may be in response to a biological or chemical weapons attack—in effect, countering an opponent's escalation of conflict to the level of weapons of mass destruction (WMD) with an in-kind response of another WMD. Another possible use of tactical nuclear weapons would be for the preemptive destruction of chemical or biological weapons storage sites. However, use of tactical nuclear weapons in such circumstances would require a willingness of military commanders and civilian decision makers to accept the effects of nuclear contamination of the targeted area and to face other battlefield and international political challenges posed by the use of these weapons. In the case of destroying storage sites, this requires additional willingness to accept the possibility of dispersion of chemical and biological agents as a result of the blast.

Unilateral Initiatives and the Difficulties of Addressing TNWs through Arms Control

The problems with tactical arsenals mentioned above and with the continued possession of these weapons by the United States and Russia are indications that the 1991–92 PNIs possess intrinsic shortcomings. Although unilateral initiatives hold the benefit that they circumvent the lengthy and complicated process of treaty negotiations (and expediency was one of the goals of the PNIs), they have the following shortcomings:

- ◆ they are not legally binding, allowing either side to modify or withdraw from the arrangement;
- ◆ they do not provide consistent means for data sharing and verification; this lack of transparency increases uncertainty regarding stockpile levels, implementation of the agreement, and the manner and timing as to when information is shared;
- ◆ they do not limit research and development into other similar, newer, or related weapons systems;
- ◆ they provide no way of assuring the Russian or American public that any reduction is taking place;

- ◆ they are vulnerable to changes in other international agreements; and
- ◆ they are vulnerable to shifts in international affairs or attitudes, undercutting long-term commitment to the terms of the agreement.[38]

Incentives for Controlling Tactical Nuclear Weapons

Incentives can play an important role in addressing the proliferation and theft of tactical nuclear weapons. In chapter 9, Jonathan Dean reviews the landscape of tactical nuclear weapons and the prospects for future arms control agreements to deal with this class of nuclear weapons. He concludes by encouraging further exploration of negotiating strategies for controlling tactical nuclear weapons. In chapter 8, David Cortright and Andrea Gabbitas take a careful look at the role of incentives as bargaining tools for disarmament and nonproliferation purposes—developing a model that emphasizes the merits of positive inducements and coercive measures, such as sanctions, to create effective bargaining dynamics.

The role for greater U.S.-Russian initiatives to address the safeguarding of tactical nuclear arsenals goes well beyond the U.S.-Russian context and could serve as a productive starting point for addressing the multilateral nature of the problem. The security architecture of Europe in the 21st century will have to address the Russian military balance, including the Russian tactical nuclear arsenal and the role of the approximately 150 to 200 U.S. tactical nuclear weapons currently based in Europe. The degree of U.S.-Russian cooperation on arms control issues will deeply affect the global strategic outlook in the post–Cold War security environment by influencing the weapons policies of other nuclear states. To reduce risks within these states, and to prevent other nations (and nonstate actors) from attaining these weapons, the United States and Russia would benefit from acting to reduce the political and military status they attach to their tactical nuclear weaponry.

2

The 1991–1992 PNIs and the Elimination, Storage, and Security of Tactical Nuclear Weapons

Joshua Handler

Introduction

One of the most important developments in post–Cold War arms control and disarmament efforts occurred in the early 1990s when U.S. President George Bush and Soviet President Mikhail Gorbachev, and then Yeltsin, took unilateral but reciprocal steps to reduce and de-alert their strategic and tactical nuclear weapons.[1] These 1991 and 1992 initiatives were announced in prominent televised public addresses that were covered widely in the international media. The announcement brought international acclaim from world leaders. French President Francois Mitterrand applauded Bush's proposals as "a real turning-point in nuclear disarmament" and said France could also participate in reducing nuclear arsenals. British Prime Minister John Major praised Bush's initiative as "bold . . . far-reaching, historic and imaginative." Japanese Prime Minister Toshiki Kaifu said, "Japan praises a bold and courageous initiative by President Bush and strongly supports the proposal as a step toward the total elimination of nuclear arms." German Foreign Minister Hans-

Dietrich Genscher hailed Bush's speech, saying, "I welcome the initiative taken by President Bush which I think is historical. We are very happy that the president decided that the nuclear weapons should be put away."[2]

In regards to tactical nuclear weapons, the presidential nuclear initiatives (PNIs) committed the United States and Russia to the following: eliminating all nuclear weapons in their respective army or ground forces; removing all tactical nuclear weapons from ships, submarines, and land-based naval aircraft; eliminating some of these weapons and storing the rest centrally; withdrawing some Air Force weapons to central storage sites and eliminating part of them; and, in the case of the Soviet Union, which still deployed such weapons, removing nuclear air defense weapons from deployment and eliminating some of them. Several years later, President Bill Clinton took the important additional step of denuclearizing the U.S. surface fleet as a result of his administration's nuclear posture review (i.e., surface ships lost their nuclear sea-launched cruise missile [SLCM] capability, and aircraft on aircraft carriers no longer were nuclear capable).[3]

The PNIs on tactical nuclear weapons were not treaties, but neither were they empty promises. They were frank pledges—for the most part unconditional pledges—to take specific disarmament steps. The key commitments were to remove, eliminate, and consolidate, either in part or in their entirety, certain categories of tactical nuclear weapons.[4] This chapter will provide an overview of the status of implementation of the PNIs, offer some conclusions about the security of tactical nuclear weapons compared to other nuclear weapons and give some thoughts on the future of tactical nuclear weapons.

United States

The particulars of President Bush's proposals were fleshed out by Department of Defense (DoD) officials, who were surprisingly open about the details of the U.S. tactical nuclear weapons to be removed, eliminated, and consolidated under the PNIs.[5] They provided, for the first time, information about the numbers and general locations of some of the U.S. tactical nuclear weapons arsenal. (See table 2.1.) In the worrisome categories of nuclear warheads for short-range tactical missiles and nuclear artillery shells, the world learned that there were 2,150 Lance and artillery warheads, 1,700 deployed overseas and 450 kept in the United States. Overall, at least 3,050 warheads in total were to be eliminated—850 Lance missile, 1,300 artillery, 900 B-57 depth bombs.[6] In 1994 President Clinton's Nuclear Posture Review denuclearized U.S. surface ships. This meant that nuclear sea-launched cruise missile capability was removed. In addition, U.S. aircraft carriers no longer carried B61 bombs for strike aircraft, and as a result the B61–2 and -5 mods were dismantled.[7]

TABLE 2.1
Summary of U.S. PNIs

Army (and Marine Corps)—Eliminate all ~2,150 missile and artillery
   weapons
Lance missile—Eliminate 850 Lance warheads (~150 ER in U.S.)
Artillery—Eliminate ~1,300 artillery shells 3 types—two 8 in and one
   155 mm
W-33 8 in ~500 to be returned to U.S.
W-48 155mm ~ 500 W-48s to be returned to U.S.
W-79 8 in—(W79-1 ER in U.S.)—all to be eliminated

Navy—Remove ~500 TNW usually at sea aboard surface ships and
   submarines
B-57 Depth Bomb—Eliminate all ~900 land and sea-deployed
SLCM ~100 usually at sea; returned to the U.S.

Air Force and Navy/Marine Corps* Strike Bombs
B-57 Strike bomb*—Keep, but some eliminated
Tactical bomb—B61-2* -5* / B61-3,-4,-10—Keep B-61

---

*Denotes Navy/Marine Corps bombs.

Withdrawals

In terms of removing tactical nuclear weapons from deployments, the United
States implemented the PNIs relatively quickly. The U.S. Army removed its
weapons from Korea by the end of 1991 and from Europe by mid-1992.[8] Army
nuclear weapons were removed from service in the continental United States
by mid-1994.[9] In terms of the Navy, withdrawal of nuclear weapons from surface ships, submarines, and forward bases for land-based maritime aircraft
had taken place by mid-1992. Air Force weapons, like their Army counterparts, were removed from Korea by late 1991. In Europe, reductions resulting
from the 1991 PNIs were completed in 1993.[10]

Eliminations

The United States did not promise to finish the implementation of the PNIs
by a particular date. It appears, however, that the United States has been making steady progress in eliminating those weapons it said it would liquidate.
(See table 2.2.) A notable exception, however, is the W-79 nuclear artillery
shell. Elimination only started in 1998 and could be completed in early 2003.[11]
Confusingly, the recent data provided by the U.S. Department of Energy
(DOE) does not entirely match the information given by U.S. officials in 1991

about the number of tactical nuclear weapons to be eliminated. For example, it appears more Lance missile warheads were eliminated than were stated to exist to be eliminated in 1991. Moreover, there are some gaps in the data that would be good to fill for the purposes of reassuring the public (e.g., the number of W-33 artillery warheads eliminated and the dates of starting and completing elimination; the number of W-79 artillery warheads to be eliminated and the total Army warheads to be eliminated; the portion of the 1,159 B-61 bomb warheads dismantled that are B61-2 and -5 mods; and answer to the question: are the 2,242 B-57 depth bombs equal to all the existing B-57 depth-bomb and strike variants?).

Consolidation

Consolidation of U.S. tactical nuclear weapons has also occurred. In general, according to the U.S. Department of Defense, nuclear weapons storage locations were "reduced by over 75 percent" between 1988 and 1994.[12] Recent reductions and consolidations have included storage sites for U.S. Navy tactical nuclear weapons—SLCMs—which were reduced from four to two. In the Atlantic, Naval Weapons Station Yorktown, Virginia, transferred its SLCMs to the Strategic Weapons Facility Atlantic in the summer of 1997. The SLCMs are stored with Trident warheads near the King's Bay, Georgia, Trident SSBN base.[13] In the Pacific, NAS North Island, San Diego, California, transferred its SLCMs to the Strategic Weapons Facility Pacific. They are stored with Trident warheads near the Bangor, Washington, Trident SSBN base.[14] Yet significantly from the perspective of worries about forward-deployed TNWs, U.S. TNWs are thought to be kept at 10 bases in seven European NATO countries. Table 2.3 summarizes the status of U.S. tactical nuclear weapons deployments.

As a result of the U.S. PNIs, there was a large and significant reduction in areas where U.S. nuclear weapons are deployed. Some of these withdrawals greatly improved the security and safety of U.S. tactical nuclear weapons and crisis stability and helped reduce tensions in certain regions of the world. Particularly noteworthy was the complete denuclearization of the Army, resulting in the removal of all Army tactical nuclear weapons—including nuclear artillery shells, which were a major security concern—from frontline locations in Europe and South Korea. Also, Navy tactical nuclear weapons were removed from warships and submarines afloat, from forward-deployed logistic surface ships such as the submarine tender in La Maddalena, Italy, and other forward-deployed locations such as Guam and Adak, Alaska, close to the Soviet Union. Finally, Air Force tactical nuclear weapons bombs also were removed from South Korea. (See table 2.4.)

Nuclear-Certified Units

Another interesting indication of the withdrawal and elimination of U.S. tactical nuclear weapons is the number of nuclear-weapons-certified units in the

TABLE 2.2
Status of Eliminations of U.S. Tactical Nuclear Weapons per the PNI Commitments

Warhead	System	Phase VII Retirement	Eliminated From	To	Dismantled FY97–FY00	Nos. Dismantled FY90–FY97	1991 PNI Commitment to Eliminate
Army (Marine Corps)							
W-70	Lance	FY 92	Feb 92	Nov 96		1,170	850
W-33	8 in	FY 92	?	?			500 at least
W-48	155mm	FY 93	Apr 92	Apr 96		759	500 at least
W-79	8 in		Jun 98[15]	FY 03	Y	3	~300?
Total Army						1,932	2,150
Navy							
B-57*	ND/SB	FY 93	Nov 89	Mar 95		2,242	900 NDB
W-80-0	SLCM				Y		900 NDB
Total Navy						2,242	900 NDB
Total Army + Navy						4,174	3,050
Air Force and Navy/Marine Corps* Strike Bombs							
B-57	See Navy						
B61-2*	Bomb		Jun 96	Mar 97		1,159 all B61 mods	
B61-5*	Bomb		Mar 97	Aug 97			
B61-3, -4, -10	Bomb				Y		

*Denotes Navy/Marine Corps bombs.

TABLE 2.3
Number of U.S. Nuclear Weapon Storage Sites 1985, 1992, 2001[16]

	1985	1992	2001
Domestic	39	34	12
Overseas	125	16	10
Total	164	50	22
Number of U.S. States storing nuclear weapons		25	12
Number of U.S. States storing tactical nuclear weapons			4

Europe—10 Bases in 7 Countries storing U.S. TNW (B61 bombs)
Kleine Brogel AB, Belgium; Buchel AB, Germany; Ramstein AB, Germany; Spangdahlem AB, Germany; Araxos AB, Greece; Aviano AB, Italy; Ghedi AB, Italy; Vokel AB, The Netherlands; Incirlik AB, Turkey; RAF Lakenheath, U.K.

U.S. military. Every unit that has a nuclear-weapons mission of transporting, storing, or firing nuclear weapons must be certified to do so by its service and by the Department of Defense. Table 2.5a presents the number of nuclear-certified units per year from 1989 to 2000. After the PNIs there was a dramatic drop in the number of nuclear-certified units in the U.S. military. With the removal of all nuclear weapons for ground forces, the Army and Marine Corps no longer had any nuclear-certified units. The removal of tactical nuclear weapons from the Navy also resulted in a large drop in the number of Navy nuclear-certified units. Those that remain are a combination of nuclear-fueled ballistic missile submarines (SSBNs), nuclear storage facilities and perhaps some 20 SSNs that retain a nuclear SLCM capability. The Air Force was least affected by the PNIs, but even so the number of nuclear-certified units has dropped by over half. Typically, Air Force nuclear-certified units are wings. Thus wings containing nuclear-capable attack aircraft such as B-2 and B-52 bombers or F-16 or F-15E fighter-bombers will receive nuclear certification. Strategic missiles are also organized into wings, and these are nuclear certified. Finally, the wings that operate C-17, C-130, or C-141 aircraft and that are responsible for the air transport of nuclear weapons receive certification. In addition, several of the munitions units (munitions squadrons or munitions support squadrons) with nuclear weapons responsibility may receive their own nuclear certification.

Soviet Union/Russia

In regards to the Soviet Union/Russia, there is some official and semiofficial data available about the status of the PNIs. In the early to mid-1990s, Russian

TABLE 2.4
U.S. TNW Consolidation from 1991 to 2001

	1991 Locations	*2001 Locations*
Army/Marine Corps		
Lance	Europe, California, New Mexico, New York, Texas	—
Artillery	Europe, Korea, California, New Mexico, New York, Texas	—
Navy		
B-57 depth bomb	Europe, Pacific, Alaska, California, Florida, Hawaii, Maine, Texas, Virginia	—
SLCM	Europe (Italy), Pacific (Guam), California, Hawaii, New Jersey, South Carolina, Virginia	Georgia, Washington
Air Force and Navy/Marine Corps* Tactical Bombs		
B-57 bomb*	Europe, Pacific, New Mexico, Nevada	—
B61-2* -5* bombs	Europe, Pacific, Korea, California, Florida, Hawaii, New Mexico, Nevada, Virginia	—
B61-3, -4, -10 bombs	Europe, Pacific, California, Florida, Hawaii, New Mexico, Nevada, Virginia	Europe, Nevada, New Mexico

*Denotes Navy/Marine Corps bombs.

TABLE 2.5a
Number of Nuclear-Weapons-Certified Units in the U.S. Military
by Service 1989–2000[17]

	CY89	*CY90*	*FY91*	*FY92*	*FY93*	*FY94*	*FY95*	*FY96*	*FY97*	*FY98*	*FY99*	*FY00*
Army	141	139	139	1	1	1	1	0	0	0	0	0
Navy	187	200	200	81	31	29	34	36	38	38	38	38
Air Force	49	44	44	35	35	30	26	22	27	21	21	21
Marines	17	18	18	0	0	0	0	0	0	0	0	0
Total	394	401	401	117	67	60	61	58	65	59	59	59

TABLE 2.5b
Air Force Units Having or Scheduled to Have Nuclear
Surety Inspections in FY 2001

Unit	Location	Aircraft, Missile, or Function
2d Bomb Wing	Barksdale AFB, Louisiana	B-52H
4th Fighter Wing	Seymour Johnson AFB, North Carolina	F-15E
31st Fighter Wing	Aviano AB, Italy	F-16C/D
48th Fighter Wing	RAF Lakenheath, U.K.	F-15C/D, F-15E
509th Bomb Wing	Whiteman AFB, Missouri	B-2
90th Space Wing	F. E. Warren AFB, Wyoming	Minuteman III and MX ICBMs
341st Space Wing	Malmstrom AFB, Montana	Minuteman III ICBM
305th Air Mobility Wing	McGuire AFB, New Jersey	C-141
752d MUNSS	Volkel AB, The Netherlands	Nuclear Weapons Storage
852d MUNSS	Buechel AB, Germany	Nuclear Weapons Storage
896th MUNS	Nellis AFB, Nevada	Nuclear Weapons Storage
898th MUNS	Kirtland AFB, New Mexico	Nuclear Weapons Storage

officials elaborated on what the PNIs included and by when Russia expected to have finished implementing them (as noted, the United States has not emphasized completion dates but has provided more information about the types and numbers of tactical nuclear weapons affected by the PNIs). Table 2.6 summarizes this information.

Withdrawals

In terms of the removal of tactical nuclear weapons from deployments, it appears that this occurred relatively quickly in the case of the former Soviet republics.[18] Although official information is lacking, it seems that tactical nuclear weapons were removed from Eastern Europe and Transcaucasus before the September–October 1991 PNIs.[19] Tactical nuclear weapons were removed from the Central Asian republics and the Baltics by December

TABLE 2.6
Types and Numbers of TNWs affected by PNIs

Division	Date of Elimination	Comments
Army[20]	2000	All nuclear warheads on three types of shorter-range missiles
	2000	All nuclear warheads for six types of artillery guns of 152mm, 203mm, and 240mm caliber
	1998	All nuclear "mines"
Navy	1995[21] or *End of* 1996[22]	One-third.
Air Force	By 1996 or *End of* 1997	One-half.
Air Defense	By 1996 or *End of* 1996	One-half.

1991;[23] from Ukraine by 5 or 6 May 1992;[24] and from Belarus in early or spring 1992.[25]

In terms of the removal by service, the data about Russia are more imprecise than in the case of the United States, but it appears that Russia was not as quick as the United States to remove tactical nuclear weapons from deployments. Withdrawals from the Navy were accomplished relatively quickly by February 1993.[26] Air Defense force withdrawals seemingly took a little longer, perhaps until September 1996.[27] Finally, only in 1997 was it mentioned that nuclear weapons for the ground forces had been completely removed from operational units.[28]

Some have worried that the seemingly slow withdrawal of Russian tactical nuclear weapons represents the preservation of some tactical nuclear weapons capability above what was implied by Russian commitments made in the PNIs. Yet, whatever residual tactical nuclear weapons capability may exist, it must be considered in the context of the declining number of nuclear-capable platforms (caused by the breakup of the Soviet Union) and the accelerated retirement of platforms (caused by aging and/or lack of maintenance). For example, the number of nuclear-capable ships in the Soviet/Russian Navy shrank from some 400 in 1990 to approximately 100 by of 2002.[29]

Eliminations

In terms of elimination, Russia has not provided any detailed information comparable to that available from the U.S. government. Of most concern is that Russia seemingly had promised to finish the elimination of its ground forces nuclear weapons by 2000, or perhaps the end of 2000. Russian Foreign Minister Ivanov claimed at the NPT 2000 Review Conference that Russia was about to complete the implementation of the PNIs. The situation with the implementation of the PNIs remained in doubt in 2001, but in the April 2002 NPT PrepCom, the Russian delegation delivered an important update. Russia said that the destruction of nuclear warheads for tactical missiles, nuclear artillery shells, and nuclear mines continues. Although it was disturbing to learn some of these weapons still existed, Russia noted encouragingly that if there is sufficient funding, Russia will finish eliminating all ground force nuclear weapons by 2004.[30] Table 2.7 summarizes some official and semiofficial statements about the status of the elimination of Russian tactical nuclear weapons.

Consolidation

The consolidation of Russian tactical nuclear weapons has also occurred. By 1995 the number of nuclear-capable bases had been reduced by over 250.[31] By 1996 the number of nuclear storage facilities declined to one-third of their 1991 levels.[32] Table 2.8 illustrates which storage facilities were consolidated. When possible, the number of facilities is indicated.[33]

Many Russian strategic and tactical nuclear weapons are stored in national or central nuclear weapon storage facilities, such as the one imaged by Spaceimaging Ikonos Satellite on 1 March 2001 near Bryansk, Russia (see page 36). Note the large bunkers within the facility.

Russian Air Force tactical nuclear weapons may be kept in storage facilities such as the one near the Kholm Air Base near Arkhangelsk Northern Russia (see page 37). If so, some Russian air-delivered tactical nuclear weapons are

TABLE 2.7
Status of the Elimination of Russian TNWs

Army	Sept. 1996—Being eliminated[34]
	Dec. 1997—Mines and TNW from FSU republics being eliminated[35]
	Oct. 1998—Being eliminated[36]
	Nov.1998—Being eliminated[37]
	April 2000—About to complete elimination[38]
Navy	By June 1996—One-third eliminated[39]
Air Force	By April 2000—One-half eliminated
Air Defense	By June 1996—One-half eliminated[40]

TABLE 2.8
Russian TNW Consolidation from 1990—2001

Nuclear Weapons Storage Facilities	1990	1995	2001	With TNW
Eastern Europe	Y	N	N	N
Soviet/Russian National Storage	Y	Y	15	Y
ICBM bases	Y	Y	19+	N
Strategic Bomber bases	Y	Y	3	?
Air Force and Navy	Y	Y	30+	Y
Air Defense/Army	Y	?	N?	N?
Total	500–600+	<100[41]	~67	~45?

neither "forward-deployed" next to aircraft on an air-strip, nor kept at national-level storage sites, but at a bunker in vicinity of airfields.[42]

Elimination and Openness

Since 1991 there has been a large reduction in the number of deployed tactical nuclear weapons. Unofficial estimates of the 1991 and current sizes of the operational tactical nuclear arsenals of the United States and Russia are given in table 2.9. From the perspective of nongovernmental organizations (NGOs), there is more uncertainty about the estimates for Russia's tactical nuclear weapons than for the United States. This is not because the United States has provided comprehensive official information about the number and types of its tactical nuclear weapons. It has not. The United States, like Russia, is secretive about this information. However, much more official and semiofficial information is available about the U.S. military concerning its nuclear weapons, nuclear weapons strategy, launching platforms, and so forth, since the dawn of the nuclear age over 50 years ago. Moreover, Western nongovernment experts have been steadily examining this material for most of this time. The accumulation of information and knowledge, therefore, gives a greater confidence in the estimates of U.S. tactical nuclear weapons.

Although the United States has not provided comprehensive information about its own stockpile size and its reductions, DoD has occasionally made public its estimate of the Russian nuclear stockpile. For example, the DoD reported in 2001 that in December 2000 the Russian nuclear stockpile "was estimated to be well under 25,000 warheads, a reduction of over 11,000 warheads since 1992."[43] DoD estimates contain a wide degree of latitude because of the lack of reliable information about the size of the Russian stockpile and the rate of Russian warhead dismantling.

More openness on the part of the United States and Russia could substitute for more rigorous verification measures and would underscore the utility of unilateral initiatives. Both countries could give the overall numbers of their tactical nuclear weapons in 1991 and the present. The United States, in particular, could provide more consistent information on eliminations and explain the discrepancies in the information released heretofore. Russia, in turn, could provide more information on types of weapons eliminated and numbers dismantled. Moreover, it is all the more important for Russia's standing to take such steps in the aftermath of the Bush administration's 2001 Nuclear Posture Review. Russia has been complaining that the Bush administration's plans will not lead to transparent, irreversible reductions in strategic nuclear weapons.[44] The same criticism could be and has been leveled at the 1991 PNIs. Russia has also been criticized for how it has acted in regards to the PNIs. To give their complaints more credibility, Russia should demonstrate as soon as possible some transparency and irreversibility concerning its commitments under the 1991 PNIs. Such actions—living up to past obligations in a more open fashion—would be very helpful for the case of transparency and irreversibility in general.

TABLE 2.9
U.S. and Soviet/Russian TNW Totals

	_1991_[45]	_2002_[46]
Estimated U.S. TNW[47]		
Army/Marine Corps	3,040	0
Navy	1,150	320 SLCMs
Air Force	2,975	800 B-61 bombs
Air Defense	0	0
Total	7,165	1,120
Estimated Soviet/Russian TNW		
Ground Forces	4,800– 6,700	0
Navy	3,400– 5,000	640
Air Force	4,000– 7,000	1,540
Air Defense	2,800– 3,000	1,200
Total	15,000–21,700	3,380

The Reversibility Problem

The U.S. inactive stockpile of nuclear warheads and Russian nuclear weapons production capacity indicate that the reduction in deployed tactical nuclear weapons as a result of elimination could be reversed relatively easily by reintroducing weapons into the active stockpile or producing new ones. In the case of the United States, a good recent example of this problem is the B61-10 bomb, which was manufactured using the W-85 warheads that were removed from Pershing II intermediate-range missiles eliminated under the 1987 INF Treaty.[48]

In addition to reducing tactical nuclear weapons, further agreements and methods should be developed to ensure that tactical nuclear weapons disarmament measures could not be easily reversed. These steps should also extend to preventing a nuclear capability to be restored to units that are no longer nuclear certified.

Security of Tactical Nuclear Weapons

Ensuring the security of tactical nuclear weapons has been a major concern of many analysts and commentators. It is frequently claimed that the security of tactical nuclear weapons is somehow worse than for strategic nuclear weapons and, thus, that special steps are somehow merited. However, one result of the PNIs is that tactical nuclear weapons are now approximately as secure as strategic nuclear weapons. It is now as good—or as bad—and this is a large change from the 1990–91 time frame.[49] Tactical nuclear weapons in the United States and Russia are in many cases collocated with strategic nuclear weapons in major nuclear weapons storage facilities that contain multiple bunkers. Moreover, major changes in deployment patterns have improved the security situation for tactical nuclear weapons. There are almost no forward-deployed or dispersed tactical nuclear weapons on land, and there are no such weapons deployed on U.S. or Russian ships or submarines. The only exception is U.S. tactical nuclear weapons aircraft bombs based in Europe, which are now kept in weapons storage vaults (WSV) set into the floor of hangers where aircraft can be located.[50] In the case of Russia, some tactical nuclear weapons may be located in storage areas in the vicinity of an airfield, but unlike the United States, they are most likely not on the airfield area proper. Lastly, many of the supposedly smaller and more easily transportable tactical nuclear weapons, such as artillery shells, may almost be or have been completely eliminated. Thus concerns about them being stolen are now (or soon to be) moot.

If a thief has the leisure to decide, there are several reasons why tactical nuclear weapons may not provide an attractive target. In terms of ease of

(text continued on page 39)

Kirtland Underground Munitions Storage Complex (KUMSC)

One of the two main Air Force nuclear weapons general depots in the United States, located at Kirtland Air Force Base, Albequerque, New Mexico, stores approximately 2,000 nuclear warheads underground and covers an area of some 40 football fields. Completed in 1994, it replaced the nearby Manzano mountain storage complex. Managed by the 898th Munitions Squadron of the 377th Air Base Wing, KUMSC also serves as a transshipment base and storage point augmenting the Pantex, Texas, assembly/disassembly plant.

An aerial photo of the Kirtland Underground Munitions Storage Complex (KUMSC), next to Albuquerque, New Mexico. *U.S. Geological Survey,* 1996

A schematic of the KUMSC, showing the interior layout. *U.S. Army Corps of Engineers*

Nuclear Weapons Storage Area at Nellis Air Force Base

The second main Air Force nuclear weapons general depot in the United States contains several hundred gravity bombs and air-launched cruise missile warheads in above-ground bunkers. Operational since 1955, it is the largest above-ground nuclear weapons storage in the United States, covering over 790 acres. It is managed by the 896th Munitions Squadron of the 377th Air Base Wing.

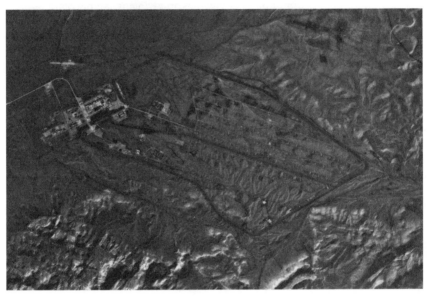

An aerial photo of the nuclear weapons storage area of Nellis Air Force Base, near Las Vegas, Nevada. *U.S. Geological Survey,* 1990

Strategic Weapons Facility, Pacific (SWFPAC)

One of two main Navy nuclear wespons storage area, SWFPAC contains over 1,000 warheads for Trident SLBMs and Tomahawk cruise missiles in above-ground bunkers. Operational since the early 1980s, it covers an area of over 5 square miles.

An aerial photo of the U.S. Navy's Strategic Weapons Facility, Pacific, near the Bangor, Washington, Trident submarine base. *U.S. Geological Survey,* 1994

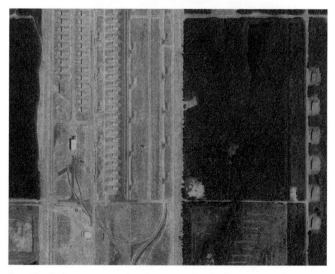

Detail of the storage bunkers in the U.S. Navy's Strategic Weapons Facility, Pacific, near the Bangor, Washington, Trident submarine base. *U.S. Geological Survey,* 1994

National-Level Russian Weapons Storage Site

One of a dozen major national level nuclear weapons storages sites in Russia. Several hundred tactical and strategic nuclear weapons from any military service may be stored in the several large bunkers located within perimeter security fence, which surrounds more than 2 square miles. Large bunkers cover an area of several football fields. Operated by the 12th Main Directorate of the Ministry of Defense.

Ikonos satellite image of a Russian national-level nuclear weapons storage site near Zhukovka in western Russia from March 2001. *Space Imaging Inc.*

Detail of two storage bunkers in the Russian national-level nuclear weapons storage site near Zhukovka in western Russia from March 2001. *Space Imaging Inc.*

Kholm Air Base and Associated Tactical Nuclear Weapons Storage Bunker

A dozen or more of such bunkers may exist near air bases with nuclear capable aircraft, serving as stores for their tactical nuclear weapons. The bunkers are several kilometers from the air strip. Unlike current U.S. practice with its aircraft in Europe, nuclear weapons are not stored in the hangar with the aircraft.

Corona satellite photograph of Kholm Air Base and an associated tactical nuclear weapons storage bunker located in Northern Russia from 1971. *U.S. National Archives and Joshua Handler*

These photographs provide an illustrative comparison of the sizes of nuclear warheads.

Figure #1: Workers remove strategic warheads from a Minuteman III reentry vehicle at F. E. Warren AFB, Wyoming. It appears that three to four people with the proper loading and transport equipment could carry off an ICBM warhead. *Courtesy of the U.S. Air Force*

Figure #2: Examples of various nuclear weapons that have been developed in the Soviet Union and Russia. Note that the nuclear artillery shell in the foreground is significantly smaller than the huge multimegaton aircraft bomb in the back and the tactical aviation bomb to the right. However, it is still probably a meter or so in length and all may soon be eliminated. *Courtesy of Chelyabinsk-70 Museum, Russia*

theft, overall, any modern nuclear weapon is not so large. If a group could gain access to a storage bunker, it would be possible for a modest number of people to carry off any type of nuclear weapon. In terms of desirability, the obstacles to creating detonation of tactical nuclear weapons that have been placed in a stored configuration or retired may be the same or greater than for strategic nuclear weapons. If the goal is to obtain fissile material, a strategic nuclear weapon may contain more fissile material than a tactical one. In terms of vulnerability, a major concern is the susceptibility of nuclear weapons to theft during transport. Today, there is perhaps even less logistical movement of tactical nuclear weapons than strategic nuclear weapons. Strategic nuclear weapons may actually be more vulnerable, since they are more often transported from remote base areas.

The photographs on page 38 provide an illustrative comparison of the sizes of nuclear warheads. On the left are strategic nuclear weapons for a U.S. Minuteman III ICBM. It appears that three to four people with the proper loading and transport equipment could carry off an ICBM warhead. The photos on the right are of various nuclear weapons that have existed in the Soviet Union and Russia. Note that the nuclear artillery shell in the foreground of the top photo is clearly smaller than the huge multimegaton aircraft bomb in the back and the tactical bomb to the right. But it is still probably a meter or so in length and all may soon be eliminated. In the bottom photo, various missile RVs are displayed.

The Future of Tactical Nuclear Weapons

The future of tactical nuclear weapons is uncertain. There is widespread disagreement on whether these weapons should remain—some advise keeping tactical nuclear weapons in the U.S. and Russian arsenals and others advocate deemphasizing and reducing them. Currently, tactical nuclear weapons are still seen as important. The United States sustains its capability, regularly holding nuclear SLCM regeneration exercises.[51] Moreover, U.S. tactical nuclear weapons are deployed in Europe for political unity and new NATO missions. In addition, in the United States the enthusiasm for stopping or countering proliferation of weapons of mass destruction (WMD)—promoted both by liberal arms controllers and conservative hawks—is creating the political space and pressure for new missions for tactical nuclear weapons and the development of new tactical nuclear weapons. As a result of President Clinton's 1993–94 Nuclear Posture Review, the decision was made to develop the B61-11 earth-penetrating bomb for attacking hardened targets. It was deployed in the mid-1990s.[52] Nuclear weapons advocates in the United States have used the continuing worries about WMD proliferation to push for development of additional new nuclear weapons. The Bush administration's 2002 Nuclear Posture Review endorsed the idea of pursuing an "Advanced Concept Initiative" within the National Nuclear Security Administration

(NNSA) that could provide options for future weapons development and deployment. The Nuclear Weapons Council, as a result of an Air Force requirement, directed the NNSA to look at a "Robust Nuclear Earth Penetrator" (RNEP) as its first advanced concept program.[53]

From Russia there are news reports about the need for tactical nuclear weapons. These reports seemingly are based on the views of the same types of people who advocate tactical nuclear weapons in the United States—hawks and nuclear weapons laboratory scientists. Although work on some sort of new weapons types undoubtedly goes on in Russian weapons labs, it does not seem to be policy to acquire new types of tactical nuclear weapons—yet.[54] (See Ivan Safranchuk's chapter 3 for an exploration of this topic.) Also, Russia, like the United States, exercises its tactical nuclear weapons capability, although its exercises have raised some questions about its commitments to the PNIs. Of particular note, a Russian general described a Russian tactical nuclear weapons exercise in March and June 1999 that involved a "rocket brigade."[55] It is not clear whether a ground force or air defense unit was involved because both could have "rockets." If it was the former, this news would be disturbing in light of the PNI pledge to denuclearize the Army. Equally worrisome are reports in 2000 that artillery troops have continued training at least with exercise versions of nuclear artillery shells.[56] Moreover, there were news reports in January and February 2001 about Russian tactical nuclear weapons in Kaliningrad. If true, this may be an indication that Russia was exercising its allowed tactical nuclear weapons capability:[57] movement of tactical nuclear weapons to airbase storage or exercise of the same, or an exercise with the Russian Navy similar to as what is done in the United States. Yet, the tactical nuclear weapons movement to or an exercise in Kaliningrad goes against the Gorbachev-era pledge to denuclearize the Baltic.

There is, however, some pressure to further reduce and eliminate tactical nuclear weapons. The United States could decrease its nuclear SLCMs following the attacks of 11 September, as attention shifts toward improving conventional forces. As a result, nuclear SLCM versions could be converted into conventional variants.[58] Also, there has been some debate in the submarine community about whether to keep SLCMs or give them up.[59] Finally, U.S. SSNs are overextended[60] and some in the U.S. submarine community are concerned about the added burden of keeping a nuclear SLCM capability.

In general, it may be possible to eliminate nuclear SLCMs. In 1991 it was a lost opportunity when President Bush did not take up President Gorbachev's offer to eliminate all naval tactical nuclear weapons. Complete destruction of naval tactical nuclear weapons would have been a good disarmament step and would have further eased the burden of verifying PNIs. However, there may be still some interest within the Russian Navy to eliminate nuclear SLCMs.

It was also reassuring that Russia stated at the NPT PrepCom in April 2002 that it was willing to finish eliminating all of its ground force nuclear weapons by 2004 if funding was available. Clearly, it should be a priority for the international community to ensure this happens. Moreover, help in this regard could lead to more openness about tactical nuclear weapons.

Are Low Numbers of Tactical Nuclear Weapons Preferable to Low Numbers of Strategic Missiles?

It is conceivable that the United States may end up with only tactical nuclear aircraft bombs, either through unilateral steps or in conjunction with Russia. If so, it may be premature to advocate the complete elimination of all tactical nuclear weapons. In fulfilling their NPT Article 6 commitments, a good way station toward zero nuclear weapons may be to set aside a small number of air-delivered tactical nuclear bombs rather than keep low levels of ICBMs on land or SLBMs on nuclear-powered submarines at sea.

A world where only a small number of tactical nuclear weapons exist would be as stable—if not more so—than a world with small numbers of ICBMs or SLBMs. Tactical nuclear weapons could be just as secure from attack and theft. There would be less concern about hair-trigger alert launches and, if launched, aircraft-carrying tactical nuclear weapons could be recalled. There would be better command, control, and communication than with SLBMs and less worry about naval nuclear accidents. It would cost less to maintain some dual-capable aircraft (or bombers in general) for carrying tactical nuclear weapons than ICBM wings and SSBNs and their bases. In the case of the United States, the overhead for maintaining a separate nuclear command, STRATCOM, could be eliminated.

In essence, the idea would be to return to a world with only a few nuclear-capable bombers. At this point, equivalent force structures may facilitate the final steps toward zero. It could be easier to obtain the final reductions if bomber weapons were balanced against bomber weapons, rather than trying to balance ICBMs against SLBMs against bombers (if each country decides to keep a different mixture of forces).

The author would like to thank the Ploughshares Foundation and the John Merck Fund in conjunction with the Natural Resources Defense Council for support for research involving satellite imagery.

Part II

Tactical Nuclear Weapons in the Post–Cold War Era

3

Tactical Nuclear Weapons in the Modern World

A Russian Perspective

Ivan Safranchuk

The debate in Russia about the role of tactical nuclear weapons is similar to tactical nuclear weapons (TNW) discussions by Western academics in the 1960s. Like past debates, Russians are trying to determine whether tactical nuclear weapons can be used to compensate for the weaknesses of its conventional force. However, the Russian discussion takes place in an information vacuum. There is a clear shortage of useful data on the quantitative and qualitative parameters of the Russian tactical nuclear weapons arsenal.

Focus on tactical nuclear weapons was initially provoked by NATO expansion. The majority of statements and publications at that time related to NATO plans, but since the mid-1990s defense experts have increasingly linked pro-tactical nuclear weapons arguments with threats from the East and the South.[1] However, in recent years debates about tactical nuclear weapons have quieted down in Russia. The last major splash of interest occurred in April 1999 during the Russian Security Council meeting on the future development of nuclear weapons. Since then, Russian statements on tactical nuclear weapons have not attracted much attention. For example, the May 2000 statement at the Non-Proliferation Treaty (NPT) RevCon and the April 2002 statement at the NPT PrepCom on the implementation of 1991–92 presidential nuclear initiatives (PNIs) passed unnoticed except by a small circle of defense experts.

This recent lack of interest in the issue of tactical nuclear weapons may be explained by two major factors. First, the argument about whether tactical nuclear weapons could be used as a substitute for weak conventional forces was mostly exhausted by the late 1990s. The paradigm of using tactical nuclear weapons for new threats (without making a direct connection to the stance of conventional arms) was not fully developed because defense experts disagreed about new threats and challenges. Second, the last two years were marked by strong interest in other arms control topics such as the Anti-Ballistic Missile (ABM) Treaty and the new strategic offensive weapons reduction agreement.

These two factors are interconnected, of course, but it is not clear which one is original or more powerful. If lack of interest is primarily caused by the second factor, then debates on tactical nuclear weapons will renew as soon as the expert community tackles current pressing issues (assuming new issues do not emerge in the meantime). If the first factor prevails, then tactical nuclear weapons will remain marginal anyway. Debates within Russia about tactical nuclear weapons are more likely to grow if there is pressure from the United States—on an official and expert level—to discuss the issue. Without that pressure, domestic motivations for debating the future of nonstrategic nuclear arms control will not be enough. Because the implementation of the 1991–92 presidential nuclear initiatives has been declared a success by the Russian government, there is little interest in the subject. However, if the Russian government were to revise its commitments, then experts within Russia would probably focus more attention on Russia's tactical nuclear weapons.

This chapter will provide an overview of the major issues shaping Russian thought on the modern role of its nuclear forces. Following an assessment of the data set, it will then discuss the problem of defining tactical nuclear weapons and explore how they emerged in the context of nuclear arms control negotiations and treaties. Russian doctrine on tactical nuclear weapons is also reviewed to provide perspective on the views of Russian officials and understand the structure of Russian forces. As will be argued, the official Russian position on tactical nuclear weapons has not been made available to the public. However, an interpretation of official statements suggests that Russia is, in fact, embarking on programs to modify existing tactical nuclear weapons or to develop new warheads. This chapter will also assess the role tactical nuclear weapons may play in regional deterrence.

Problems of Classifying Nuclear Weapons

In the late 1980s it was possible to encounter an understanding of certain terms and criteria for classification of a nuclear weapon as a tactical nuclear weapon, versus a strategic nuclear weapon.[2] However, in later discussions this issue was generally ignored, although it has remained topical. The need for continued attention to defining tactical nuclear weapon has been evident in recent discussions of arms control matters. George Lewis and Andrea Gabbitas, for example, note at least seven criteria by which a nuclear weapon could be defined as "tactical." These include range, target, yield, ownership (whether in terms of command structure or national ownership), delivery vehicle, and a definition by exclusion (meaning any nuclear weapon not already covered by strategic arms control treaties). However, the authors conclude that "none of these approaches is entirely suitable . . . [because of] the overall similarity between some types of strategic and tactical weapons."[3] Ambiguities surrounding various terms and notions, implying different meanings, are unacceptable for serious discussions on nuclear issues. They should ideally be based on an adequate and clear understanding of a set of terms used by all involved parties.

Defining Tactical Nuclear Weapons in an Historical Context

In the late 1960s, when the SALT talks started, the USSR and the United States urgently needed to determine what weapons systems would become subject to negotiations and define the category of strategic arms. The Soviet Union proposed to regard as strategic all systems of the two states capable of reaching the territory of the other superpower. However, because Washington considered its nuclear arms in Europe to be tactical and not subject to the arms control agreements, this would have meant the commitment to negotiate its nuclear weapons forward deployed in Europe (hence, making the process of limitation asymmetrical for the two states).

At the completion of negotiations, the parties could not come to any agreement on the universal definition for the strategic weapons. They did agree, however, that the treaties would cover the nuclear arms deployed on the national territory and capable of hitting the enemy's territory.

SALT I was a unique agreement, because it provided only vague terms defining the subject matter of the treaty. Articles I and III included some indication of the scope of the treaty: intercontinental ballistic missile (ICBM) launchers (Art. I) and submarine-launched ballistic missiles (SLBM) launchers (Art. III). Nonetheless, at that time, the parties had no clear notion of what the ICBMs and SLBMs were. They agreed that ICBMs were land-based missiles deployed on the territory of one state and capable of reaching the territory of the other, although ambiguity in defining differences on the minimal flight trajectory remained. It proved even more difficult to define the SLBMs, since their ability to hit the enemy's territory depends on the distance between the submarine and the coastline of the potential adversary. At that time, the parties failed to solve the problem and, despite the implementation of the treaty, they provided an inadequate definition of strategic arms.

SALT II gave a more detailed and better-thought-out description of the weapons to which the agreement pertained. In SALT II the parties came to a mutual understanding of what criteria to apply to the ICBMs, which they agreed was a range of 5,500 km and more. Moreover, the treaty also covered SLBMs, the heavy bombers, the air-launched cruise missiles (ALCMs) (with a range over 600 km), air-launched ballistic missiles (with a range exceeding 600 km), and the land-based and sea-based cruise missiles (with a range exceeding 600 km).[4]

START I and START II were increasingly specific, but still excluded entire groupings of nuclear weapons. According to START I and START II, the provisions of the treaties apply to ICBMs, SLBMs, heavy bombers, sea-based cruise missiles (with a range over 600 km), and air-launched ballistic missiles (with a range over 600 km; these weapons have been prohibited under the treaty).[5] The new treaty between Russia and the United States on nuclear potentials is also vague on the subject of the arrangement. It applies to "strategic nuclear warheads," which is a term that had not been used in previous treaties and remains undefined in the May 2002 treaty.

Thus, proceeding from the scope of SALT and START agreements, types of nuclear weapons can be singled out that are not considered to be strategic. Specifically, according to these agreements, nonstrategic nuclear weapons are the following:

◆ warheads attributed to nonstrategic bombers and tactical air force units;

◆ nuclear armaments on surface ships and submarines (except long-range, sea-based cruise missiles and SLBMs);

◆ warheads attributed to naval aviation, nuclear artillery, and ballistic missiles with a range not exceeding 5,500 km;

◆ land-based cruise missiles and ALCMs with a range not exceeding 600 km; and

◆ sea-based cruise missiles, atomic demolition munitions, and interceptor nuclear warheads.

The majority of the above weapon systems became the object of the unilateral presidential nuclear initiatives launched by the United States and Russia in 1991–92. Therefore, taking into account the course of negotiations, strategic weapons could be considered as those covered by SALT I and II and START I and II. Nonstrategic nuclear weapons are those not covered by these treaties.

However, such classification is not universal. These treaties actually contain no definitions of any weapons systems; they merely list weapons systems that are to be eliminated or limited, in accordance with the agreement between the parties. Because the scope of the START treaties has been expanding, the current list of weapons identified in START I and START II cannot be regarded as a final version. Russia for many years insisted on negotiating the issue of the long-range, sea-based cruise missiles, which proves that at least one party to the START process does not consider this list to be final. Thus, it is not quite correct to base the classification into tactical and strategic weapons on the scope of the treaties dealing with strategic offensive arms.

Other ways to divide nuclear arms into tactical and strategic have been proposed. For example, it has been suggested that strategic nuclear weapons are those that reach the territory of the potential enemy (Russia and the United States) when launched from the national territory or submarines; all other weapons are nonstrategic.[6] Some U.S. experts suggested a more detailed classification based on the same fundamental principle. Their main criteria were the territory of launch and targeting. According to these experts, strategic nuclear weapons were based in Soviet and U.S. territory and on the class of nuclear-fueled ballistic missiles (SSBNs) of naval fleets, and were designated for targeting each other's territory. Intermediate-range nuclear arms were U.S. nuclear weapons in Western Europe targeted at the Soviet Union and Soviet nuclear weapons on Soviet territory targeted at Western Europe. Tactical nuclear arms were U.S. nuclear weapons in Western Europe targeted at Eastern Europe and Soviet nuclear weapons on Soviet territory targeted at Western Europe.[7] The shortcomings of such classifications were obvious. On the one hand, the difference between Soviet intermediate-range and tactical weapons was unclear. On the other hand, under such classification, the USSR/Russia could not differentiate between U.S. strategic and intermediate-range nuclear weapons.

At the start of the SALT talks, the Soviet leadership indicated to the United States that its intermediate- and short-range nuclear forces in Europe could perform strategic tasks against the USSR. At that time, Washington disagreed. Nonetheless, a substantial part of the U.S. arms control community later agreed that the U.S. intermediate-range nuclear weapons deployed in Europe were strategic for the USSR.[8] At the same time, Soviet specialists emphasized that, for Europeans, there was practically no difference between strategic and tactical nuclear weapons as far as the consequences of their use were concerned. This was a paradox: the same type of weapon was tactical and strategic for different parties.[9]

In the 1990s a new classification emerged based on the nuclear warheads yield. This variant provided for numerous interpretations, since the yield threshold could be selected arbitrarily. Nonetheless, the classification was logical because it was a modification of the system based on definitions of "tactical" and "strategic." The meaning depended on the scale of combat operations and, thus, the classification proceeded from this assumption. Tactical operations are of a smaller scale, so they require nuclear weapons with lower yields. Unfortunately, this method cannot be used in practice, because some tactical nuclear weapons (in accordance with the general classification) have higher yields than strategic nuclear weapons (as defined in the START treaties). For instance, the U.S. tactical bomb B-61 has a yield of 300 KT, whereas the warheads mounted on Trident strategic missiles have a yield of 150 KT.

Some researchers proposed to make the strategic and tactical classifications dependent on the designation of the weapons. For instance, it was suggested that counterforce weapons be called "tactical" and countervalue weapons called "strategic."[10]

If the classification based on range has a known criterion subject to verification, the functional classification produces more difficulties. This is because reliable data about nuclear weapons and their use can be found only in the strategic plans of the General Staff, and this information has never been disclosed (and is very unlikely to be disclosed in the future), unlike the technical characteristics. Nonetheless, the designation of a particular type of nuclear weapon can be discerned by analyzing its characteristics. However, this assessment is not foolproof, because practical experience demonstrates that there can be different interpretations of the same characteristics. For example, Western experts have long portrayed SLBMs as nuclear weapons designed for retaliatory strike and have maintained that they cannot be used for preemptive strikes to "disarm" the enemy. Russian specialists, in contrast, hold the opposite point of view (at least in public debate). Another example is the difference in approaches to the designation of SS-18 heavy missiles. Americans have always believed that these missiles serve as a preemptive "disarming" strike,[11] while Russians have criticized this position and rightly point out that, until the late 1970s, SS-18 did not have the required accuracy to accomplish such tasks. For all of these reasons, the classification can exist only if there are objective and verifiable data. Otherwise, the problem of criteria cannot be resolved, since lack of reliable information generates some subjective interpretations and conjectures.

The classification of nuclear weapons into strategic and tactical has traditionally been combined with the range criterion. As a result, long-range missiles are more often named strategic missiles and tactical nuclear weapons have become synonymous with shorter-range missiles There is no single opinion on whether to include the intermediate-range nuclear weapons in the tactical classification.[12] They are frequently referred to as the intermediate-range nuclear force (INF) only, that is, they have been left out of the tactical-strategic classification. However, U.S. reasoning on this point is questionable, because the U.S. military divides classification into strategy and tactics only, which implies that all nonstrategic weapons should be automatically referred to as tactical and vice versa. The Soviet military singled out one more intermediate level between strategy and tactics, known as "operational art." With this nomenclature, it might be possible to refer to INF weapons as operational, since they have never been regarded as strategic and have not always been referred to as tactical.

Russia refers to nuclear weapons with the following terms:

Strategic offensive arms. As a rule, these contain launchers that are covered by START I and START II provisions. This term is widely used in various official documents.

Strategic nuclear forces (SNF). According to the federal law "On Financing the Strategic Nuclear Forces" of 1999, the SNF are "the strategic offensive weapons of the Strategic Missile Forces (SMF), the Navy, and the Air Force, the means and systems of the Aerospace Missile Defense (AMD) (early warning of missile attack, control over outer space, missile defense) and the SNF's command and control systems." The law has a reservation that the aforementioned definition is legally applicable only to the provisions of this law. Normally, the term "SNF" is used as a synonym for the strategic offensive arms. The term is widely used in various official documents.

Substrategic nuclear forces. This term, which is not used officially, usually refers to medium-range heavy bombers and missiles with a range of 3,500–5,500 km.

Tactical nuclear weapons (TNW). There are several usages of this term. First, it can refer to all nonstrategic nuclear weapons. In this case the term is used as a synonym for nonstrategic nuclear weapons and also covers intermediate-range and shorter-range missiles. Second, the term can also mean battlefield nuclear weapons, which are nuclear weapons with a range of several hundred kilometers. Hence, in this meaning, tactical nuclear weapons are regarded as a type of nonstrategic nuclear weapon. Third, tactical nuclear weapons are also defined as all types of nuclear weapons that are covered by the 1991–92 presidential nuclear initiatives between the USSR/Russia and the United States. Generally, the term is used in official documents normally in its second and third meaning. Nonofficial research papers use this term in all three meanings.

Operational-tactical nuclear weapons. There is no clear understanding of this term. It is known that operational-tactical nuclear weapons included "Oka" missiles, which were covered by the INF Treaty. It is more likely that this class of weapons included missiles with ranges not exceeding 1,000 km; SS-20 missiles, presumably, were not referred to as operational-tactical. Many experts believe that the lowest range for such weapons is 500 km, which may lead them to conclude that all operational-tactical missiles that the USSR possessed were eliminated under the INF Treaty. However, "Oka" missiles had a shorter range, so the USSR may have included in this category missiles with a range of about 400 km and, perhaps, even 300 km. Therefore, Russia may still possess operational-tactical nuclear weapons, in accordance with the Russian inner classification. Moreover, this category comprises tactical aircraft armed with nuclear weapons. The term "operational-tactical" is rarely used in official documents. One exception is the 1996 *Presidential National Security Address to the Federal Assembly of the Russian Federation*, which states that Russia's arsenal contains strategic nuclear forces as well as operational-tactical and tactical nuclear weapons.[13]

Intermediate-range nuclear weapons. At present, this term is rarely used in Russia. It was more popular in the mid-1980s during the negotiations on nuclear arms limitations in Europe. Later, when the parties defined the scope and framework of the INF talks, this term was no longer used in the Soviet Union. Although in English the treaty is called INF, the Russian translation is "The Treaty on Intermediate-Range and Shorter-Range missiles." The terms "medium-range missiles" and "shorter-range missiles" were used deliberately to define the missiles covered by the INF Treaty: 1,000–5,500 km and 500–1,000 respectively.

All above-mentioned terms imply that the classification of nuclear weapons depends on the range of missiles. Moreover, land-based missiles defy clearer description in accordance with various categories. Thus, there are no universal definitions for tactical and strategic nuclear weapons. It is under the conditions of this ambiguity that the debate on classification continues.

In theory, the most logical way to proceed with international arms control negotiations is to work out universally applicable terms. However, in practice, the accepted classification, which uses range as the standard but employs the terms "tactical" and "strategic," rules out chances for elaborating the common terminology even for the U.S.-Russian dialogue. For nuclear forces of other states it is even more difficult.

The Role of Substrategic Nuclear Weapons after the Cold War

The breakup of the bipolar world resulted in dramatic changes in the global geopolitical situation, which affected the perceived role of nuclear weapons in international security arrangements. The employment of tactical nuclear weapons has always been called into question.[14] At the same time, it was useful during the Cold War to preserve and modernize TNWs, because these weapons served as an additional *field of competition* and expanded the capabilities of the states to project their power, making the process of exerting pressure (the escalation of confrontation) more flexible.

In the USSR, tactical nuclear weapons were believed to be a viable option in a strategic war with the United States,[15] and that this employment would take two forms. First, they might have been used to conduct strategic operations in the theater of war (TOW). In the past the views concerning the form and character of strategic warfare were different from contemporary concepts. During the time of the Cold War, the military believed that a strategic war between the two superpowers would be nuclear but would not be limited to nuclear missile warfare using strategic nuclear forces only.[16] The military planning of both parties included conducting large-scale operations in continental and sea areas of war with the use of conventional forces,[17] which would have been grouped into strategic units. Tactical nuclear weapons were aimed at reinforcing these units if strategic nuclear weapons were used. Thus, the dominating view on the form of strategic nuclear war was that tactical nuclear weapons formed a systematic element of the strategic conflict.

This concept was extremely popular in the USSR, because a large part of the theater of war, which would have served for the strategic operations in case of global conflict, was adjacent to Soviet borders. The success of hostilities in this area (in accordance with the logic of the past) would have been decisive for the outcome of the conflict (i.e., the strategic mission). Moreover, successful operations would have enabled the USSR to divert the strategic forces of the enemy from Soviet territory and, thus, the tactical mission would have been accomplished.

The United States was less inclined to regard tactical nuclear weapons as a systematic element of the strategic conflict. The problem of diverting the enemy's strategic forces from U.S. territory was solved with the peculiar deployment (functional and territorial) of its strategic nuclear arsenal. In addition, the United States preferred to accomplish strategic missions without the large-scale use of conventional forces on the TOW, and without tactical nuclear weapons employment. Nonetheless, some systems we consider to be tactical were to be used in strategic nuclear conflict in accordance with the U.S. military plans. These were short-range and intermediate-range nuclear missiles, which were designed for early stages of the conflict. The plans for their use in combat led Russia to conclude that the missiles deployed in Europe transformed into a strategic resource in the hands of the United States and its allies.

The second way in which tactical nuclear weapons might be used is in the course of the conflict before it even reaches the military phase: as a foreign policy resource and a bargaining chip. Tactical nuclear weapons enabled the resolution of differences using fewer resources, in other words, at a lower price.[18] It is noteworthy that this scenario of the tactical nuclear weapons use was possible only because the parties did not doubt the readiness of each other to employ the tactical nuclear weapons.

Nowadays, another vision of strategic nuclear warfare prevails, which is confined to nuclear missile warfare. (Of course, the prevailing political view is that no strategic nuclear conflict is possible, but remaining warfare plans have been largely unaltered since the end of the Cold War.) This variant fits the conditions of strategic nuclear weapons employment better than the aforementioned concepts, because it is hardly possible that conventional forces will be able to accomplish any combat missions once the SNF become the major means of combat. In the early 1990s it became clear that Russia was not able to conduct large-scale conventional military operations. This is why Russian and U.S. military commanders regard this option as unlikely, although military planning may continue to envisage the conducting of strategic operations in the theater of war.

However, the United States and Russia are now reportedly working on fourth- or fifth-generation nuclear warheads: the so-called *pure* selective warheads (with the low collateral damage). Their development is designed to remove the obstacles for the actual combat use of tactical nuclear weapons on the battlefield, because the supposed inapplicability of the tactical stems from the *dirty* character of the present-day tactical nuclear warheads.[19]

Now researchers in the United States and Russia, favoring the further development of tactical nuclear weapons, usually refer to them as the best way to maintain nuclear deterrence on a regional level. However this rationale cannot help but to raise serious questions and doubts. The issue is not only how successful new research work on low-yield nuclear weapons will be. A more serious problem is the deterrent paradigm for these new weapons and for situations in which they are supposed to be engaged. The military component of deterrence consists of two elements, meaning that it is possible to prevent the enemy's victory in two ways. The first is by demonstrating the ability to repel the enemy's aggression. The second is by demonstrating the ability to increase the resources that the enemy must expend (outside the battlefield) so that it lessens its advantages. In the first case, the enemy's victory is prevented, in the second case, the enemy is deprived of a true victory.

At a regional level, threats to Russia are possible from all directions. The peculiarity of the eastern and southern *fronts* is that those threats will originate from authoritarian (totalitarian) regimes. The western direction has its peculiarities as well, since the adversaries are democratic regimes with a low *threshold of pain*. (This will be discussed later in the chapter.) Threats can be characterized in different ways. For shaping a policy of deterrence, principal importance should be placed on the source of the threat. The psychological nature of deterrence makes it necessary to assess the behavior of the opposite side and its leaders, that is, the source of the threat, which becomes the key criterion.

In democratic and nondemocratic regimes, there are different mechanisms for obtaining and holding on to power. The ruling elites assess the level of damage they are ready to sustain in order to keep the power. In fact, this is similar to the problem of unacceptable damage, not only for the country (its ability to survive and restore the economy) but also for the ruling elite (its ability to stay in power). As for the unacceptable damage to the country, it is practically the same in democratically and nondemocratically governed states, and its formula, if calculated, can be applied to both. As for the damage to the elite, the situation is different: in nondemocratic states the leadership may be ready to put up with a higher level of damage, and this should be taken into account. Here the *threshold of pain* would be higher, and hence, an efficient deterrent can be maintained only with the threat of higher damage to the population and the country on the whole.

This logic of unacceptable damage for the nondemocratic regimes runs counter to the logic of reliance on tactical nuclear weapons. Tactical, not strategic, weapons are supposed to compensate for weak conventional forces to prevent overkill. Tactical nuclear weapons advocates suggest that the weapons be used against the enemy troops engaged in combat but with certain limits. They believe that the enemy's leadership will retreat after such attack. However, in the case of nondemocratic regimes, it would be more difficult to get away with limited tactical nuclear forces.

The peculiarities of power legitimization in nondemocratic states hamper the task of containing such regimes with the threat of war, that is, with the threat of hostilities and combat operations against the army. If this threat fails, the nondemocratic leader will evidently benefit: the leader will gain what he or she wanted. If the threat succeeds, the nondemocratic regime may lose the war, the population will suffer, and the country will be ruined, but the leadership could survive. Moreover it may even use foreign aggression or its threat to consolidate support internally. The 1991 war against Iraq is a good example of this. Besides that, threatening the use of tactical nuclear weapons in such cases against totalitarian regimes inevitably meets resistance from the international community. This resistance may be effectively used by a target regime to prevent use of any force against it and, therefore, may help the regime survive.

In nondemocratic elite decision making under such a situation, the relative possible gains are always higher than the relative possible losses. The scheme below demonstrates the peculiarity of the situation.

$$-1 \qquad - \qquad 0 \qquad + \qquad +1$$

0   the situation before the conflict, that is, status quo;

$(-)$ the area of failure of the threat, that is, the nondemocratic regime wins or avoids the armed conflict;

$(+)$ the area of efficient threat, that is, the nondemocratic regime loses the armed conflict;

(-1) extreme value on the $(-)$ area, when the nondemocratic regime gains what it wanted to gain in the conflict or avoids the conflict;

$(+1)$ extreme value on the $(+)$ area, when the nondemocratic elite loses power after the armed conflict.

The nondemocratic regime usually reaches the extreme value of the $(-)$ area (other things being equal, there are not any evident obstacles for that and, hence, this may be regarded as an average value). To make it cross the extreme value of the $(+)$ area, it is necessary to totally defeat the country and capture the elite or to focus on the physical destruction of the elite instead of destroying the army. The first scenario is impossible in the modern world, with its international law commitments: the regime can always seek a compromise solution, negotiations, or surrender so as not to cross the $(+1)$ threshold.

This is why the relative possible gains are always higher than the relative possible losses. To correct the situation, it is necessary to facilitate the crossing of the $(+1)$ threshold, which can be done by exerting pressure on the elite and by destroying it. So, the more probable the destruction of the elite, the more effective the deterrence against the nondemocratic regime will be. This kind of deterrence can be called *deterrence through defeat of the elite.*[20]

Categories of Russian Tactical Nuclear Weapons

The nomenclature of tactical nuclear weapons is based on the armed services they are attributed to, or in accordance with the type of basing. This study will sort out tactical nuclear weapons according to the latter, since this pattern does not require any reservations about the changes in the structure of the Russian Army that have occurred or have been proposed. There are three basic categories: land, sea, and air.

Land-based tactical nuclear weapons:

♦ warheads on short-range ballistic missiles and land-based short-range cruise missiles (or, in one term, surface-to-surface short-range missiles);

♦ artillery-fired atomic projectiles;

- atomic demolition munitions (their existence has been long denied by the USSR);
- warheads of interceptor missiles (surface-to-air missiles).

Sea-based tactical nuclear weapons:

- depth bombs;
- torpedoes;
- sea-based cruise missiles.

In the 1970s the Soviet Union actively developed sea-based cruise missiles, which may account for a large part of Russia's current sea-based tactical nuclear arsenal. They were interested in developing the means for antisubmarine warfare and focused on production of depth charges for the battleships and the Navy aviation units (land-based air force units and deck helicopters), which were engaged in antisubmarine warfare. The Soviet specialists also praised the high efficiency of mine fields in antisubmarine warfare.

Airborne tactical nuclear weapons:

- air bombs;
- air-launched short-range cruise missiles;
- depth bombs;
- torpedoes.

Air bombs and short-range cruise missiles served to arm tactical aviation and medium-range bombers assigned to the Air Force. Depth charges and torpedoes armed the naval aviation units and deck helicopters.

After the 1991–92 PNIs are implemented, Russia will have only those tactical nuclear weapons assigned to the Air Force, the Navy, and the Strategic Missile Forces.[21] (The Russian Navy, besides having sea-based depth bombs, torpedoes, and cruise missiles, may also maintain tactical nuclear weapons in the naval aviation units and deck helicopters.) However, the Air Force will be the only armed service possessing active tactical nuclear weapons (airborne), because the Navy and the SMF will have to store their arms.

It is practically impossible to give a full rundown of this distribution, because the structure of unilateral reductions is unknown. For example, it is known that Russia had to eliminate one-third of its sea-based tactical nuclear weapons by 1995. But these reductions might cover all sea-based weapons, or they might deal with torpedoes and mines without covering cruise missiles. Decommissioned tactical nuclear weapons to be eliminated are normally transported to the Ministry of Defense (MOD) storage facilities and only then to the Minatom enterprises. In 1997 Russian sources confirmed the decommissioning of artillery-fired atomic projectiles and atomic demolition munitions. The head of the 12th GUMO, Lieutenant-General Igor Valynkin, said in 1997 that the mines "were decommissioned from the Army, moved from the deployment sites, and are being stored under reliable control."[22] Perhaps, the actual structure of tactical nuclear weapons may contain air bombs, ALCM warheads, depth charges, torpedoes, warheads of the interceptor missiles, and warheads of the sea-based cruise missiles.

There is also ambiguous information about the production of tactical nuclear warheads in Russia. On the one hand, a senior MOD official has stated that production stopped in 1992.[23] On the other hand, some ministry officials have, in off-the-record interviews, either evaded the issue or indirectly confirmed that production goes on. In 1996 members of the Russian delegation at the Conference on Disarmament stated that "the production of nuclear munitions for land-based tactical missiles, artillery-fired atomic projectiles, and atomic demolition munitions has been canceled."[24] This could mean that Russia continues to produce tactical nuclear warheads for the Air Force, the Navy, and, perhaps, for the interceptors of missile defense system stationed around Moscow. The latter may be particularly true, because the Russian missile defense system around Moscow remains operational.

Tactical Nuclear Weapons Totals

The total number of tactical nuclear weapon is still not known. In the late 1980s and the early 1990s, U.S. and Soviet tactical nuclear arsenals were estimated at 15,000 to 25,000 warheads each.[25] In 1994 U.S. Secretary of Defense William Perry numbered the Russian tactical nuclear arsenal at 6,000 to13,000 warheads.[26] The possible margin of error (uncertainty) is more than 100 percent. And it is not clear whether he meant the total amount of tactical nuclear arms or only commissioned weapons. There have been other widely varied estimates of Russian arsenals: 7,000[27] to 7,740[28] warheads; 3,800[29] to 4,400[30] warheads. The most up-to-date estimates appear in this book in Joshua Handler's chapter.

There is no open data on the quantitative parameters of the Russian tactical nuclear arsenal. Attempts to calculate them come up against certain difficulties. The primary obstacle is the lack of starting point for the calculations. Before the inception of unilateral initiatives by Presidents George H. W. Bush and Mikhail Gorbachev, the gap in the data was at average 50–100 percent from either side of the lower figure. Since that time, in accordance with official statements, the parties have been implementing the commitments under the PNIs. The peculiar feature of the initiatives is that all commitments are stated in relative figures without absolute numbers.

Tactical Nuclear Weapons Command and Control System

There are two views on who controls the command and control of Russia's tactical nuclear weapons. The first is that the whole system (SNF and tactical nuclear weapons) is under the control of the president, who authorizes nuclear arms employment with the help of his *nuclear briefcase,* among other means.[31] The second is that the chain of command of tactical nuclear weapons is less centralized and the order can come from lower levels of command.

The specific patterns of decision making concerning tactical nuclear weapons employment have not been revealed. However, one cannot preclude that the role of the military in this system has recently increased, and the commander of the military district (strategic direction) may take an independent decision on the time and place of their use (presumably after obtaining the principal consent of the political leadership for nuclear weapons employment). This may mean that there are no technical safeguards against or limitations to using tactical nuclear weapons at this level of command.

In 1998 President Yeltsin signed a decree changing the structure of the armed forces, the system of command, and the chain of command. This document, *Basic Provisions of the RF State Policy in the Area of Military Construction until 2005,* has not been publicly released, although it was supposed to appear in the press immediately after its adoption. Six military districts were established: Leningradsky (including the Komi Republic), Moskovsky (without changes), Privolzhsko-Uralsky (the combination of the Privolzhsky and the Uralsky military districts; the implementation of this plan has a vague deadline), Siberian (including a part of the Zabaikalsky military district; the Siberian military district should be established in the near future), Far Eastern (including Yakutia, which was previously in the Zabaikalsky military district), and North Caucasian.

Earlier that year, President Yeltsin had approved these divisions with his decree *Statute of the RF Military District,* which had been prepared by the General Staff. The statute refers to the military district as "the primary military-administrative unit and the operational-tactical territorial unit of the Russian Armed Forces." This meant that each of these districts could be regarded as a strategic *direction* but with different names. The Northwestern strategic direction corresponds with the borders of the Leningradsky military district; the Western with the Moskovsky district; the Southwestern with the North Caucasian district; the Central Asian with the Privolzhsko-Uralsky district; the Siberian with the Siberian district; the Far Eastern with the Far Eastern district.

The 1998 concept means that military districts become basic units in the system of command and control. It increased the independence of the district commander. Now the commander can put troops on alert and issue the order to use these forces in local conflicts. It is not quite clear how much the tactical nuclear weapons command and control system has changed, because they are assigned to the Air Force and the Navy (the Army's tactical nuclear weapons were decommissioned and stored at storage facilities at the MOD and the Minatom).

Implementing the 1991–92 Presidential Nuclear Initiatives

The Soviet Union/Russia launched two unilateral initiatives in the early 1990s. In October 1991 President Gorbachev set forth an initiative in response to U.S. steps;[32] in January 1992 President Boris Yeltsin reaffirmed and expanded the Russian commitment to the earlier initiative.[33]

In September 1991 President George H. W. Bush laid down a unilateral initiative on tactical nuclear weapons limitations and reductions.[34] President Gorbachev put forward a reciprocal unilateral initiative, which repeated the provisions of Bush's document and were confined to the following:

- ◆ elimination of artillery-fired atomic projectiles and nuclear warheads of the tactical missiles;
- ◆ de-alerting and storing at central storage facilities of the warheads of interceptors, and their partial elimination;
- ◆ elimination of all atomic demolition devices;
- ◆ decommissioning and storage of tactical nuclear weapons attributed to surface ships and attack submarines; some of these are subject to elimination; and
- ◆ storage and partial elimination of tactical nuclear weapons attributed to the Navy's land-based aviation units.

Moreover, the Soviet leader also proposed to carry out the following additional reciprocal measures with respect to the tactical nuclear weapons:

- ◆ elimination of the naval tactical nuclear weapons;
- ◆ de-alerting and storage of the tactical nuclear weapons assigned to the tactical air force units.

In 1992, during his visit to the United States, President Yeltsin reiterated Russia's commitment to the Gorbachev unilateral initiatives and stated that all warheads of the short-range missiles, artillery-fired atomic projectiles, atomic demolition devices, one-third of sea-based tactical nuclear weapons, half of the warheads attributed to the interceptor missiles, and half of the Air Force tactical nuclear weapons would be destroyed.

President Yeltsin's statement was perceived not as replacing the commitments, which constituted Russia's legacy from the Soviet Union, but as a set of additional measures. There were no objections from the Russian side. Thus, to realize the full scope of Russian commitments, the two initiatives should be combined.

The result is the following:

- ◆ warheads of short-range missiles, artillery-fired atomic projectiles and atomic demolition munitions are subject to complete elimination;

- ◆ warheads of interceptors should be decommissioned and stored at central bases; half of them are subject to elimination;
- ◆ tactical nuclear weapons attributed to surface ships and attack submarines are to be decommissioned and stored; one third is subject to elimination;
- ◆ tactical nuclear weapons attributed to the Navy's aviation units are to be decommissioned and stored, partly eliminated;
- ◆ tactical nuclear weapons attributed to the Air Force (tactical air force units and medium-range bombers)—half of them are subject to elimination (in accordance with the *open* plan—only half of the bombs).

The combination of the two initiatives poses several questions concerning the structure of tactical nuclear forces. According to some sources, naval tactical nuclear weapons were also attributed to the deck helicopters (Ka-25, Ka-27), beside the intermediate-range bombers, surface ships, and submarines. The Soviet initiative dealt with the surface ships, and it is not clear whether it covered deck helicopters. Regardless of Gorbachev's intended meaning, today the interpretations vary. President Yeltsin spoke about sea-based tactical nuclear weapons. This definition allows for the inclusion of deck helicopters, but it is still not clear whether they are covered or not. These commitments cannot be translated into concrete figures and one can speak only of relative figures and the reduction by the armed services.

Although the PNIs did not indicate a timescale for their implementation, in 1994 Russia announced a schedule for the work to be carried out. The schedule included: elimination of all mines by 1998; artillery ammunition by 2000; warheads of land-based missiles by 2000; half of the warheads of interceptors by 1996; one-third of the sea-based tactical nuclear weapons by 1995; and half of the air bombs by 1996.[35]

The Air Force units were supposed to possess not only air bombs but also ALCMs, with a range not exceeding 600 km. These arms were mounted on the medium-range bombers assigned to the Air Force. The Soviet fighter-bomber aircraft could carry only bombs (no more than one), but it is presumed that they had no nuclear arms on board. In this connection, it is not clear why the *open* plan speaks only about bombs.

According to this schedule, the implementation should have been finished by 2000. This was endorsed by Ministry of Foreign Affairs spokesman A. Demurin in 1996.[36] In October 1998, the head of the 12th GUMO, Igor Valynkin, reaffirmed that "Russia strictly adheres to international obligations to destroy some kinds of tactical nuclear weapons." He also maintained that "nuclear mines and shells are being destroyed according to plan" and "when there is an agreement with the United States on destroying the remaining part of tactical weapons, Russia will embark on their destruction."[37]

However, in 2000 the Russian minister of foreign affairs, during the NPT

Review Conference in New York, reaffirmed the Russian commitment to the unilateral initiative with a slightly different deadline—by the end of 2000. Neither the absence of Russian reporting in late 2000 about successful implementation of the initiatives nor the statement on extending the deadline, nor the lack of reporting by the expiration date of this new deadline, produced any visible uneasiness with the U.S. administration or expert community. The former may be explained by preliminary bilateral consultation, which presumably was taking place between Russian and U.S. representatives on tactical nuclear weapons. However, the latter may be attributed only to lack of interest.

Moreover, unilateral initiatives did not have a schedule of implementation, so Russia was free to produce whatever public deadline it wanted and then alter and re-alter it (as actually happened in April 2002). The Russian statement on Article VI at the NPT PrepCom reads: "Russia plans to complete implementation of the initiatives in the sphere of NSNW (nonstrategic nuclear weapons), by 2004. . . ." However, the end of this phrase, "on condition of adequate financing," does not exclude further extending the deadline in part because of domestic reasons not conditioned to any international military affairs. The latter proves Russia's commitment to be generally unconditional.

The shifting of this deadline is very likely to be the result of Russian financial constraints, as it is reflected in the previous citation. Nonetheless, it is incorrect to say that Russia does not have money to implement the initiatives. More likely, Russia decided to save on the implementation by correlating 1991–92 commitments with internal plans on weapons destruction. The prominent Russian strategist Alexei Arbatov, who is currently deputy chief of the Defense Committee in the State Duma and whose estimates on tactical nuclear weapons prove to be the most reliable, wrote in 1999: "Most [Russian] tactical nuclear munitions earmarked for destruction by 1997, in accordance with the commitments of the Soviet Union and Russian Federation, were to be eliminated anyway by 2003 because their design lives will have expired. This means that the undertakings with regard to tactical nuclear weapons would boil down to the obligation to limit production of new weapons to replace physically obsolete ones."[38] This assumption of Russia to correlate internal plans and international commitments is also supported by the language of the "Russian statement on Article VI" of April 11, 2002: "These initiatives of the Russian Federation are being implemented in accordance with the Federal objective-oriented program of elimination and disposal of nuclear warheads for strategic and tactical arms." The program mentioned is an internal document without direct links to international obligations, because it refers to warheads for strategic missiles, which are not subject to treaty-scheduled dismantlement.

The status of the implementation as of April 2002 was outlined in the above-referred "Russian statement on Article VI" of 11 April 2002:

♦ all nonstrategic nuclear weapons have been dismantled from surface ships and multiple-purpose submarines, as well as from ground-based Naval Air Force and placed for centralized storage; more than 30 percent of nuclear munitions of the total number designed for tactical sea-launched missiles and naval air force have been eliminated;
♦ all tactical nuclear munitions previously deployed outside Russia have been brought back to her territory and are being eliminated;
♦ production of nuclear munitions for tactical ground-launched missiles, nuclear artillery shells, and nuclear mines has been completely stopped; the destruction of nuclear reentry vehicles for tactical missiles and nuclear artillery shells, as well as nuclear mines, continues;
♦ 50 percent of nuclear reentry vehicles for surface-to-air missiles and 50 percent of nuclear air bombs of their total number have been destroyed;
♦ all Russian nonstrategic nuclear weapons have been placed only within national territory.

Although the latter item is not the obligation of the 1991–92 initiatives, it should be regarded as a Russian free and goodwill addition, rather than the reason to doubt the whole status report. The document concludes: "Russia has practically implemented all the declared initiatives to reduce NSNW with the exception of elimination of nuclear weapons of the Army."

It is difficult to undertake any independent assessment of the implementation process, however, because there are no accurate data and verification mechanisms. So far no one has doubted the fact that the initiatives are being carried out, although there might have been some obvious difficulties relating to the elimination of tactical nuclear weapons. The process of elimination may be impeded by the lack of funding and the Russian military's belief that the schedule of nonverified commitments can be adjusted. Incidentally, in that case there would be no need to finance them as top-priority programs, as presumably did happen.

The other factor that may hamper the process is the insufficient capacity of Minatom enterprises. Most likely, the capacity of Minatom enterprises and the lack of funding did not allow the dismantlement of strategic warheads eliminated in accordance with the internal plans (following elimination of missiles under START I) and tactical warheads eliminated under the 1991–92 initiatives within the initial time framework. It may be that the arms mentioned in the initiatives are decommissioned and not dismantled. The implementation of the initiatives may be reduced to ceasing the implementation of combat plans involving the delivery of tactical nuclear weapons to the combat zones. Like the implementation of the initiatives, none of these details can be verified.

Russian Policy on Tactical Nuclear Weapons

Most publicly available Russian documents related to military and foreign policy planning (*Concept of National Security*, *Basic Provisions of the Military Doctrine* and *Military Doctrine*) do not mention tactical nuclear weapons. The only official Russian document in which they are mentioned is the *Presidential National Security Address to the Federal Assembly* (1996),[39] where tactical and substrategic nuclear weapons are referred to as means to pursue the policy of nuclear deterrence on local and regional levels.

In the 1990s, there has been a heated discussion in Russia on the role and place of tactical nuclear weapons in military planning. A view gaining popularity with the Russian academic community is that Russian tactical nuclear weapons should compensate for the weaknesses of its conventional force. This belief stems from the NATO position adopted in the late 1950s, which held that nuclear weapons could be used to compensate for the USSR's superior conventional forces. At that time, the USSR had superiority in conventional forces in Europe and, to deter the Soviets, the Alliance relied on substrategic nuclear weapons.[40] Thus, to prove the advisability of tactical nuclear weapons development, contemporary Russian experts employ an argument that was valid thirty years ago. Presumably, this argument is considered to be pertinent today, since tactical nuclear weapons provide reliable and efficient compensation for the underdevelopment of conventional forces. However, this assumption is not an axiom, because NATO's reliance on tactical nuclear weapons may not have been responsible for Europe's success in preventing large-scale war. And even if it were, it would be unwise to automatically extrapolate the mechanisms of the past on the current situation. Moreover, in the late 1950s and in the early 1960s, the Western strategic planners doubted the efficiency of such TNW employment. This resulted in the concept of flexible response and in the buildup of conventional arms.[41]

At the official level, Russian authorities are silent on the matter, though they occasionally make declaratory comments. For instance, in March 1992 Russian Foreign Minister Andrei Kozyrev stated that Russia was ready to discuss the possibility of *global zero* in tactical nuclear weapons.[42] In 1996 Defense Minister Igor Rodionov, on the contrary, proposed to reinforce the tactical nuclear weapons arsenal on the Western border of the Russian Federation in response to expected NATO enlargement.[43]

Russian officials say the lack of information about Russia's tactical nuclear weapons is necessary. However, the lack of a clear position on this issue can be interpreted two ways. The absence of such a position may be accounted for by the lack of consensus in the military-political establishment or by a lack of interest in this matter. Or Russian officials might have come to a consensus, but it may run counter to the U.S. approach, and so they keep their position secret. It is also possible that they are planning to hold the information for use later as a bargaining chip, to exert pressure during negotiations.

However, substantial information on Russian attitudes toward nuclear weapons was released in April 1999. It was done in a heavily coded way, which is not unusual for Russian defense policy. Despite this, it can be decoded through a general understanding of the Russian decision-making process. On 29 April 1999, the Security Council of the Russian Federation held its regular meeting, which focused on the Russian nuclear weapons complex and strategies for its improvement. The council's decisions took the form of three top-secret documents: two presidential decrees and one program. After the meeting, Vladimir Putin, who was serving as secretary of the Security Council at that time, stated that President Yeltsin had endorsed "a blueprint for the development and use of nonstrategic nuclear weapons."[44] However, Russian and foreign experts would be incorrect to take Putin's words literally and apply them to weapon systems that had become the object of the 1991–92 presidential nuclear initiatives. Such understanding of Putin's words would inevitably lead to the conclusion that Russia had abandoned the implementation of the PNIs, but that would be incorrect. Putin had emphasized during the meeting that Russia would not refuse to comply with its commitments on any level. Putin did not distinguish between unilateral (i.e., not implying verification, and voluntarily taken) commitments and legally binding obligations within the framework of international treaties. If there is no reservation about the status of these commitments, and if there is no statement about refusal to fulfill them, international and unilateral obligations have, in fact, the same legal force.

If one was to charge Russia with abandoning its 1991 commitments, one would be interpreting Putin's words to mean that Russia has defied the international community. Yet it is unlikely that the Russian political elite would tolerate such a deception. In this vein, Putin's words must be understood as a new confirmation of Russian commitments, including those of 1991–92.

What then is the meaning of Putin's statement? When we assess the Security Council Secretary's remarks, we should take into account that there is no clear classification of nuclear weapons into either tactical or strategic arms. In practice, strategic weapons are those provided for in the START treaties; the remaining weapons are tactical. However, when we take into consideration the methods of nuclear weapon employment, such classification is no longer acceptable, because strategic arms can be used to destroy tactical targets and vice versa (although with some exceptions).

Presumably, this issue was discussed by the Security Council—not from the point of technicalities but with regard to plans and methods of combat use. More precisely, they discussed the possibility of conducting limited nuclear war with strategic means in order to deter the enemy, requiring the infliction of preplanned but limited damage. This fits the concept popular in the late 1990s within Russian military establishment (the so called "Sergeev community") of engaging strategic nuclear forces not only in "big war," but also in regional and even local conflicts (the way of engagement was not specified, at least actual use was not articulated).[45]

Hence, the Security Council discussion took place within the framework of limited strategic nuclear war. Because of the lack of clear terminology for nuclear arms classification and the lack of a satisfactory classification system, this nuclear war scenario might have been called *tactical* at the Security Council meeting. Russian military science divides military operations into tactical and strategic, using two major criteria: scale of combat operations and their consequences. Following the logic of Russian military science, this scenario could be considered tactical, taking into account that the range of combat operations and means to conduct such a war were considered tactical.

Therefore, Putin's usage of the phrase "tactical nuclear weapons" implies a new generation of nuclear munitions with regulated low-yield and super low-yield delivered to the target by strategic launchers. Some Russian media reports referred to the official bodies and reported on the intentions to modernize the current-generation nuclear munitions. In some cases, the press mentioned Minatom, in other cases, the 12th GUMO. Thus, we can draw a conclusion that there are concrete plans to perform appropriate activities using the potential of Minatom (which develops nuclear munitions) and the 12th GUMO.

Conclusion

Official Russian views on tactical nuclear weapons remain vague. However, the conclusion may be drawn that the Russian government chose to develop a new generation of nuclear warheads in the late 1990s: low-yield warheads for strategic launchers. It did so by planning to create a new warhead and modernize existing munitions to regulate their yield. In other words, Russia appeared to be embarking on the development of new versions of tactical nuclear weapons. All this seems to have been codified by the 1999 Russian Security Council meeting specifically devoted to the development of nuclear weapons.

Since that time there has been no official action taken to implement proposed changes in Russia's tactical nuclear weapons doctrine. The 1990s decision to develop or redesign low-yield warheads technically remains in place. However, subsequent developments have rendered this policy less viable. The policy decision was made under the influence of a nuclear lobby within the Russian political elite—the Strategic Missile Force—that is no longer powerful or respected.

In the summer of 2000, intermilitary disagreements in Russia culminated in a struggle between Minister of Defense Marshal Igor Sergeev (who was head of the SMF lobby) and Chief of the General Staff General Kvashnin (who was advocating conventional forces—a position supported by the heroes of the second Chechen conflict). Aside from personal motivations, their debate focused on Russia's nuclear policy. The views of the SMF lobby were inconsistent with the military establishment and prompted distrust. In the end, the SMF lost. A presidential decree was announced reforming the SMF. The SMF lost its status and major reductions in the agency were planned. Sergeev was also dismissed. This defeat was unprecedented for the SMF lobby, which had enjoyed the support of the political elite through most of the 1990s.

The SMF's downfall appears inconsistent with the Russian government's 1999 policy decision to develop new nuclear weapons, particularly tactical nuclear weapons. The obvious outcome of the nuclear lobby defeat should have been to revise Russia's nuclear policy, but this apparently did not happen. One explanation for this apparent lack of action may be that the responsibility for implementing the 1999 nuclear policy was transferred to the Russian Ministry for Atomic Energy of the Russian Federation (Minatom), where it has been given less priority. Therefore, the SMF's loss of status did not actually lead to revised policies per se.

Lowering the Threshold
Nuclear Bunker Busters and Mininukes

Robert W. Nelson

In the 2002 Nuclear Posture Review (NPR), the Defense Department recommended to Congress that the United States develop a new generation of precision low-yield nuclear warheads, "mininukes," with equivalent yields of a few kilotons of TNT or less.[1] These smaller nuclear weapons are needed, the Pentagon argues, to destroy hardened underground command bunkers and chemical or biological weapons storage sites that are otherwise inaccessible with conventional weaponry. By putting a nuclear warhead in a hardened missile casing that impacts the ground at high velocity, these weapons would penetrate into the ground before detonating so as to "threaten hard and deeply buried targets."

Proponents have argued that these smaller warheads, one-tenth the explosive size of the Hiroshima bomb, but still equivalent to over 1,000 tons of TNT, would reduce nuclear fallout and limit "collateral damage."[2] Others have argued that smaller nuclear weapons could be used in otherwise conventional conflicts against "rogue" states possessing weapons of mass destruction.[3] Indeed, in "setting the requirement for nuclear strike capabilities," the Nuclear Posture Review specifically mentions Libya, Iran, Iraq, Syria, and North Korea as potential adversaries where low-yield nuclear weapons might be used.

Some nuclear advocates have even suggested that earth-penetrating weapons could be used near urban population centers without massive civilian casualties. As one anonymous Pentagon official put it to the *Washington Post*, "What's needed now is something that can threaten a bunker tunneled under 300 meters of granite without killing the surrounding civilian population."[4]

Statements like this one have resulted in the common perception that low-yield earth-penetrating weapons could be used to make clean, surgical strikes against military targets without the usual destructive effects of blast and radioactive fallout. This is a dangerous myth. In fact, shallow buried nuclear explosions produce far more local fallout than air or surface explosions of the same yield. When used in this mode, mininukes are truly dirty weapons. Moreover, as shown in more detail below, it is not physically possible for an earth penetrator to drill deep enough into the ground to contain the explosion and fallout. Any nuclear weapon capable of destroying a buried target that is otherwise immune to conventional attack will necessarily produce enormous numbers of civilian casualties if used near an urban environment. The explosion simply blows out a massive crater of radioactive debris that rains down on the local region with an especially intense and deadly fallout.

The Pentagon's proposal to introduce low-yield warheads into the world's nuclear inventory has far broader implications for nuclear arms control. If smaller nuclear weapons are perceived as less destructive, they will be more likely to be used in otherwise conventional conflicts. Mininukes lower the nuclear threshold and make nuclear war more likely. For this reason, Congress passed an amendment to the 1994 Defense Authorization Act that prohibits U.S. nuclear laboratories from undertaking research and development that could lead to a precision nuclear weapon of less than 5 kilotons, because "low-yield nuclear weapons blur the distinction between nuclear and conventional war." This legal restriction would have to be overturned by Congress if the United States decides to build a new low-yield warhead.[5]

The immediate concern, however, is the threat that new nuclear weapons pose to the Comprehensive Test Ban Treaty (CTBT) and other arms control agreements. Although the CTBT failed Senate ratification in October 1999, and the Bush administration continues to oppose the treaty, the United States continues to abide by the world moratorium on nuclear testing. A truly new low-yield warhead—designed to survive the punishing impact shock of an earth-penetrator—would likely need to be fully tested before the weapons labs could certify that the warhead will perform according to the required military characteristics. If the United States tests, the Russian and Chinese nuclear-weapons establishments would put great pressure on their governments to allow them to do so as well. With the United States "taking the heat" for breaking the moratorium, the Chinese and Russian governments would probably not see a high international price to be paid in following suit. This will destroy any prospects for eventual entry into force of the CTBT. Collapse of the treaty would also weaken support for the already fragile Non-Proliferation Treaty (NPT).

Buried Nuclear Explosions

Deeply buried and hardened structures, like a command bunker or a missile silo, are difficult to destroy, even with an aboveground nuclear explosion. Most of the air shock energy from a nuclear blast is reflected back into the atmosphere (the large density contrast between the air and ground creates a mechanical "impedance mismatch"), and only a small fraction of the total energy is transmitted into the ground. Several meters of dirt will protect most hardened structures from all but the highest-yield weapons. Consequently, before the introduction of the earth penetrating B61-11 bomb in 1996, the 9-megaton B-53 warhead was required to destroy hardened underground targets, such as Soviet command and control bunkers.

A nuclear explosion buried by only a few meters, however, drives a much more intense and damaging seismic shock into the ground than would an air burst of the same yield. Less than 1 meter of burial increases the energy coupling by more than an order of magnitude. The warhead is thus more likely to destroy a buried hardened structure if it first penetrates into the ground near the target before detonating.

There seems to be widespread confusion, however, between this effect and the very deep earth penetration that would be required for an appreciable containment. The required depth of burial to fully contain an underground nuclear explosion depends on the particular type of rock or soil and other aspects of the geology. At the U.S. Nevada Test Site (NTS), a 1-kiloton explosion must be buried deeper than about 92 meters (300 feet). In practice, many tests at this equivalent depth have leaked radioactivity and caused carefully sealed shafts to rupture. These problems led the NTS to add an additional safety precaution, so that 1-kiloton explosions would be buried deeper than 122 meters (450 ft). A weapon of much lower explosive energy would still have to be buried at a substantial depth, because the required containment depth is only weakly sensitive to the weapon yield. Nuclear weapons as small as 0.1 kiloton still would have to be buried at a depth greater than 43 meters (140 feet) to be fully contained. As discussed below, an earth-penetrating weapon simply cannot bury itself this deeply.

The Limits to Earth Penetration

The United States already has a nuclear earth penetrator in its arsenal, the B61 Mod 11 bomb with a variable yield of 0.3–300 kilotons. The B61-11 replaced the aging B53, a 9-megaton weapon, in 1997 by putting the nuclear explosive from an earlier B61 bomb design into a hardened steel casing with a new nose cone to provide ground penetration capability. Its earth-penetrating capability is quite modest, however. In two drop tests from

Underground nuclear tests must be buried at large depths and carefully sealed in order to fully contain the explosion. The 1970 10-kiloton Baneberry nuclear test occurred 910 feet beneath the surface. Nevertheless, the explosion ruptured its stemmed shaft, and a large quantity of radioactive debris vented into the atmosphere. The cloud reached a height of 10,000 feet. Following the Baneberry venting, new containment procedures were adopted to prevent similar occurrences. Even a 0.1-kiloton explosion must be buried deeper than about 43 meters (140 feet) to be fully contained.

approximately 2.5 km (40,000 ft) near Fairbanks, Alaska, an unarmed B61-11 penetrated into frozen tundra only 2–3 meters.

An earth-penetrating weapon acts in many ways like a high-velocity nail or spike driving itself into the ground. In general, the penetration depth increases with increasing impact velocity. A missile cannot penetrate to arbitrarily large depths, however, simply by impacting at higher and higher velocities; the missile will eventually crumple—like a bending nail—because of the severe impact stresses on the missile casing. To explain this point, we can do no better than to quote George Ullrich, the civilian deputy director of the Defense Special Weapons Agency (now DTRA):[6]

> There is a limit to how deep you can get with a conventional unitary penetrator. . . . Fundamentally, you're not going to come up with a magic solution to get 100 feet or deeper in rock. If you go to higher velocities you reach a fundamental material limit where . . . the penetrator will eat itself up in the process, and in fact that will achieve less penetration than at lower velocity. So you get into these different regimes where you are really just fundamentally limited, physically, in how deep you can get into rock.

The stated goal here of 100 feet is almost certainly too optimistic. The penetration depth and crater formation of a missile impacting on a solid target depends on the mechanical response of both the target and penetrator at high-dynamic stress levels. Detailed calculations show that a missile made of the strongest steels cannot penetrate further than about four or five times the length of the missile—about 12 meters for a missile 3 meters long.[7] The most successful conventional penetrating weapon—the GBU-28—is advertised to have a penetrating capability of about 6 meters of concrete.[8]

As described above, the burial depth required to contain a nuclear explosion is very much larger than the maximum penetration depth. No earth-penetrating weapon (EPW) can penetrate a hardened site to the depths necessary to contain an explosion even as small as 0.1 kiloton. The missile will destroy itself from the intense impact stresses well before it could reach the depths required for nuclear containment.

Radioactive Fallout and Casualties

Surface and shallow-buried nuclear explosions produce much more intense local radioactive fallout than an equivalent-yield high-altitude burst, where the fireball does not touch the ground.[9] When the fireball breaks through the surface of the earth, it carries with it into the air large amounts of dirt and debris. In addition to the radioactive fission products from the weapon itself, this material contains nuclei made temporarily radioactive by the large num-

A conventional GBU-24 earth-penetrating weapon is capable of penetrating approximately 10 feet of reinforced concrete. Note that at this depth the explosion from the warhead containing about one-half ton of conventional high explosive—one thousand times smaller than a 1-kiloton mininuke—is not contained.

The 2.3 kiloton Cabriolet Plowshare test was buried at a depth of 170 feet in hard tuff. It produced a crater 120 feet deep and 360 feet in diameter. The highly radioactive base surge reached a diameter of approximately 2 miles.

ber of neutrons produced from the nuclear detonation. The resulting radioactive dust cloud does not rise as high as a classic mushroom cloud, but typically consists of a narrow column of vented hot gas surrounded by a broad base surge of radioactive ejecta and suspended dust particles.

A nuclear explosion occurring at depths less than required for containment produces a crater. The size of the crater depends sensitively on the depth of detonation, the type of soil or rock, and the depth of the local water table. A 1-kiloton weapon detonated at a depth of 30 meters in dry soil or soft rock will produce a crater with an apparent radius of about 55 meters—more than a football field in diameter—and with an extended lip of ejecta 2 to 3 times this radius.[10] Much of the mass ejected from the crater will settle as local radioactive fallout. This means that people living within a few kilometers of a relatively low-yield explosion will suffer from almost immediate exposure to a high-radiation field.

The number of fatalities resulting from the use of an earth-penetrating nuclear weapon depends on a large number of variables: the weapon yield, the depth of penetration, the population density, evacuation time, weather conditions, and local terrain. Without a detailed model, only approximate "back of the envelope" estimates can be made. The results are nevertheless striking. If a 1-kiloton earth-penetrating weapon were used in a densely populated environment like Baghdad, several tens of thousands of people would likely receive a lethal dose of radiation, and potentially more would die from the effects of the uncontained blast and heat. It is clear that earth-penetrating weapons are not the clean, surgical weapons that some government officials and members of the media have been promoting. In this case, according to proponents from U.S. weapon laboratories, "minimal collateral damage" simply means tens of thousands of deaths rather than the hundreds of thousands of casualties associated with larger yield weapons.

The Robust Nuclear Earth Penetrator

The Bush administration's 2001 Nuclear Posture Review calls for "improved earth penetrating weapons to counter the increased use by potential adversaries of hardened and deeply buried targets." In response, the National Nuclear Security Administration (NNSA) requested in FY2003 $15.5 million to initiate a Design Definition and Cost Study (Development Phase 6.2A) for a new "Robust Nuclear Earth Penetrator" (RNEP), described as a 5,000-pound weapon that uses an existing warhead. Recent news stories indicate that both the Livermore and Los Alamos labs are already at work suggesting design improvements to the B61-11 or the B83 gravity bombs.[11] By increasing the weight of the bomb with a heavy internal ballast material and manufacturing the bomb casing from a stronger high-strength steel alloy, these weapons could be modified to increase their penetration ability somewhat. Testimony by NNSA Administrator General John Gordon indicates that the agency would still be restricted to existing warheads with yields greater than 5 kilotons, so it would not violate the 1994 Furse-Spratt amendment.

Even with a modest improvement in penetration ability, it is nevertheless impossible for an improved penetrator to contain even a small nuclear explosion. In fact, until depths of 150 feet are reached for a 1-kiloton explosion, increased penetration actually increases the size of the crater and the amount of radioactive debris dispersed. Moreover, since the greatest increase in seismic coupling occurs from the first few meters of earth penetration, further penetration does not increase the strength of the seismic shock, and the subsequent destructive power of the weapon does not help much more in destroying deeply buried targets. Indeed, as the NPR states, "For defeat of very deep or larger underground facilities, penetrating weapons with large yields would be needed to collapse the facility." We estimate that a warhead with a yield greater than 100 kilotons would be required to destroy a bunker beneath more than 100 feet of hardened concrete. Thus, low-yield nuclear weapons (i.e., 5 kilotons or less) remain ineffective for all but a very narrow range of depths.

The Real Issue: The Threat to the
Comprehensive Test Ban Treaty

Perhaps more significant, the Nuclear Posture Review states that the NNSA will also "reestablish advanced warhead concepts teams at each of the national laboratories" in order to "train our next generation of weapon designers and engineers. DoD [Department of Defense] and NNSA will also jointly . . . [assess] whether nuclear testing would be required to field such warheads." The eventual goal "is to maintain sufficient R&D and production capability to be able to design, develop, and begin production on the order of five years from a decision to enter full-scale development of a new warhead"—roughly the same length of time it took to design and produce a new nuclear weapon during the Cold War. Furthermore, the NPR restates an earlier recommendation by the Foster Panel "that DOE/NNSA assess the feasibility and cost of reducing the time [to resume testing] to 'well below the Congressionally-mandated one year.'"

The NNSA's proposed budget would move the United States toward a return to full-scale testing of nuclear weapons, which have been suspended since the previous Bush administration. If the agency gets the green light, it has the capability to return to nuclear testing within 24 to 36 months. At President Bush's direction, the NNSA and DoD are conducting a study to reexamine "the optimum test readiness time." Pending the results of that study, the budget requests $15 million to reduce the time needed to conduct a nuclear test. Any move to shorten the test readiness time would be a dangerous sign, especially when combined with activities such as the design of a new earth-penetrating nuclear weapon, a rush to certify newly produced plutonium pits for the W-88, and plans to modify every warhead in the stockpile, any of which may provide rationalization for a return to full-scale testing.

The most vocal proponents of new small-yield weapons come from the nation's nuclear weapons laboratories at Los Alamos and Livermore. A cynical interpretation of these statements would be that the laboratory staff and leadership simply feel threatened by the current restrictions on their activities and want to generate a new mission (and the associated funding) to keep them in operation indefinitely. Indeed, beginning in 1990 with the collapse of the Soviet Union and the end of the Cold War, there was serious discussion of closing one of the bomb labs.

In the 1990s U.S. nuclear weapons test explosions came to an end when President Bill Clinton signed a test moratorium in 1993 and the Comprehensive Test Ban Treaty (CTBT)—a permanent worldwide ban on nuclear testing—in 1996. Despite the Senate's failure to ratify the CTBT in 1999, its proponents believe the treaty will eventually come into force. The major nuclear powers continue to abide by the world moratorium on nuclear testing, and even India and Pakistan appear to have joined the moratorium after their May 1998 nuclear tests.

The nuclear weapons labs are particularly threatened by the CTBT, since it will probably limit them to maintaining the stockpile of weapons already in our arsenal. Keeping young scientists interested in the weapons program is especially difficult when their main job is the relatively mundane task of assuring reliability. The labs desire the challenge of designing new nuclear weapons, simply for the scientific and technical training experience the effort would bring. Hence, there is tremendous pressure to create a new mission that justifies a new development program.

But could the United States deploy a new low-yield nuclear earth-penetrating weapon without testing it? Under continued political pressure to support the CTBT and its related Stockpile Stewardship Program, Los Alamos Associate Director Steve Younger has stated, "one could design and deploy a new set of nuclear weapons that do not require nuclear testing to be certified. However . . . such simple devices would be based on a very limited nuclear test database."

Conversely, it is unlikely that a warhead capable of performing such an extraordinary mission as destroying a deeply buried and hardened bunker could be deployed without full-scale testing. First, even if the missile casing were able to withstand the high-velocity ground impact, the warhead "physics package" and accompanying electronics must function under extreme conditions. The primary device must detonate and produce a reliable yield shortly after suffering an intense shock deceleration. Second, there must be great confidence that the actual nuclear yield is not greater than expected. Since the natural energy scale for a fission nuclear weapon is of order 10 kiloton, much-lower-yield weapons must be sensitive to exacting design tolerances; the final yield is determined by an exponentially growing number of fission-produced neutrons, so the total number of neutron generations must be finely tuned. These physical considerations are generally ignored by policymakers, who assert that mininukes can be developed without full-scale testing. Given that these weapons may be used near population centers, it is highly unlikely that designers could certify a low-yield nuclear warhead without actually testing it.

What would be the consequence if the United States decides to test a new generation of nuclear weapons? As House Democrats expressed in a letter to Rep. Ike Skelton, the ranking Democrat on the House Armed Services Committee, "The resumption of nuclear test explosions that will result from such a program involving nuclear weapons would decrease rather than increase our national security and undermine U.S. and international non-proliferation efforts." If the United States abandons the test moratorium, Russia and China will almost certainly respond in kind—destroying prospects for eventual passage of the CTBT.

Discussion

Proponents of the Bush administration's plan to build new low-yield nuclear weapons have seldom been specific about situations where nuclear devices would be able to perform a unique mission. The one scenario that has been outlined involves using these warheads as a substitute for conventional weapons to attack deeply buried facilities. It is hard to imagine a realistic scenario, however, where any U.S. president would actually use a nuclear weapon against a nonnuclear state. Certainly, he or she would not order such an attack in an urban area. If located well outside an urban area, a U.S. president would likely use special forces to capture the site. Also, the Bush administration's hypothetical target—an underground bunker in a rogue state that is filled with all that state's chemical and biological weapons and whose underground geometry is known exactly but which we can't attack by any other means (e.g., the entrances and air shafts)—is a highly implausible concoction. Based on the analysis here, this type of mission appears to be impossible without causing massive radioactive contamination.

Developing nuclear weapons to be used in the developing world would be a momentous reversal of U.S. policy. All previous presidents have regarded them as weapons of very last resort. Presidents Harry Truman, Dwight Eisenhower, Lyndon Johnson, and Richard Nixon refrained from using nuclear weapons in Korea and Vietnam even when U.S. troops were in danger of being overwhelmed. Indeed, U.S. nuclear restraint became a model for the other seven nations that have acquired nuclear weapons. As a result, despite the production of tens of thousands of nuclear warheads during the last 50 years, none has been used since the United States gave the world a glimpse of nuclear hell in Hiroshima and Nagasaki. Congress understood the danger of crossing the nuclear threshold when it banned research on new nuclear warheads with yields below 5,000 tons of TNT equivalent in 1994.

More than ten years ago, President George H. W. Bush decided that the United States had no need for new nuclear weapons. This policy made it possible for the United States to push for an end to the development and testing of new nuclear weapons by all countries. The original five nuclear powers continue to abide by a world moratorium on nuclear testing, and even India and Pakistan appear to have joined the moratorium after their May 1998 nuclear tests. If the United States returns to underground nuclear testing, Russia, China, and other countries might resume nuclear testing as well. Their weaponeers surely have many improvements that they would like to make in their nuclear arsenals. Their testing would send the same signal as ours—an interest in making nuclear weapons more useable and threats of their use more credible.

Given its overwhelming superiority in conventional weaponry, U.S. security would be undercut—not enhanced—by actions encouraging nuclear proliferation or nuclear use. The world has avoided the catastrophe of nuclear warfare for over 50 years precisely because the use of nuclear weapons remains unthinkable. Attempts to develop smaller and more usable nuclear warheads would inevitably make nuclear war appear to be a feasible solution to conflict and, thus, more likely. It would also return us to the dangers of Cold War nuclear competition, but now with a larger number of nations participating.

5

Russia, NATO, and Tactical Nuclear Weapons after 11 September

Alistair Millar

Since the end of the Cold War, there have been concerns that terrorist organizations sponsored by states or individuals are actively attempting to procure improperly secured nuclear weapons, particularly from Russia, where thousands of nuclear weapons may not be adequately controlled.[1] Awareness of this potential threat has increased in the aftermath of the attacks on 11 September 2001, particularly among policymakers in Washington and its NATO allies. President George W. Bush told the American public that the Al-Qaeda network was seeking nuclear weapons and ways to deliver them against American and other Western targets.[2] Secretary of Defense Donald Rumsfeld then testified before the U.S. Senate that "it is only a matter of time before terrorist states, armed with weapons of mass destruction, develop the capability to deliver those weapons to U.S. cities, giving them the ability to try to hold America hostage to nuclear blackmail."[3] NATO was also quick to respond by considering the attack on the United States as an attack against the Alliance, pledging "to improve the Alliance's capability to cope with the possible use by terrorists of chemical, biological, radiological, and nuclear materials."[4]

Former officials in the United States have highlighted concerns about one class of these weapons that could be acquired by terrorists: Russian tactical nuclear weapons. Former Sen. Sam Nunn (D-Ga.), former Clinton administration Defense Secretary William J. Perry, and former commander of U.S. strategic nuclear forces retired Air Force Gen. Eugene E. Habiger, argued that an accurate accounting of both U.S. and Russian tactical nuclear arsenals should be a priority as efforts ensue to prevent terrorists from obtaining and using weapons of mass destruction, noting that "[t]hese are the nuclear weapons most attractive to terrorists—even more attractive to them than [radioactive bomb-making] material, and much more portable than strategic warheads."[5]

This chapter will focus on this potential threat stemming from uncertainties surrounding the security of Russian tactical nuclear weapons, deployed against NATO during the Cold War. It will focus on the efforts by the United States and its NATO allies to reduce risks associated with this class of nuclear weapons. First it will briefly assess the threats posed by the theft, sale, or unauthorized use of tactical nuclear warheads (TNW) and delivery vehicles deployed in the United States, on NATO territory, and in Russia.

Assessing the Threat

Aside from the smuggling incidents reported by the International Atomic Energy Agency (IAEA) and at least one case where two Lithuanian arms brokers were accused of offering to sell Russian tactical nuclear weapons to U.S. undercover agents, to date there is no publicly available evidence to corroborate claims that terrorists have procured intact tactical nuclear weapons.[6] Russia is the most likely source for the procurement of weapons-grade materials or intact nuclear warheads. These materials may, nonetheless, be extremely difficult to obtain.[7]

An influential commission report released before the 11 September attacks concluded that "[t]he most urgent unmet national security threat to the United States today is the danger that weapons of mass destruction or weapons-usable material in Russia could be stolen and sold to terrorists or hostile nation states."[8] Other analysts have pointed out that the confluence of corruption and increased sophistication of organized crime has made the theft of entire weapons more likely.[9]

Tactical nuclear weapons are arguably more susceptible to unauthorized or accidental use than nuclear strategic weapons. They are often deployed near the front line; they are far more sensitive to communications problems under crisis conditions; and they can be fired by an individual combatant on the battlefield without employing stringent safety precautions that govern the launch of strategic nuclear weapons.

According to the Canadian Security Intelligence service, for example, "Theft of an intact nuclear weapon is not considered very likely, given the stringent security measures in place in most of the nuclear-weapon states, although political instability and socioeconomic decay in some of them—including the former Soviet Union—must remain of some concern. Tactical nuclear weapons, whose security features may be more vulnerable to tampering, are of greater concern than strategic nuclear weapons in this regard."[10]

Since the end of the Cold War, lack of information confirming the location and safety of these weapons is perceived, particularly among Western experts and officials, to be a serious security problem. Without reliable data on a vast number of Soviet-era tactical weapons, no one can be sure if they have, or could have, fallen into the wrong hands. It is very difficult to determine whether the security threats posed by Russian tactical weapons have become more acute since the end of the Cold War. In hearings in July 2002 before the Senate Foreign Relations Committee, U.S. Secretary of State Collin Powell explained:

> Tactical nuclear weapons remain an issue. Secretary Rumsfeld is particularly interested in this issue, because while we have not many left, and we have—we have complied with what we said we were going to do on a unilateral basis back in 1991 and '92, the Russians still have quite a few in various states of repair, disrepair, in need of maintenance, and operational. And will be pressing them in our discussions, in the four-party discussions that I will be having with Secretary Rumsfeld and the two ministers Ivanov—Sergei Ivanov, defense minister, Igor Ivanov, my foreign ministry counterpart. These are the kinds of issues we'll start to talk about. How can we get into the problem of theater nuclear weapons, and how do we get a handle on this issue as well? This is more of a problem with proliferation, I would submit, than are the strategic warheads. And so all of these issues will have to be worked as part of moving forward.[11]

As Powell noted, the "loose nuke" problem in Russia has been a source of concern for some time. Since the 11 September attacks, however, Russia's slack nuclear security is a more pressing concern. For example, Colonel General Yevgeniy P. Maslin, chief of the 12th GUMO, which is responsible for nuclear munitions, claimed in 1996 that theft from Russian nuclear weapons facilities is "impossible." But he qualified his statement by noting that, during transport, Russia's nuclear weapons could be vulnerable to theft by criminals or terrorist groups. Maslin expressed concern about the potential theft of nuclear weapons by insiders, rhetorically asking, "What if such acts were to be undertaken by people who have worked with nuclear weapons in the past? For example, by people dismissed from our structures, social malcontents, embittered individuals?"[12] Indeed, some basic needs had not been met for 12th GUMO nuclear storage sites. There have been reports of pesonnel shortages and poorly functioning alarm systems. The U.S. Nuclear Intelligence Council's Annual Report to Congress on the Safety and Security of Russian

Nuclear Facilities and Military Forces noted in February 2002 mentioned these problems and noted that:

> Much like other parts of the military, the Strategic Rocket Forces and the 12th GUMO have also suffered from wage arrears as well as shortages of food and housing allowances. In 1997, the 12th GUMO closed a nuclear weapons storage site due to hunger strikes by the workers; in 1998, families of several nuclear units protested over wage and benefit arrears. According to Russian press, the Ministry of Defense addressed most of the arrears by early 1999, and wages are now paid regularly. Even when paid, however, officers' wages rarely exceed $70 a month and wives cannot earn a second income because the storage sites are usually located far from cities, according to the anonymous 12th GUMO officer.[13]

As Matthew Bunn, a senior researcher at Harvard University, has pointed out, Russia's security problem can be traced in part to its communist past in which Russia had "a closed society; closed borders; pampered, well-cared-for nuclear workers; everyone under close surveillance by the KGB. Now, it's largely the same security system having to face a world with an open society; open borders; rampant theft; crime; corruption; desperate, unpaid nuclear workers. It's a totally different situation that the system was never designed to address."[14] In a February 2002 report, the Central Intelligence Agency (CIA) explained, "The [Russian nuclear weapons] security system was designed in the Soviet era to protect weapons primarily against a threat from outside the country and may not be sufficient to meet today's challenge of a knowledgeable insider collaborating with a criminal or terrorist group."[15]

In the early 1990s the limited time that Moscow had to remove its tactical force from Soviet republics into Russia led to substandard accounting of the number and exact location of those weapons. "Dozens of small nuclear weapons, ideal for terrorist use, may have fallen into the wrong hands, or perhaps not," said Congressman Curt Weldon, chair of the U.S. House of Representative Military Research and Development Subcommittee. "The important point is that crime, corruption, incompetence, and institutional disintegration are so advanced in Russia that the theft of nuclear weapons, unthinkable in the Soviet era of the cold war, seems entirely plausible in the Russia of today. The mere possibility that terrorists or rogue states may have acquired some Russian nuclear weapons should be a matter of the gravest concern to the governments and the people of the West."[16]

Delivery Vehicles

It is not only the characteristics of TNW warheads that can cause a proliferation problem, but their delivery vehicles could also be vulnerable to theft or use by terrorist entities. These delivery vehicles are often dual capable and have been exported on the international market for decades. TNW warheads could possibly be mated with dual-capable delivery vehicles manufactured in Russia, which have been exported to "states of concern" in the Middle East and Asia. Many of these delivery systems, including air defense missiles, land-based missiles, and sea-launched cruise missiles (SLCMs), are now located in third-party states. These systems were designed to carry corresponding nuclear warheads (generally classified as tactical or substrategic nuclear weapons) that are now under questionable control in Russia and could be attached to exported delivery vehicles—enabling a terrorist, or state sponsor of terrorism, to use a nuclear capable missile at short or medium range.

Severe economic problems and related systemic difficulties, such as a poorly functioning state bureaucracy, have led some Russian government officials, organizations, and private sector individuals to use military hardware exports to raise funds to prop up a failing defense industry. According to CIA Director George J. Tenet, "Russian state-run defense and nuclear industries are still strapped for funds, and Moscow looks to them to acquire badly needed foreign exchange through exports. We remain concerned about the proliferation implications of such sales in several areas . . . Russian entities last year continued to supply a variety of ballistic missile-related goods and technical know-how to countries such as Iran, India, China, and Libya."[17] The 2001 CIA National Intelligence Estimate concluded that "Russia has the most technologically evolved and best-equipped, maintained, and trained theater ballistic missile force in the world today. The SS-21 and SS-26 short-range ballistic missiles (SRBMs) provide Russian general-purpose ground forces with a rapid, precision-guided, theater deep-strike capability."[18]

Perhaps Russian political leaders use exports, or the threat to export missiles, as a form of political influence. Yet, in some cases, it may be difficult for Russian officials to control these exports by cash-starved Russian enterprises. In some cases, shipments have been exported by nongovernment business enterprises that were able use false labeling to clear customs in Russia.

Whether or not it is approved by the Russian government, there is a connection between delivery vehicles, exported regularly to nations on the State Department's list of states of concern, and the warheads that are unaccounted for in Russia. Overall, there are at least 19 nations that possess Russian or Soviet-made short- or medium-range missiles, not including the FROG (free rocket over ground) series of rockets.[19] The Soviet-designed Scud ballistic was originally built as a tactical battlefield support weapon, yet many countries view it—along other SRBM systems—as strategic weapons that can be used against urban areas.

FROG missiles have been proliferated to more countries than any other ballistic missile.[20] In the 1970s and 1980s, the Soviet Union exported FROG, Scud, and SS-21 surface-to-surface missiles, which can carry nuclear or chemical payloads, to nations such as Libya and Syria. It is possible that Syria could have passed on to Iran some of the Scud-B missiles it procured from the Soviet Union. Other Russian missile components have also been found by UN inspectors in the Tigris River near Baghdad in Iraq. In recent years it has become increasingly common for future threat assessments to conclude that states of concern have developed or are developing methods of weaponizing missile warheads "either through concerted autonomous development programs, or the acquisition or theft of warheads and warhead technology from the former Soviet Union."[21]

Cruise Missiles

According to the U.S. Defense Advanced Research Projects Agency (DARPA), there are 75 cruise missile systems in service and 42 more in development worldwide. Over 82 countries have cruise missiles in their inventories. All of these systems are capable of delivering conventional weapons and chemical/biological agents.[22] Using the Missile Technology Control Regime (MTCR) payload of 500 kg as the nuclear-capable threshold, as many as 10 production models of cruise missiles can accommodate nuclear payloads.[23] Two variants of the Russian land-attack cruise missile, the air-launched AS-15 and the submarine-launched SS-N-21, have ranges of over 1,500 miles and are nuclear capable.

The United States and Russia have discussed linking controls on SLCMs and TNWs, which has further underlined uncertainties on behalf of both parties about the extent to which the PNIs had been fulfilled. In 1997, at the Helsinki summit, the *Joint Statement on Parameters of Future Reductions in Nuclear Forces* stated that "in the context of START III negotiations their experts will explore as separate issues, possible measures relating to nuclear long-range sea-launched cruise missiles and tactical nuclear systems." If the 1991–92 PNIs have been completed as promised, neither Russia nor the United States has deployed nuclear long-range SLCMs.

SLCMs are also susceptible to illegal procurement, enabling a terrorist organization or state to acquire them for use in more crude applications. The United States and Russia have produced large numbers of them, and they can be armed with nuclear warheads. Russia exports the conventional version, while the tactical warheads are possibly insecure and could be procured by the same parties that own the missiles. Russia's P-700 Granit long-range supersonic antiship missile (SS-N-19 "Shipwreck"), a nuclear-capable antiship cruise missile, is being marketed for export by its manufacturer, NPO Mashinostroyeniye.

The Granit was conceived in the late 1970s specifically to interdict U.S. carrier battle groups. Both conventional and nuclear warheads can be deployed.

Granit entered service with the Soviet Navy in the 1980s and is capable of striking targets 500 km away.[24] There are thought to be hundreds of warheads in the SLCM class.[25] The Russian dismantlement initiatives were to be completed in 2000, but whether the schedules were met is unknown. Several thousand tactical nuclear weapons may be retained as spares or reserves. They also could have been retired but await dismantlement. The weapons that have been removed from ships are believed to be consolidated at regional or central storage sites, but without assurances that the nuclear warheads for these missiles have been dismantled or safely secured, it is possible that exported missiles could be mated with nuclear warheads.

The problems associated with a dual-capable delivery vehicles—many varieties of which have been legally, and possibly illegally, exported by Russia and other nations on the international market—illustrates the shortcomings in including delivery vehicles when accounting for or negotiating controls for tactical nuclear weapons. Applying the standard of accounting for delivery vehicles, employed for strategic nuclear weapons, is far too complicated for tactical nuclear weapons. It would therefore be more efficient to focus on the warheads as the appropriate method of accounting.

Reminiscent of the doctrine and strategic concept of NATO at the height of the Cold War, Russia has increased its emphasis on tactical weapons in its doctrine. In relation to Russia's security concerns to its western-most borders, this shift has occurred in an effort to counterbalance the conventional superiority of an enlarging NATO and bridge a "generational" gap with rapidly improving high-tech weapons capabilities (mainly from the United States).[26]

Addressing the Problem

What are the United States and NATO doing to prevent Russian tactical nuclear weapons from getting into terrorist hands? For many of the reasons listed above, the United States and NATO have become increasingly concerned about nuclear safety, particularly surrounding the battlefield models of these weapons. U.S. Secretary of State Colin Powell has claimed that

> the president [G. W. Bush] is still very interested in theater Nuclear weapons and tactical nuclear weapons. And so this is going to be an area of discussion with the Russian side. It has been discussed in all of our meetings, but it was not ready for the kind of deliberations and the kind of decisions that we were prepared to make with the strategic part of it. So, yes, he is interested, and yes, we're concerned—concerned with them more from the standpoint of we really don't want these nukes loose anywhere; and as a proliferation problem more so than a war-fighting problem. It's almost a disposal problem more so than a war-fighting problem.[27]

In June 2002 the G-8—the informal group of eight countries: Canada, France, Germany, Italy, Japan, Russia, the United Kingdom, and the United States and representatives from the European Union—met in Canada and established a "G8 Global Partnership against the Spread of Weapons and Materials of Mass Destruction" by pledging $20 billion over 10 years to address nuclear security and counter terrorism issues. The initial phase of the initiative will focus on improving Russian security issues as they relate to weapons of mass destruction and terrorism, including improving the security of storage and transport of Russian nuclear weapons.[28]

NATO has also acknowledged that it has had concerns about the uncertainty of Russian tactical nuclear weapons. On several occasions NATO has openly expressed its concerns about the large number of Russian tactical nuclear weapons and has called on Russia "to bring to completion the reductions in these forces announced in the 1991–1992, and to further review tactical nuclear weapons," acknowledging that there could be serious problems with Russia's TNW arsenal and the Alliance. There have also been reports that NATO diplomats were displeased when they attempted to cooperate with the Russians in an exchange of information on tactical nuclear weapons. "NATO officials said they had hoped to learn how many weapons the Russians still have and what safety procedures they use, but that the information presented by the Russians was extremely vague."[29]

A few NATO member states have expressed concerns about the problem of Russian tactical nuclear weapons. For example, in the general debate at the First Committee of the United Nations in October 2001, Norway stressed the need for further reductions in nonstrategic weapons and called for increased transparency, adding that "NATO recently proposed a set of transparency measures to Russia, and supported efforts by NATO and Russia and the US to pursue dialogue on this important subject."[30]

The set of measure referred to by the Norwegian U.N. delegation were proposed by NATO in a December 2000 report titled "Options for Confidence and Security Building Measures (CSBMs), Verification, Non-proliferation and Arms Control." The document was the result of an agreement reached at NATO's Washington Summit in April 1999 to conduct an internal review of its nuclear weapons policies, with specific attention to the adoption of CSBMs. This review became informally known as the *Paragraph 32 Process*— referring to the relevant paragraph of the NATO summit communiqué."[31] The NATO report had more to say on the issue of Russian substrategic nuclear weapons than any previously released publicly available document from NATO. "Given the extensive Russian nuclear arsenal," the report called for the following

> specific CSBM proposals to enhance mutual trust and to promote greater openness and transparency on nuclear weapons and safety issues:

A. Enhance and deepen dialogue on matters related to nuclear forces.
B. Exchange information regarding the readiness status of nuclear forces.
C. Exchange information on safety provisions and safety features of nuclear weapons.
D. Exchange data on U.S. and Russian sub-strategic nuclear forces.[32]

NATO also noted that "this proposal would involve conductng a reciprocal data exchange with Russia within the Permanent Joint Council (PJC) context. The objective would be to enhance transparency and knowledge of the size of the U.S. and Russian stockpiles."[33]

The final communiqué from the foreign ministers meeting in December 2001 tasked ambassadors with exploring "effective mechanisms for consultation, cooperation, joint decision, and coordinated/joint action." At the defense ministers meeting later that month, NATO exclaimed that it has reached agreement with Russia on the need for dialogue on nuclear weapons safety and security issues, noting that "improved transparency, predictability and growing mutual trust between NATO and Russia in this important field . . . is in our mutual interest."[34]

After the Cold War, NATO made some attempts to address the security concerns about its own tactical nuclear weapons. In 1991 the Alliance adapted its overall strategy, policy, and force posture. NATO reduced its nuclear forces by over 85 percent and the number of storage sites in Europe by 80 percent. It removed systems such as nuclear land mines, nuclear artillery, and air-to-surface missiles. NATO has left up to 180 land-based, substrategic nuclear gravity bombs in storage in seven European countries[35] capable of being delivered by dual-capable aircraft (DCA). Readiness levels of its dual-capable aircraft have also been reduced from being measured in minutes to weeks or months. NATO now regularly reminds the public that these weapons are not only in fewer locations but they also "are stored safely in very few storage sites under highly secure conditions."[36]

By contrast, while there have been significant reductions in the number of weapons and their locations in the former Soviet Union, there are at least 100 warhead and weapon-grade storage facilities, and most of them are reportedly not properly secured.[37]

According to the Congressional Research Service:

> The United States would like further restrictions on Russian tactical nuclear weapons both because it believes these might pose a proliferation risk and because Russia has a far greater number of these weapons than does the United States. Russia has resisted formal limits. However, in late April 1998, officials from NATO and Russia exchanged information about their nonstrategic nuclear weapons. This effort was designed not only to ease Russia's concerns about NATO's nuclear weapons, but also to pro-

vide NATO with information about the thousands of tactical nuclear weapons still in service in Russia.[38]

Proposals and agreements initiated by NATO and the United States have not yet, however, achieved many tangible results. Substrategic nuclear forces continue to be viewed as an essential security guarantee in both Europe and Russia. There are several reasons given for the lack of movement between NATO and Russia on controlling tactical nuclear weapons. The collapse of the Soviet Union, and the core threat to NATO that it embodied, enabled radical reductions in substrategic forces in Europe.[39] While NATO found that it became increasingly difficult to argue that tactical nuclear weapons in NATO were needed to provide a counterbalance to Soviet conventional superiority and the numbers of NATO weapons have been reduced in the immediate post–Cold War period, the political significance attached to the remaining weapons has remained essentially the same as it did during the Cold War, as the 1999 Strategic Concept explains:

The fundamental purpose of the nuclear forces of the Allies is political: to preserve peace and prevent coercion and any kind of war. They will con-

TABLE 5.1
NATO Nuclear Systems Deployed in Europe

	1971	1981	1987	1991	1999
Mines	X	X			
Nike Hercules SAM	X	X	X		
Honest John SSM	X	X			
Lance SSM	X	X	X	X	
Sergeant SSM	X				
Pershing IA	X	X	X		
Pershing II			X		
GLCM			X		
15mm Howitzer	X	X	X	X	
8-inch Howitzer	X	X	X	X	
Walleye ASM	X				
ASW Depth Bombs	X	X	X	X	
DCA Bombs	X	X	X	X	X
Total Systems	11	9	9	5	1

Source: NATO Fact Sheet, "NATO's Nuclear Forces in the New Security Environment" 27 January 2000.

tinue to fulfill an essential role by ensuring uncertainty in the mind of any aggressor about the nature of the Allies' response to military aggression. They demonstrate that aggression of any kind is not a rational option. The supreme guarantee of the security of the Allies is provided by the strategic nuclear forces of the Alliance, particularly those of the United States; the independent nuclear forces of the United Kingdom and France, which have a deterrent role of their own, contribute to the overall deterrence and security of the Allies. . . . The Alliance will therefore maintain adequate nuclear forces in Europe.[40]

NATO posits that it heavily depends on widespread participation in nuclear roles by its European allies. For the Alliance, the presence of tactical nuclear weapons on European soil ensure that Allies on both sides of the Atlantic are sharing the risk and the burden associated with NATO's nuclear mission. There are concerns that efforts to implement controls with Russia on tactical nuclear weapons would be based on the condition by Russia that NATO remove its remaining nuclear weapons from Europe. For NATO such withdrawal would weaken the value of the alliance substantially, because the European allies desire both a tactical and strategic nuclear umbrella as part of NATO's defenses, which in tandem makes the alliance much more credible.

Indeed, the U.S. European-based TNW arsenal possesses a strong symbolic value in the European defense establishment that should not be underestimated.[41] The political landscape surrounding these weapons is volatile. Politicians in Europe are said to prefer to keep the issue of allowing the arsenal to remain in Europe off the table altogether to quell public awareness and concern.

The deadlock on this issue remains because NATO and Russia have diametrically opposed positions on the continued presence of NATO nuclear weapons in Europe. Moscow has repeatedly asserted that it will not consider negotiations to control its tactical nuclear arsenal if the United States will not remove its nuclear weapons from Europe. As NATO expands eastward toward the boarders of mainland Russia, there are also anxieties about the deployment of NATO nuclear weapons on the territory of new member states. Russia has continually refused to enter into TNW talks until stipulations on the withdrawal of the U.S. nuclear weapons from Europe and the nondeployment of nuclear weapons on the territory of new NATO members are met.[42]

Part of this disagreement stems from Moscow's ability to continue to use nuclear weapons as a bargaining chip, a remaining symbol of Russia's once powerful status as a superpower. Another aspect stems from military strategic concerns. Russia's conventional inferiority is an issue of increasing importance and is particularly germane as NATO continues to expand eastward. The very likely prospect that NATO will offer an invitation to at least one

Baltic nation at the Prague Summit in November 2002 is inevitably going to raise concerns about the forward deployment of NATO (U.S.) and Russian TNWs. Former U.S. Secretary of Defense James Schlesinger, for example, sparked a heated debate in 1997 during the last *tranche* of enlargement when he asserted that the Baltics would certainly be "indefensible without nuclear weapons."[43] It is conceivable that these kinds of arguments will increase and make tactical nuclear weapons politically urgent if Lithuania or Latvia are placed on the short list for NATO membership. Questions will also surface about what role former Soviet states bordering mainland Russia might play as new NATO members in the Nuclear Planning Group (NPG) or as nuclear-capable members (first-class members).

In an effort to gain Moscow's acquiescence to NATO enlargement, the Alliance offered Russia two incentives in 1997 containing the promise of closer partnership. The first was an essentially symbolic document, referred to as a "Founding Act," which outlined areas of common interest and cooperation between the former Cold War enemies. The second incentive came with the establishment of a NATO-Russia Permanent Joint Council, which provided a discussion forum but had no mechanism for substantive joint decision making. Given Russian concerns regarding further enlargement, NATO's expansion may augment that offer with additional palliatives in a more contentious second round. Statements by Russian President Putin in the wake of the 11 September attacks suggest a greater willingness to accept NATO expansion. This could provide an opportunity for greater cooperation. Some adjustment to the symbolic reliance on and status quo of NATO nuclear weapons and/or a more enhanced role for the Permanent Joint Council (PJC) on nuclear issues could be such an incentive.

Even if the improvement in relations between NATO and Russia since 11 September bears fruit and both parties manage to get past the contentious issues surrounding the future of weapons deployments in Europe and west of the Ural Mountains, a host of other problems could continue to complicate efforts to reduce the threat of nuclear weapons.

Conclusion

On a scale of potential nuclear threats posed by terrorist organizations, it is much more likely that someone could illegally procure a tactical nuclear weapon than threaten the world with a nuclear-tipped intercontinental ballistic missile. Despite this fact, the dangers posed by Russia's tactical nuclear weapons arsenal receive far less attention than the perceived threat of WMD-capable ICBM development. Uncertainty is a major factor in assessing the hazards posed by tactical nuclear weapons. A completely accurate assessment of this threat is, however, insufficient without verifiable information about the quantity, security, and safety of the weapons in question. To date there is no confirmed evidence that tactical nuclear weapons are missing or have been stolen by terrorists. Nonetheless, it is a possibility. Poor data also make the problem more complicated and, therefore, a less attractive agenda item for negotiation. Officials in Western Europe and North America acknowledge the potential risks associated with these weapons but do not rank the issue a priority. According to U.S. Under Secretary of Defense for Policy Douglas J. Feith: "The issue of Russian tactical nuclear weapons . . . gets very little attention. The Russians have lots of tactical nuclear weapons. We view them at this point not as a big military headache for us but as a [sic], more from the point of view of the danger of nuclear proliferation."[44]

However, the opportunities to control tactical nuclear weapons are improving. After a series of low points in NATO-Russian relations during the 1990s (marked by Balkan conflicts, the first post–Cold War round of NATO enlargement, two wars in Chechnya, and NATO's Kosovo campaign), relations between the two former adversaries have grown warmer. The cooperative sprit established after the 11 September attacks has helped to solidify their relationship, allowing both parties to make some progress on the issue of tactical nuclear weapons. In late 2001 NATO and Russia announced that they had "decided to give new impetus and substance to our partnership, with the goal of creating a new council bringing together NATO member states and Russia to identify and pursue opportunities for joint action at 20."[45] Simply recasting the relationship between NATO and its former enemy will not be enough to alleviate the dangers posed by Russia's nuclear weapons arsenal. More needs to be done. A more fruitful outcome than what the Permanent Joint Council has produced in the past five years is absolutely essential. A common sense of purpose in the campaign against terrorism would provide a better backdrop for enduring relations and generate a level of confidence between both parties necessary to tackle the issue of tactical nuclear weapons. The creation of a new NATO Russian Council (NRC) in the fall of 2001 has already shown signs of progress under the circumstances. The NRC working group meetings have enjoyed more enthusiastic Russian participation.

Building confidence in this area, however, will take time. On the U.S. side, officials have stated that they are willing to discuss the problem, but it is not at the top of the list of their priorities when working with Russia on nuclear security issues. For example, according to U.S. Undersecretary of State for Arms Control John Bolton, missile defense and strategic weapons are higher on the list.[46] In addition, the Bush administration has made it clear, evident with its decision to withdraw from the ABM treaty and its desire to discontinue a bilateral commitment to the START process, that it would prefer to avoid the legal constraints of arms control treaties.

On the Russian side, officials have opposed discussing accounting or control issues related to tactical nuclear weapons. Statements from Russian officials that NATO enlargement would force Russia to rely more heavily on its nuclear arsenal have been toned down and are fewer in number. Russia politicians are likely to raise this issue in the next round of NATO enlargement, but Moscow is becoming less concerned with the deployment of weapons in Europe as their relationship with, and acceptance of, NATO has grown. Russia is also keen to work more with Western institutions in an effort to improve its financial situation. Neither side would view the concession of withdrawing tactical nuclear weapons from Europe as a symmetrical gesture. It would therefore be unwise to put aside this important issue as an initial step in order to control tactical nuclear weapons.

Since the PNIs were announced, the United States and NATO have provided more assurances than the Russians on the status of their tactical nuclear weapons. However, the political and military functions that these weapons continue to play are ambiguous, particularly since strategic weapons are now in an active reserve force according to the 2002 Nuclear Posture Review.

There is increasing pressure from outside the U.S. government to encourage officials to address the problems associated with Russian tactical nuclear weapons and terrorism since 11 September 2001. In testimony before the Senate Foreign Relations Committee, former Senator Sam Nunn summarized the problem and offered succinct advice to his former colleagues about how the government ought to tackle the problem:

> Tactical nuclear weapons are another piece of unaddressed business. These weapons have never been covered in arms control treaties. We can only guess at the numbers in each other's inventories as well as the locations. Yet these are the nuclear weapons most attractive to terrorists—even more valuable to them than fissile material and much more portable than strategic warheads. The United States and Russia should insist on accurate accounting and adequate safeguards for tactical nuclear weapons, including a baseline inventory of these weapons with sufficient transparency to assure each other that these weapons are being handled in a safe and secure manner. This type of agreement may be hard to achieve, but it is difficult for me to envision keeping the "U.S.-Russian/Bush-Putin positive spirit" for the duration of this Treaty unless we deal with the tactical nuclear weapons question. One hypothetical illustration, Mr. Chairman: Suppose a terrorist tactical weapon was detonated in an American or Russian city—would either of our two nations be able to confidently determine its origin in a timely fashion? Could good relations survive this horror if the fundamental question of weapon origin remained unanswered? Or worse, what if the isotopic fingerprint of that weapon showed it to be of Russian origin? I submit that it would be far better to prevent the catastrophe by cooperation on tactical nuclear weapons beginning now and to work together to be able to answer this question accurately and quickly if, God forbid, a weapon is missing or if the event occurs.[47]

Attractive inducements can be offered to Russia with an eye toward building confidence and reducing threats associated with its tactical nuclear weapons. Discussions on less intrusive steps (for example, actions that do not involve inspections and focus on the attainment of basic information about Russia's TNW arsenal) could be an intermediate objective. Incentives could be offered as an exchange for a warhead inventory without rigorous verification. Other steps could follow the contours of more formal threat-reduction programs, such as the Nunn-Lugar program, emphasizing the establishment of a U.S-funded computerized data management system. In the context of a new dialogue between the United States/NATO and Russia, the details of this "transparency for currency" or "debt for data" could be worked out in a manner that satisfies both sides in mutually beneficial ways. The "Debt Reduction for Nonproliferation Act of 2001" may be a useful model. With this policy the U.S. *forgave* portions of Russian debt in exchange for Russian commitments to use the savings to underwrite nonproliferation activities, such as efforts to improve the physical security and dispose of weapons-usable materials.[48]

Despite the Bush administration's reticence to address tactical nuclear weapons and the less-than-outstanding success of NATO's transparency initiatives, the improving relationship between Russia and the West provides an opportunity to make progress on tactical nuclear weapons. Statements by Putin in the wake of the 11 September terrorist attacks suggest a greater willingness to accept NATO expansion. And in late 2001 NATO and Russia announced that they had "decided to give new impetus and substance to our partnership, with the goal of creating a new council to bring together NATO member states and Russia to identify and pursue opportunities for joint action at 20." Building NATO-Russian relations and cultivating a common sense of purpose in the campaign against terrorism could generate a level of confidence between both parties necessary to tackle the issue of tactical nuclear weapons. In April 2002 NATO and Russian nuclear experts held a joint seminar on nuclear safety and security. NATO noted that "the Seminar represented the first step in further advancing consutations and cooperation on NATO proposals for confidence and security building measures to enhance transparency between the two sides on nuclear weapons issues."[49] But NATO and the United States must offer more incentives to encourage Russia to deal with its tactical nuclear weapons.

In the final analysis, Russia will not increase transparency without viable inducements from the West. These could include financial incentives or preconditions for loans in exchange for increased transparency, such as data on warhead security and weapon dismantlement. Other incentives could provide verifiable (possibly legally binding) assurances from the United States on qualitative and quantitative reductions in its strategic force, which the Russians have repeatedly asked for in recent years.

The Buddha Frowns?

Tactical Nuclear Weapons in South Asia

Timothy D. Hoyt

The successful tests of nuclear weapons by both India and Pakistan in May 1998 raise troubling questions for analysts of international security.[1] The de facto "induction," to use an Indian term, of nuclear weapons into the militaries of the subcontinent raises serious questions of doctrine, deployment, command and control, and actual nuclear use. These concerns are exacerbated by long-standing tensions between the two states, the ongoing insurgency in Kashmir, disparities in national resource endowments, and adverse trends in the balance of conventional forces.

It is quite possible that India and Pakistan already possess weapons that could be used for tactical purposes. Both India and Pakistan claim to have tested subkiloton nuclear weapons in their May tests. If correct, these weapons are relatively optimized for tactical nuclear use in the subcontinent. Close proximity of major cities to the Indo-Pakistani border and line of control (in Kashmir) makes fallout a serious concern, particularly as the prevailing winds switch according to season. Collateral damage can be effectively minimized through use of low-yield weapons, which may be of interest to both sides. Even if subkiloton devices do not exist, the consensus of most analysts is that Indian and Pakistani weapons designs have yields in the low-kiloton range, roughly equivalent to the fissions weapons used on Hiroshima and Nagasaki. In appropriate terrain, like the desert regions in Rajasthan, these weapons could still be used as battlefield weapons.

The existence of "usable" battlefield weapons raises the crucial issue of doctrine. Under what circumstances might either side resort to nuclear use, and what form might that nuclear use take? The Indian government has published a "Draft Nuclear Doctrine" reaffirming India's commitment to no first use of nuclear weapons, calling for a secure retaliatory capability based on land-, sea-, and air-based nuclear forces, and suggesting that nuclear weapons are useable only as a deterrent—a political capability, rather than a military one. Recent statements have hinted at a policy of massive nuclear retaliation in the event of tactical nuclear use by Pakistan, but military and defense officials are also speaking of the potential for "limited war" in the subcontinent—a concept disturbingly close to the striving for escalation dominance that fueled the U.S.-Soviet arms race. Pakistan's nuclear doctrine is similar to NATO's, using nuclear weapons to help redress conventional inferiority and deter conventional attack. Unlike NATO, however, Pakistan also carries on an aggressive campaign of support for insurgency and terrorism in Indian territory and relies on nuclear deterrence to limit or prevent Indian retaliation.

Analysts tend to look at both intelligence and capabilities in an effort to determine risk or threat. In both India and Pakistan, these issues remain unclear. Both states clearly have *some* nuclear capability, and Pakistan apparently *intends* to use this capability to deter Indian conventional attack. Both Indian and Pakistani authors have explored the possibility of tactical nuclear use, but only in the abstract. As the two states continue to develop their doctrines and command and control mechanisms, in an atmosphere of heightened tension and suspicion, nuclear use on the battlefield and the problems of controlling escalation remain critical concerns.

The introduction of nuclear weapons into a conflict environment fundamentally raises the dangers and uncertainties for both sides.[2] The awesome destructive power of nuclear devices, whether fission or fusion, and regardless of the means of delivery, represents a potent political force. Some analysts regard the mere possession of nuclear weapons as a fundamentally stabilizing force in conflicted regions—rational opponents, knowing the capability of their adversaries, will not dare risk the possibility of nuclear conflict.[3] Other analysts are less sanguine, detecting multiple opportunities for miscommunication, misperception, or simple mistakes to bring competing states to the brink of disaster or beyond.[4]

Nuclear weapons also represent a significant military capability—if they are actually used. Nuclear weapons can be used against cities and population centers—"countervalue" targets, in the lexicon of nuclear strategy—or against opposing nuclear or strategic forces—"counterforce" targets. The former capability helps to determine the political or deterrent value of nuclear forces. Most adversaries are dissuaded from possible attack by the realization that it could lead to the deaths of hundreds of thousands or millions of civilians as a result of nuclear strikes. The latter capability, however, tends to undermine deterrence, particularly if an adversary gains confidence in their ability to eliminate or severely degrade enemy nuclear retaliation through an efficient counterforce strike. Both of these roles—counterforce and counter-value—are familiar to students of the U.S.-Soviet nuclear competition during the Cold War.[5] It is not clear, however, how relevant these concepts, particularly counterforce and the concept of "first strikes," are in the study of emerging nuclear arsenals.[6]

The use of nuclear weapons on the battlefield, or for some operational purpose against conventional military forces, remains a possibility in the subcontinent. Although the nuclear doctrines of both countries remain ill-defined, the consensus of most analysts is that Pakistan's nuclear arsenal represents a response to India's superior resources and stronger conventional military capabilities. To some analysts, Pakistan's nuclear arsenal remains existential—it will be deployed when the survival of the country is at risk. This means, at a minimum, that nuclear weapons *might* be used against Indian ground or air forces in the event that Pakistani political or territorial integrity is threatened. India's rationale for tactical nuclear use is less clear, but nuclear strikes might be considered against either select Pakistani targets or against Chinese forces on the still-contested Sino-Indian border in the event of a renewal of that conflict.[7]

This chapter, therefore, will focus on assessing the capabilities and intentions of the two states. First, what are the capabilities of both sides? How long have they had nuclear weapons, and what do we know about their yields and size? The answers to these questions are far from definitive, but they do provide some insight into what *might* be possible in terms of tactical weapons designs and use.

The second section will briefly review possible doctrines and uses for these emerging arsenals. This discussion is particularly timely and important because of recent events. The massive movement of Indian armed forces to the border after the 13 December 2001 terrorist attack on India's Parliament prompted both sides to make more explicit pronouncements on nuclear weapons and doctrine.

The combination of regional tension, evolving doctrine, and increasing numbers of weapons may lead both sides toward a doctrine more permissive of nuclear use, particularly on the battlefield. Both sides currently deny any intention of using tactical nuclear weapons. As nuclear red lines are drawn more clearly and as Indian conventional and nuclear advantages increase, Pakistani leaders may be increasingly drawn toward a policy of "flexible response," including the consideration of battlefield nuclear strike. Indian military planners may be forced to seek to clarify their own military options to maintain or undermine deterrence, depending on the situation.

Nuclear Capabilities: India and Pakistan

India

On 11 and 13 May 1998, India tested a series of five nuclear devices. This was not India's first nuclear test but it was the first test in which India publicly acknowledged that it was actually testing a nuclear *weapon*. The Shakti 1 test of May 1974 was described as the test of a "peaceful nuclear explosive"—a bizarre concept permitted under the Nonproliferation Treaty—although a leading Indian nuclear scientist later admitted that it was an attempt to test a weapons design. The yield, originally claimed at 12–15 kilotons, remains disputed—the initial estimate was later restated as 8–12 kilotons, and then 8–10 kilotons, with Western intelligence estimates as low as 4–6 kilotons.[8]

India's current nuclear capability can be extrapolated from existing data on the May 1998 tests and India's potential production and separation of weapons-grade plutonium. India announced on 11 May 1998 that it had tested a fission weapon, a thermonuclear weapon, and a "low-yield weapon."[9] Two additional subkiloton tests were reportedly carried out on 13 May 1998.[10] According to official spokesmen, the reason for the subkiloton tests was to provide additional data and to aid in achieving the capability to carry out subcritical tests, if necessary. Subkiloton warheads also can be used for battlefield or tactical purposes, because of their low yield, modest collateral damage, and limited fallout. The results of India's tests, particularly its claim of a successful thermonuclear test, continue to be challenged by analysts.[11]

India's stockpile of nuclear materials is sufficient for development of a considerable arsenal. The Institute for Science and International Security estimates that in late 1999 India had 240–395 kg of separated weapons-grade plutonium (93 percent or more Pu-239), sufficient for 45–95 nuclear devices. India also possessed an additional 8,300 kg of reactor-grade plutonium,[12] 4,200 kg of which is not subject to international inspection and might be used to create 500 or more additional warhead equivalents over time.[13] India's current nuclear stockpile is estimated still to be under 100 weapons. India's large civilian nuclear infrastructure and current fissile stockpiles will allow India to dwarf Pakistan's potential nuclear arsenal. Currently, however, some comparative estimates suggest that India's arsenal may be smaller than Pakistan's.[14]

Pakistan

Pakistan responded to India's nuclear tests on 28 and 30 May 1998. Pakistan claims to have tested six weapons on those dates—five on 28 May and an additional weapon on 30 May.[15] Indian experts immediately dismissed the

Pakistani claim.[16] At least one weapon—the sixth weapon, tested on 30 May—was reportedly a "miniaturized device."[17] Analysis of the seismic data suggests that Pakistan clearly detonated a 1–3 kiloton weapon, described as a fission device, on 30 May. The yields of the 28 May tests are disputed—Pakistan claimed to have detonated a boosted fission device with 25–36 kilotons yield (too large for tactical use in most circumstances), a fission device of 12 kilotons, and three low-yield devices. Seismic data confirms that at least two weapons were detonated, with lower yields.[18]

Pakistan's stockpile of nuclear materials is substantially smaller than India's, partly because of the lack of a civilian nuclear infrastructure. The Institute for Science and International Security estimated Pakistan's 1999 fissile material stockpile as 1.7–13 kilograms of weapons-grade plutonium (possibly enough for 1 or 2 warheads), 585–800 kilograms of highly enriched uranium (HEU), and 600 kilograms of unseparated Pu-240 still subject to International Atomic Energy Agency inspections and safeguards. This would be enough fissile material for 30–52 warheads (weapons based on HEU require larger amounts of fissile material than weapons based on Pu-239), with an additional 75 if reactor-grade plutonium were used.[19] Pakistan may have additional sources of fissile material. It was initially believed that all of the weapons Pakistan tested in May 1998 used HEU, as the Khushab reactor that processed weapons grade plutonium only went on line in April 1998. U.S. reports suggest, however, that at least one Pakistani test may have used plutonium.[20]

Intentions: India and Pakistan

India

India's nuclear program dates back to the late 1940s, when Prime Minister Jawaharlal Nehru and his chief science adviser, Dr. Homi Bhabha, began an ambitious dual-use nuclear energy program that would provide for India's energy and, if necessary, security needs.[21] The program has been largely removed from public scrutiny, although occasional crises have brought the debate to the public eye. More important, perhaps, is the fact that the program has remained largely beyond the influence or input of India's military services. Decisions on the nuclear issue were made by the prime minister and a handful of advisers, none of whom were military officers. It was not until 1988 that the then-chief of staff of the Indian Air Force and a small cadre of Air Force officers independently initiated notional planning for a nuclear force.[22]

The relative absence of military input into India's nuclear program has led to considerable confusion. One of the most outspoken advocates, and serious students, of Indian nuclear capability was the former Chief of Army Staff General Krishnaswamy Sundarji, and Indian Army officers have desired a voice in the program since the 1960s.[23] Despite these rare exceptions, India's strong tradition of civilian dominance of civil-military relations has largely isolated nuclear debates from professional military advice.[24] This, in turn, has led to an idealistic, highly symbolic, and deeply secretive nuclear program.

India's nuclear debates have been dominated by a succession of political leaders and by a scientific community dedicated to the development of the nuclear program.[25] Development of nuclear weapons demonstrates advanced technological and scientific capacity, symbolizes the strength of the Indian state and civilization, and fulfills a primarily political function in deterring possible hostile acts by outside powers. Indian analysts point primarily to China as a rationale for Indian nuclear policy, but Sino-Indian relations have improved substantially since the 1962 Himalayan war, and China has shown little interest in expanded confrontation with India.[26] The ongoing political conflict with Pakistan represents the most likely threat of physical invasion, but this is a scenario that India has proven capable of handling easily well short of the nuclear threshold.

Given the relative lack of significant military threat, and the absence of military advice, it is hardly surprising that India has "muddled through" with a series of nuclear policies (they can hardly be called doctrines) that appear highly idealistic. India followed a policy later described as "recessed" or "opaque" deterrence—an assumption that the nuclear demonstration of 1974 was sufficient to warn off nuclear adversaries. Indira Gandhi canceled nuclear tests in 1982 as unnecessary. Although her son, Rajiv Gandhi, encouraged research into more-advanced nuclear weapons designs, neither he nor his successors found it necessary to test or deploy actual nuclear devices. India carried out no systematic planning for using nuclear weapons, for their command and control, or for operating in a nuclear environment, until after the May 1998 tests.

In the eyes of many analysts, the 1998 nuclear tests and, more important, Pakistan's prompt countertests, actually degraded Indian security in the near term. The overt demonstration of nuclear weapons in the subcontinent increased international attention to the region and the Kashmir issue. India assumed that the presence of nuclear weapons led to stability and peace and initiated the Lahore peace process. Pakistan, however, took advantage of the "stability-instability" paradox brought about by the presence of nuclear deterrence—the notion that high-intensity conflict that might threaten the survival of states is deterred, but not lower-level conflict.[27] The result was Pakistan's covert invasion of Kargil in early 1999, which was rebuffed at great cost by Indian forces. Significantly, during Kargil, India did not escalate or expand the conflict by crossing the Line of Control or the border—a tactic India had first used in 1965 and had threatened after the nuclear tests. In short, it appears that India was deterred from escalation by Pakistan's nuclear capability.

India released the Draft Nuclear Doctrine (DND) in August 1999, conveniently timed to coincide with domestic political elections.[28] This doctrine was clearly the compromise of a number of different points of view regarding the size, potential targets, and utility of India's emerging nuclear arsenal. The DND articulated a need for a survivable second-strike force, but it also suggested that, unlike the U.S.-Soviet competition, retaliation did not need to be immediate—only assured. This would permit lower levels of readiness, and perhaps smaller nuclear forces, than the superpower competition. Minister of Defense George Fernandes announced a new "limited war doctrine" in early 2000. This new doctrine recognized that there was a "strategic space" in which conventional combat could take place without triggering nuclear deterrence.[29] Both concepts aimed at denying the Pakistanis any advantage through the threat of nuclear escalation in the future.

The 13 December 2001 terrorist attack on Indian parliament prompted an angry Indian response, including an unprecedented military buildup on the Indo-Pakistani border and the Line of Control in Kashmir. India also began a careful campaign to undermine confidence in Pakistan's nuclear deterrent. In late December a leading figure in the Bharatiya Janata Party (BJP) stated that India would not be deterred by Pakistani nuclear threats and that attacks on Indian troops would be treated as attacks on Indian soil. Minister of Defense Fernandes repeated this threat on 3 January 2002.[30] Most ominously, it was echoed by Chief of Army Staff General Padmahnaban on 11 January 2002.[31] According to reports, the general remarked that if Pakistan used nuclear weapons against Indian soldiers on the battlefield, "the continuation of the existence of Pakistan as a nation would be in doubt." Given the limited role of the military in formulating nuclear policy, this clearly suggested that his statements were made at the behest of the government. The testing of the 700–800 km Agni-1 missile in January reinforced the idea that India had nuclear-capable forces postured for use against Pakistan.[32]

The interaction between India and Pakistan *since* the nuclear tests, therefore, suggests that Indian nuclear doctrine is evolving rapidly, and perhaps in predictable directions. The role of the military is likely to increase in nuclear preparations, because credible deterrence will become increasingly important in the subcontinent. This will be discussed further in the conclusion.

Pakistan

The driving factor behind Pakistan's nuclear capability is the perceived threat from India.[33] A peaceful nuclear research program was initiated in the 1950s, but it was not until the 1960s that a civilian—then Foreign Minister and later

President and Prime Minister Zulfikar Ali Bhutto—made the nuclear program a national issue. Bhutto saw the nuclear weapon as a substitute for failed alliances with the United States, as a symbolic counterweight to India's much larger and more advanced nuclear program, and as a means of undercutting the domestic political power of the Pakistani Army.[34]

The program accelerated after the disastrous 1971 war with India, and particularly after India's nuclear test in 1974. When General Zia-ul-Haq deposed Bhutto in a 1977 coup, the nuclear program was put firmly under military control. It quickly became a fixation in the Indo-Pakistani relationship—the 1980–90 period saw at least three Indo-Pakistani crises with a nuclear component—as well as an irritant to the renewed U.S.-Pakistani partnership against the Soviet Union's invasion of Afghanistan.[35]

Nuclear crises in 1984, 1986–87, and 1990 brought troubling aspects of South Asia's new nuclear dimension to the attention of international observers. Poor intelligence capabilities nearly caused a crisis in 1984.[36] The 1986–87 Brasstacks exercise and the associated Operation Trident raised fears that India might seek to use its conventional superiority to alter the regional status quo.[37] Finally, the 1990 crisis reportedly included the actual deployment of Pakistani weapons to air bases, although this has been disputed by many of the key players in India, Pakistan, and the United States[38]

Throughout this period, Pakistani nuclear doctrine and policy remained deliberately opaque and ill defined. Leaders spoke openly of Pakistan's nuclear capability when in opposition: Benazir Bhutto, for instance, reported that she had no control over Pakistan's nuclear forces in the 1990 crisis.[39] Officials implied that the capacity to make nuclear weapons existed, but they continued to officially deny the existence of actual weapons.[40] Nevertheless, the most authoritative study of Pakistani nuclear doctrine emphasizes that no serious effort was made to develop either a doctrine or a secure command and control system until *after* the nuclear tests—even though Pakistan had been nuclear capable for a decade.[41] Like India, therefore, Pakistan also followed a laissez-faire nuclear doctrine until after the tests forced more serious reconsideration.

The core of Pakistani nuclear doctrine, however, has focused on using the existence of nuclear capability to deter superior Indian conventional forces—in the words of one author, "a doctrine of minimum nuclear deterrence and conventional defense to balance India's nuclear and conventional forces."[42] Pakistan maintains sufficient conventional force to successfully defend the country for short periods, which raises the threshold for nuclear use and makes this combination credible for defensive purposes. The value of nuclear weapons as "cover" for more aggressively pursuing Pakistani ambitions at lower levels of intensity, however, was both recognized and publicly addressed. Shortly before the Kargil operation was discovered, then Chief of Army Staff General Pervaiz Musharraf announced that while nuclear weapons had made large-scale conventional wars obsolete in the subcontinent, proxy wars were very likely.[43]

As mentioned above, Indian declarations since Kargil have attempted systematically to undermine the viability of and confidence in Pakistan's nuclear deterrent. India's efforts to achieve a rhetorical form of escalation dominance were met with a series of equally belligerent Pakistani responses. A delegation of Italian visitors from the Landau Center met with prominent Pakistani political and military leaders shortly after the 13 December 2001 mobilization crisis peaked, and Lieutenant General Kidwai, director of the Pakistani Strategic Plans Division, articulated a more comprehensive, if still vague, set of conditions under which Pakistan would use nuclear weapons. These conditions were defined in terms of Indian threats to Pakistani national existence, and included:

- ◆ *Space Threshold:* loss of significant territory
- ◆ *Military Threshold:* destruction of large parts of the Army or Air Force
- ◆ *Economic Strangling:* blockade, manipulation of water supply, or other acts of economic warfare
- ◆ *Domestic Destabilization:* creation of large-scale internal subversion or other threats to Pakistani domestic political stability.[44]

The concept of Pakistani nuclear use in the face of a threat to national survival was recently reiterated by now-President Peryez Musharraf, in interviews with newspapers and the German magazine *Der Spiegel*.[45] At a time when conventional mobilization on both sides of the border has reached unprecedented peacetime levels, this rhetorical dueling raises the possibility that at some point, one state might test the other's commitment and credibility. If this is the case, it is worth briefly exploring how and why nuclear weapons might be used in the subcontinent, and the relevance of Cold War concepts of strategic and tactical use of nuclear weapons.

The Specter of Nuclear Use

Many of the assumptions regarding the South Asian nuclear confrontation are derived from the U.S.-Soviet competition. Often, these "nuclear lessons" stem from theories and observations developed later in the Cold War, when both sides possessed enormous arsenals governed by reasonably flexible command and control arrangements and deployed in secure, triadic forces.

The South Asian competition is, in some ways, fundamentally different. The adversaries are closely linked, culturally and geographically, and the primary "prize" in the competition (Kashmir) remains divided between them. Pakistan's major cities lie, for the most part, very close to the border, as do its major nuclear facilities. Nuclear forces are not clearly separated from conventional forces—most of the delivery systems of both sides (aircraft and mobile short-range missiles) are at least theoretically dual use. The proximity of major bases and nuclear facilities to urban population centers on both sides raises high risks of collateral damage from nuclear strikes on military targets, and the seasonal shifting of prevailing winds makes fallout and radiation a long-term concern. As a result, there is little practical distinction, particularly for Pakistan, between "strategic" and "tactical" nuclear weapons, or between "counterforce" and "tactical" use.[46]

The reportedly low yields of the weapons of both sides actually makes battlefield use more plausible, although the United States deployed "tactical" weapons with warheads of several hundreds of kilotons in Europe during the 1970s.[47] The limited testing programs of both states probably precludes certain types of weapons deployed in Europe during the Cold War. These would include artillery shells, which require significant miniaturization and are subject to extraordinarily high stresses and therefore probably substantial additional testing.[48] However, recent reports cite Indian Army generals as stating that Pakistan has low-yield devices useable by artillery and aircraft—specialized tactical weapons designed specifically for battlefield use.[49] According to one report, the weapons and/or manufacturing technology were probably acquired from a third party.

Another option is enhanced radiation weapons—the so-called "neutron bomb"—which proved highly controversial in Europe, but which might be attractive in the fallout-averse South Asian environment.[50] Both of these options, however, would probably require further nuclear tests. Warhead yields for these kinds of weapons, in the U.S. case, ranged from 0.1 to 15 kilotons—well within the range that both sides claim to have available. It is reasonable to assume that resumed testing or other interest in these battlefield-dedicated types of weapons would demonstrate a move toward a doctrine that included the possibility of tactical nuclear use.

How might nuclear weapons be used in a conflict? Again, nuclear weapons are viewed by both sides as primarily political weapons, so the first possibility is use as a symbolic act—as a demonstration of seriousness and to indicate that the conflict was reaching much higher levels of potential risk.[51] This demonstration effect would also encourage international attention and possibly intervention, preventing one side from achieving a decisive victory.[52] This demonstration could take the form of a nuclear detonation at a remote site, or perhaps something near the conflict area.

Low-yield nuclear weapons also can be used for battlefield effect, even if artillery shells are not available—aircraft and missile delivery remain a distinct possibility, and both India and Pakistan have these systems in their arsenals. Compared to artillery, these types of delivery suffer from two key disadvantages: relatively long lag times between the request for nuclear use and the delivery of the weapon and relative inaccuracy compared to an artillery round.[53]

Nuclear weapons can also be "demonstrated" with military effect. For Pakistan, which seeks to use nuclear weapons to deter India or to terminate conflicts where national survival may be at risk, such a strike could take a number of forms, including:

- attack on Indian naval forces;
- attack on Indian ground forces inside Pakistan;
- attack on Indian ground forces in India ("follow-on forces" or logistics);
- attack on Indian airfields;
- preemptive attack on Indian nuclear assets.

A tactical nuclear attack on Indian naval forces has several advantages over an attack on ground or air forces or installations. First, it would limit fallout and collateral damage. Second, it would attack a substantial Indian military asset that Pakistan cannot match conventionally. Third, it would fit easily into the calculus of nuclear use articulated by General Kidwai—India used its Navy in 1971 to blockade Pakistan, and Indian analysts believe that movements of the Indian fleet in 1999 and again in late 2001 had substantial political effect on Pakistani decision making.

An attack on Indian ground forces inside Pakistan would also represent, in the eyes of the international community, an essentially *defensive* use of nuclear weapons. In many regions of the Indo-Pakistani border, battlefield use of nuclear weapons would pose substantial fallout and collateral damage hazards because of the proximity of Pakistani cities to the border. In the south, however, where Indian armored forces massed in 1986–87, 1990, and 2001–2002, large open areas and vulnerable supply lines make battlefield use a more plausible option. Indian doctrine and exercises focus on this as an area where substantial territorial gains are possible, and one where India can use its superior armored and mechanized forces to maximum advantage. Therefore, this front is a high-risk possibility for battlefield nuclear use in crisis, either as a demonstration or in the event of an Indian breakthrough.[54]

Pakistan might also find itself tempted to use nuclear strikes either on Indian follow-on forces—a second echelon of troops threatening to exploit a potential breakthrough—or on Indian supply and logistic services, which would limit India's ability to exploit its quantitative advantages. This attack, however, would take place on *Indian* soil—a substantially different issue in terms of international opinion and escalation control. Another option, similar to this scenario, would be a nuclear attack on Indian forces in an effort to support a Pakistani cross-border offensive. This would be much more aggressive, and would be unlikely to gain the sympathy of the international community.

Pakistani analysts also recognize the long-term asymmetry between the Indian and Pakistani air forces. While Pakistan can put up a fight for a few days, in a longer, several-week campaign, Pakistan will be forced to preserve its Air Force for crucial engagements—a practice followed in 1971, and also used by a number of Arab air forces in the Arab-Israeli and Persian Gulf wars. Attacking the Indian Air Force, therefore, might become a necessity in a longer war, particularly if India proves capable of exploiting its air advantage.

Attack on air and missile facilities might also become imperative if Pakistani intelligence perceived, rightly or wrongly, substantial risk of an Indian preemptive strike. Since India is developing a significantly improved precision-strike capability, the threat to Pakistan's facilities may not be a nuclear threat. Destroying key Indian strike aircraft at their airfields may be beyond the capability of the Pakistani Air Force (PAF), particularly if the PAF relies on conventional weapons. Nuclear-tipped missile strikes might then become a serious option for a Pakistani regime faced with significant military pressure.

At this level of engagement, there is little difference between "battlefield" use of nuclear weapons and more traditional Western notions of "counterforce" strikes on enemy strategic forces. From airfield strikes, it is only a short leap to preemptive nuclear attacks on missile installations or command and control centers. Because of the geographic proximity of the combatants, however, these strikes may be carried out by what would have been described in the Cold War as "tactical" systems, and escalation may occur very rapidly from the conventional to the strategic level. The final option for Pakistan, of course, is "countervalue" strikes against Indian population centers.[55]

Indian options are similar, but India is also less likely to initiate nuclear use. First, India has formally declared, and reasserted, a no-first-use doctrine. Second, India has substantial conventional superiority over Pakistan— comfortable enough that it needn't worry about significant territorial loss, and a superiority that allows it the upper hand in terms of escalation. India can always choose simply not to accept a cease-fire, relying on its superior resources to eventually force Pakistan to negotiate through attrition.

This does not mean that India will not prepare nuclear weapons— according to Indian reports, four short-range Prithvi and one medium-range Agni missiles, along with an unnamed number of Mirage 2000 aircraft, were prepared for nuclear strikes during the Kargil crisis.[56] Leading Indian experts on military weapons have considered the possibility that China might use tactical nuclear weapons in a conflict in the Himalayas.[57] According to anecdotal reports, a 1986–87 crisis with China at Somdurong Chu in the Himalayas led the military leaders to ask what nuclear options India had to respond to a Chinese tactical nuclear attack.[58] The writing in India on tactical nuclear weapons or tactical nuclear use is limited, but what there is suggests a wide range of opinion.[59] The most sophisticated Indian analyses of nuclear strategy, however, reject the tactical weapon option.[60] The most exhaustive study of Indian nuclear policy suggests that India is unlikely to deploy tactical nuclear warheads.[61]

India has considered the problems of Pakistani nuclear threats, despite its stated belief that nuclear war will not occur. Indian responses have come in two forms—first, in a series of highly publicized conventional military exercises and doctrines, and second, by a more recent change in rhetorical policy aimed at reestablishing stable nuclear deterrence. Indian planners have deliberately sought to acquire capabilities, both material and operational, that will allow them to threaten or rapidly destroy Pakistan's nuclear capability. These include Indian Air Force targeting of Pakistani nuclear facilities and delivery vehicles (both aircraft and missiles) with conventional strikes. These capabilities, if acquired, raise the potential of conventional preemption of Pakistani nuclear capabilities in crisis. The ground forces have attempted to reorganize and adapt their doctrine to the difficulties of fighting in a nuclear environment and have also attempted to acquire the ability to rapidly seize or threaten targets of great value to Pakistan in an effort to undermine the nuclear threat.[62] These capabilities are insufficient, despite a recent series of expensive and widely publicized exercises.[63]

As a result, and because of Pakistan's continuing use of the nuclear umbrella to provide cover for a proxy war, India has now chosen to pursue escalation dominance. The announcements of Minister of Defense Fenandes and Chief of Army Staff General Padmanabhan that any Pakistani nuclear strike on Indian forces will meet with massive retaliation and the possible destruction of Pakistan may be an operational fix that temporarily erodes Pakistani confidence in their nuclear deterrent. It also encourages Pakistani leaders, both military and political, to reexamine their assumptions about nuclear use. Some Pakistani analysts have already drawn the conclusion that, given India's new policy, the only option for Pakistan is to commit to a nuclear doctrine of massive countervalue strikes—a position that would certainly ensure, in the event it was ever carried out, massive if not fatal damage to both Indian and Pakistani society.[64] Another consequence, partly the result of the winter 2001–2002 crisis, is the likely devolution of control of nuclear weapons to operational military commanders at earlier points in crisis or conflict, with a subsequent increased danger of accidental, unauthorized, or premature nuclear use.[65]

Conclusion

South Asia remains a terribly dangerous part of the world, despite the hopes of some analysts that nuclear weapons would bring regional stability. The core political issues that divide India and Pakistan remain unresolved, and the crucial issue of Kashmir continues to be a significant flashpoint. The growing disparity in conventional force capability, and in economic development more generally, places tremendous stress on Pakistan—stress that is only exacerbated by the Pakistani government's continuing covert assistance for the Kashmir insurgency.

This disparity in resources will lead Pakistan to place increasing reliance on its nuclear deterrent. At a minimum, Pakistan can be expected to continue expanding its nuclear stockpile and increasing the survivability and number of potential delivery systems. This is a natural reaction to India's increasing nuclear and conventional power.

Some analysts have argued that Pakistan should reduce its conventional forces and move resources to a larger, more survivable nuclear arsenal.[66] Even if implemented, this is unlikely to provide a stable solution to Pakistan's security problem, for three reasons. First, every state has harbored some hope that creation of a nuclear deterrent will lead automatically to lower requirements for conventional forces and, as a result, lower defense spending. This has not proven true, primarily because in most cases—and certainly in the Pakistani case—possession of nuclear weapons alone does not resolve the underlying political conflict that made them necessary in the first place. Second, reduction of conventional forces will only place increasing pressure on the credibility of the nuclear force if Pakistan continues its current support for the Kashmiri insurgency. As long as Pakistan remains a state with revisionist intentions in the region, an existential nuclear arsenal will not achieve them. It will provide only some level of security cover under which to pursue those ambitions with other means. But India might choose to call that bluff in the future. Third, the Pakistani Army plays an important role in Pakistani society and is unlikely to make choices that will undermine its organizational structure, self-image, or capabilities.

Since Pakistan will almost certainly continue to rely on the nuclear force to deter higher-intensity conventional conflict while enabling continued support for covert and low-intensity conflict in Kashmir, South Asia is likely to see a continuing action-reaction spiral not unlike the 1999–2002 period. India will seek to undermine Pakistani confidence in its nuclear deterrent through a combination of new conventional threats, improved nuclear capability, and development of increasingly sophisticated military doctrine—all efforts that will require greater professional military input into Indian security policy. Increasing military input could also lead to increased consideration of the battlefield utility of small nuclear weapons in seeking a decisive victory over Pakistani military forces.

Pakistan, in return, will be forced to focus on the survivability of its nuclear forces, which will be the lynchpin of their security policy. This will require mobile forces and increasingly devolved command and control procedures—efforts that ensure that Pakistan's weapons and doctrine always work when leaders want them to.[67] Weapons or their components will be more widely scattered throughout the country to limit the risk of preemption, and weapons may be stored in an assembled state. Control will be devolved downward through the chain of command earlier in crisis to make sure that the weapons are useable. Weapons and delivery systems will be dispersed earlier in crisis to ensure survivability and retaliation. All of these actions will increase the risk of accidental or unauthorized use, or perhaps even seizure of weapons by nonstate groups.

Sadly, the "logic" of nuclear deterrence in South Asia appears to be all-too-closely following the escalating and destabilizing role it played in Europe in the 1950s. At some point, arsenals on both sides will get large enough to ensure a devastating second strike. Until that point is reached *and recognized* by both sides, however, the risk of nuclear use remains, through deliberate action, escalation, or miscalculation. So long as Pakistan maintains its policy of destabilizing Kashmir, the conditions for a potential nuclear conflict exist in the subcontinent.[68]

7

Chinese Tactical Nuclear Weapons

Charles D. Ferguson, Evan S. Medeiros, and Phillip C. Saunders

China's nuclear weapons have long been an issue of significant interest to international policymakers and analysts. After China exploded its first nuclear device in 1964, its nuclear capability became a central factor in Asian security. Since the 1980s, China has gradually sought to improve the reliability and survivability of its strategic nuclear deterrent and, as a result, its nuclear weapons have assumed increased relevance to global stability. The pace and scope of China's ongoing nuclear modernization efforts have accelerated, which has raised concerns throughout the world about major changes in its nuclear doctrine and nuclear force structure. Such shifts hold implications for global strategic stability and regional security in Asia.

In analyzing China's current and future nuclear capabilities, the subject of tactical nuclear weapons (TNWs) is by far the most opaque aspect. This chapter seeks to shed a brighter light on these issues by systematically analyzing the available open-source data on China's tactical nuclear weapons capabilities. To do this, we examine questions regarding China's tactical nuclear capabilities and Chinese military doctrine and war planning that have a direct bearing on China's possible possession of tactical nuclear weapons. The first part of this chapter examines the technical issues related to tactical nuclear weapons, and the second half assesses changes in Chinese military doctrine since the 1980s.

Three broad considerations are important in assessing China's tactical nuclear capabilities. First, there is a paucity of consistent and reliable information on this topic. Unlike China's strategic nuclear capabilities, China has never officially acknowledged possessing a tactical nuclear capability. Most of the information on its tactical nuclear weapons comes from Hong Kong–source materials of uncertain reliability and Western publications, including some declassified U.S. intelligence reports. There are some articles from mainland Chinese sources (especially in the early 1980s) that discuss tactical nuclear weapons in general terms; yet, these open publications seldom address China's research, development, or deployment of tactical nuclear weapons. Most notably, the Chinese Academy of Military Sciences' *Military Encyclopedia* acknowledges China's possession of strategic nuclear weapons and defines them; regarding tactical nuclear weapons, the encyclopedia simply provides a generic definition with no acknowledgment of such a capability.[1]

Second, since the beginning of China's nuclear weapons development program in the 1960s, its nuclear efforts have been heavily focused on developing and deploying strategic nuclear weapons. China's initial motivations to develop nuclear weapons stemmed from U.S. nuclear threats against China in the 1950s and the desire to acquire nuclear weapons to prevent nuclear coercion or blackmail by the major powers in the future. The bulk of the nuclear program's technical and financial resources have been devoted to developing nuclear weapons and delivery systems that would ensure a credible second-strike capability. Tactical nuclear weapons were never a priority for China's political leaders. The limited and scarce resources devoted to nuclear weapons development and modernization were focused on ensuring the acquisition and maintenance of a survivable and credible nuclear deterrent.[2]

Third, the lack of reliable information about China's tactical nuclear weapons capabilities does not necessarily imply the absence of such capabilities. Rather, the public data on this issue are sufficiently limited that only qualified claims can be made, and more research is needed to make definitive conclusions about China's past and current tactical nuclear weapons capabilities.

Assessing China's Tactical
Nuclear Weapons Capabilities

In assessing China's tactical nuclear capability, two questions are relevant: does China possess the capability to design and produce tactical nuclear weapons, and has China weaponized and deployed such weapons. This distinction between design/production capability and weaponization/deployment is critical to accurately assessing China's tactical nuclear arsenal. This distinction has been overlooked in much of the existing literature on Chinese tactical nuclear weapons.[3]

This chapter argues that there are multiple indications that China has long possessed the capability to design and produce tactical nuclear weapons, both low-yield weapons useful in battlefield environments and miniaturized nuclear weapons. However, it is far less clear that the People's Liberation Army (PLA) actually weaponized and deployed tactical nuclear weapons. Some data suggest that in the early 1980s the PLA possessed and trained with tactical nuclear devices, but this information is contradictory and inconclusive. In addition, even if one concludes that the Chinese military weaponized and deployed such weapons in the 1980s, it is unclear whether the Chinese military currently deploys tactical nuclear weapons. Given the demise of the Soviet threat and the new warming in Sino-Russian relations, the most valuable role for such weapons (to deter or respond to a Soviet blitzkrieg across China's northern and western borders) has vanished. In recent years, the majority of China's resources devoted to nuclear modernization have been allocated to improving the size and capabilities of China's strategic missile forces. Growing Chinese concerns about U.S. missile defense plans and a possible conflict over Taiwan have prompted Beijing to accelerate the pace and scope of its strategic nuclear modernization program.[4]

Parsing the Estimates

Several open-source estimates of China's tactical nuclear weapons address questions of design/production capability and weaponization/deployment. These estimates provide a mixed and narrow picture of China's development and operationalization of tactical nuclear weapons. The most commonly cited estimate of China's tactical nuclear weapons comes from the Natural Resources Defense Council (NRDC), a Washington, D.C.-based research organization. In its authoritative 1994 volume on *British, French and Chinese Nuclear Weapons,* NRDC estimated that China possesses some 150 tactical nuclear weapon systems, "including artillery shells and atomic demolition munitions."[5] Yet, in subsequent updates to the volume, NRDC analysts heavily qualified their earlier assessment. In November 2000, a senior NRDC analyst noted that "information about China's tactical nuclear weapons is limited and contradictory, and *there is no official evidence of their existence.* China's interest in tactical weapons may have been spurred by worsening relations with the Soviet Union in the 1960s and 1970s [emphasis added]."[6]

Declassified estimates by the U.S. Defense Intelligence Agency (DIA) provide more detailed data. The DIA information offers perhaps the best open-source data on China's past tactical nuclear weapons capabilities. DIA reports indicate an enduring Chinese interest in and capability to design and develop tactical nuclear weapons. However, these reports do not confirm China's weaponization or deployment of tactical nuclear weapons. The DIA estimates also provide no data on China's current tactical nuclear arsenal—if one exists. A 1972 DIA report, titled *People's Republic of China: Nuclear Weapons Employment Policy and Strategy,* stated that China's interest in "developing a tactical nuclear capability . . . can be traced back to 1961."[7] The report noted that, although during the 1960s and 1970s Chinese nuclear doctrine was focused on deterring threats from major nuclear powers, some internal discussions about doctrine referred "to use of tactical nuclear weapons." An appendix to the report noted that in 1972 China may have possessed "0–25 tactical bombs for delivery by F-9 [Q-5] or IL-28."[8]

A declassified 1984 DIA Defense Estimative Brief titled *Nuclear Weapons Systems in China* offers additional information.[9] This report's conclusion confirms China's capability to design and produce tactical nuclear weapons but is less definitive about the PLA's weaponization and deployment of them. DIA believed in 1984 that China possessed such weapons even though no direct proof existed. In discussing China's overall nuclear program, the report stated that "no direct evidence exists on the actual size of China's present nuclear stockpile . . . , [yet] indirect evidence derived from Chinese nuclear tests and estimates of the characteristics of deployed delivery systems give some basis for estimating types, yields, and approximate numbers." In reference to tactical nuclear weapons, the DIA estimate noted that "the Chinese nuclear weapons technological capability would limit the current ground force nuclear support to atomic demolition munitions (ADMs), bombs, and missiles; it would not include artillery-fired nuclear projectiles. . . . We also estimate that the Chinese maintain ADMs in their inventory, although there is no evidence confirming their production or deployment." At the end of the estimate, DIA *projected* that by 1989 China's nuclear arsenal could include 50 ADMs and 200 tactical bombs. Yet, the report caveated these estimates by noting "we know very little, however, about the extent of tactical or theater nuclear weapons for use by the Chinese People's Liberation Army (CPLA)."

Additional Factors in Assessing China's Tactical Nuclear Weapons Capabilities

Beyond these broad estimates, there are a number of technical dimensions of China's nuclear weapon program that shed more light on China's capability to develop and deploy tactical nuclear weapons. The key indicators are:

◆ China's nuclear testing program
◆ Chinese and U.S. data on a neutron bomb program
◆ Chinese military exercises

◆ China's fissile material production
◆ China's delivery systems

Each of these factors is addressed below. An assessment of these five factors suggests several conclusions: 1) for several decades China has had the ability to design and produce different types of tactical nuclear weapons; 2) tactical nuclear weapons research and production were never a priority in China's nuclear weapons program; 3) China's ability to design and produce tactical nuclear weapons was largely an outgrowth of the natural evolution of its broader nuclear weapons development program (which placed priority on acquiring strategic weapons for deterrence purposes); and 4) by the 1980s China may have weaponized and deployed tactical nuclear weapons in its military, including the development and deployment of a neutron bomb (also known as an enhanced radiation weapon). Furthermore, no open-source data demonstrate China's current weaponization or deployment of tactical nuclear weapons.

Information on Chinese nuclear tests since the mid-1960s provides much evidence of the capability to develop low-yield weapons and to miniaturize nuclear designs for more efficient tactical delivery. Testing data are less clear on the question of China's weaponization and deployment of tactical nuclear weapons. Since 1964 China has conducted some 20 (of 45) tests at the level of 20 kilotons (KT) or below. It is likely that many of these tests, especially from the 1980s onward, were used to develop smaller, more efficient nuclear weapons designs. According to DIA's 1972 analysis, China's twelfth nuclear test (in November 1970) marked a new phase in which China developed a low-yield (15 KT) device employing a "boosted plutonium primary." The report noted this may indicate development of "plutonium primarys [sic] or pure fission weapons for tactical uses." Lending additional credibility to the development of a tactical nuclear weapons capability, a Qian-5 (Q-5/Fantan) attack aircraft dropped a low-yield bomb just two years later, in 1972, as part of a test.[10]

Additional U.S. and Chinese data further elucidate China's past tactical nuclear weapons capabilities. China clearly developed the ability to design and build neutron bombs—one type of tactical nuclear device. The 1984 DIA study noted that "the Chinese might find Enhanced Radiation (ER) weapons particularly appropriate for use in defense of their border area in Northeast China, especially in the Sino-Soviet border area in Northeast China." These claims were buttressed by China's own statements. According to a prominent study on Chinese nuclear weapons, in the late 1970s and early 1980s Chinese leaders and military publications expressed "an unusual degree of fascination with" the neutron bomb. Senior Chinese military officials openly discussed the value of neutron bombs against large concentrations of Soviet tanks.[11] In the early 1980s, the PLA Daily printed several articles on the tactical and economic benefits of neutron bombs in combat. A 1981 *PLA Daily* article specifically argued that a neutron bomb, which costs $900,000 USD (a curious Chinese estimate), could incapacitate hundreds of Soviet tanks.[12] In the early 1980s, when Deng Xiaoping was reorienting China's national priorities away from national defense construction to economic development, this economic argument may have been persuasive in internal discussions.

The most definitive evidence of China's development of a neutron bomb capability emerged in recent years. (Though evidence of actual weaponization and/or deployment of such a weapon is far less certain.) In 1999, in response to a U.S. congressional report that China had stolen U.S. nuclear and missile secrets, China issued a technical rebuttal that detailed its own efforts at mastering nuclear and missile technologies—without resorting to espionage from the United States. In its response, China acknowledged for the first time the development of a neutron bomb capability. Its report stated, "China had no other choice but to continue to carry out research and development of nuclear weapons technology and improve its nuclear weapons systems, mastering in succession *the neutron bomb design technology* and the nuclear weapon miniaturization technology . . . through its own efforts over a reasonable period of time [emphasis added]."[13] To date, this statement is the closest the Chinese government has come to admitting developing tactical nuclear weapons.

Furthermore, Chinese reports of PLA training and exercises using tactical nuclear weapons offer perhaps the best evidence of China's TNW weaponization and deployment.[14] According to Chinese sources, the PLA began as early as 1979 to conduct military training and exercises that simulated operations on a nuclear battlefield. In January 1979 the PLA conducted exercises simulating defense against the first-use of nuclear weapons. In 1980 the PLA apparently conducted its first offensive exercise simulating China's use of a 5 KT warhead against enemy forces invading the mainland.[15] A large and very public nuclear training exercise occurred in June 1982 in Ningxia Province. In reporting the simulated retaliation against Soviet first-use of tactical nuclear weapons, a *Ningxia Daily* article said, "Our troops' nuclear strike capability zeroed in on the targets, took the enemy by surprise and dealt his artillery positions and reserve forces a crushing blow."[16] Chong-pin Lin, in his seminal study on Chinese nuclear strategy, emphasized several unique aspects of China's military exercises involving tactical nuclear weapons. He argued that the PLA's tactical nuclear warfare training was widespread in China, having been conducted in 9 of 11 military regions in the early 1980s. He argued that Chinese exercises involving tactical nuclear weapons not only simulated enemy attack with them but also simulated PLA attacks using tactical nuclear weapons. The most well-known "offensive exercises" were held in 1982 in Ningxia, in 1983 in the Beijing Military Regions, and in 1984 in the Jinan Military Regions.[17]

An assessment of China's fissile material production and delivery systems is also relevant to analyzing China's tactical nuclear weapons capabilities. This analysis, unlike the discussion of nuclear tests and military exercises, does not provide direct evidence of a tactical nuclear capability. Rather, it simply indicates that China's fissile material production and delivery systems were not constraints on the development of tactical nuclear weapons. In this sense, these two dimensions of China's nuclear program provide indirect evidence of such a capability but do not shed much light on the distinction between design/production capability, on the one hand, and weaponization/ deployment, on the other. In terms of fissile material production, various estimates indicate that China has a large enough stockpile of weapons-grade material to produce or to have produced several hundred more nuclear warheads for both strategic and tactical roles.[18] Indeed, even though China stopped producing both plutonium and highly enriched uranium over 10 years ago, the U.S. government estimates that the size of the fissile material stockpile is not a constraint on China's current nuclear modernization efforts.[19]

Furthermore, for decades China has possessed an array of delivery systems that could facilitate delivery of tactical nuclear weapons—if China actually operationalized its TNW capability. By the 1970s the PLA possessed several attack aircraft and bombers, such as the Q-5 Fantan and Hong-6 medium-range bomber, which were used to conduct airdrop tests of low-yield nuclear weapons. China deployed about 100 to 120 H-6s and about 500 Q-5s (with only about 30 reportedly devoted to a nuclear role). The H-6 could carry up to three gravity bombs, and the Q-5 could hold only one gravity bomb. While these platforms were widely used in the 1970s and 1980s, they are far too antiquated to be effective today. During the 1990s, China initiated a major Air Force modernization effort by purchasing some 200 SU-27s fighters from Russia. In 1999 China also bought 50 more-capable SU-30s from Russia.[20] These multirole aircraft are meant to serve as effective fighters or ground-attack aircraft in conventional conflicts, and there is no evidence of these platforms having been converted to nuclear roles. Some of China's missiles could serve as delivery vehicles for tactical nuclear weapons as well. The 600-km-range DF-15 (M-9/CSS-6) and the 300-km-range DF-11 (M-11/CSS-7) became fully operational in the 1990s. China has deployed several hundred of these missiles (believed to be armed with conventional explosives) within striking distance of Taiwan. Both missiles are nuclear capable. According to John Lewis, the DF-15 could carry a 10 KT neutron warhead or a 20 KT nuclear warhead. Yet, there is no evidence that either has been deployed with such warheads.

The preceding analysis provides firm and consistent evidence that China has long possessed the capability to design and produce tactical nuclear weapons. Yet, none of the preceding data provides definitive or consistent evidence that China actually weaponized or deployed tactical nuclear weapons or that the PLA currently deploys such weapons. The preceding technical analysis must be mated with an assessment of changes in China's military doctrine and possible scenarios of usage to further elucidate China's past and future TNW capabilities. It is to the issues of Chinese military strategy, doctrine, and war planning that this chapter now turns to further clarify questions surrounding China's tactical nuclear weapons capabilities.

Chinese Military Doctrine and Tactical Nuclear Weapons

The preceding sections have presented open-source estimates of Chinese tactical nuclear weapons, examined how the development of China's strategic nuclear weapons program produced a degree of inherent capability to produce tactical nuclear weapons, and surveyed the available evidence of the existence of operationally deployed Chinese tactical nuclear weapons. This section explores how changes in China's military doctrine and external security environment have affected China's interest in tactical nuclear weapons. It concludes with speculation about scenarios in which tactical nuclear weapons might have military utility for China.

Despite Mao Zedong's public statements in the 1950s denigrating nuclear weapons as a "paper tiger," Chinese leaders have long been acutely aware of the geopolitical importance of nuclear weapons and China's vulnerability to nuclear threats. As a result, China launched a nuclear weapons program in January 1955. The initial Chinese program relied heavily on Soviet technical assistance, but the Soviet Union ultimately reneged on a secret agreement to provide China with design information and a sample atomic bomb. As a result, China was forced to rely on its own scientific capabilities and technological infrastructure. These efforts ultimately produced a successful test of a highly enriched uranium fission bomb in October 1964 and a hydrogen bomb in June 1967.[21]

China announced its nuclear capability in October 1964 with a statement that it had developed nuclear weapons for defensive purposes, a proposal to work for the "complete prohibition and thorough destruction of nuclear weapons," and a pledge that China would not be the first to use nuclear weapons.[22] Although these principles have continued to guide China's declaratory nuclear weapons policy, China did not issue a definitive public statement explaining its nuclear doctrine or the conditions under which it might use nuclear weapons. Alastair Iain Johnston argues that "for about 30 years after China exploded its first nuclear weapon there was no coherent, publicly articulated nuclear doctrine."[23] This doctrinal vacuum appears to have also existed within the Chinese military and defense industrial complex. China's nuclear and ballistic missile development programs were guided by a handful of Mao's aphorisms rather than a coherent, comprehensive strategic doctrine.[24]

Despite the lack of doctrinal sophistication, it is clear that Chinese leaders thought of nuclear weapons mainly within a broad geopolitical context. For decades, Chinese leaders repeatedly stated that China possessed nuclear weapons and their delivery means in order to prevent blackmail and coercion by the other nuclear powers, especially the United States and the Soviet Union. This statement, combined with the small and relatively unsophisticated nature of China's strategic nuclear force structure, has led most analysts to conclude that China subscribes to a policy of minimum deterrence that relies on countervalue targeting, that is, aiming at population centers. Deng Xiaoping's 1983 statement suggests the political role of nuclear weapons: "China only wants to adhere to this principle: we must have what others have, and anyone who wants to destroy us will be subject to retaliation." China's nuclear weapons and ballistic missile programs appear to have been driven mainly by general geopolitical concerns and technological factors rather than by detailed strategic analysis. Only in the 1980s did the Chinese military begin to conduct serious strategic research that sought to link China's nuclear arsenal to its foreign policy and national security objectives.

The Chinese leadership's emphasis on the strategic role of nuclear weapons and no-first-use declarations left relatively little role for tactical nuclear weapons in Chinese military doctrine. The smaller payloads and shorter delivery ranges of tactical nuclear weapons make these weapons best suited for a war-fighting role rather than a broader geopolitical role. Moreover, China's public commitment to the goal of complete nuclear disarmament and no-first-use pledges meant that overt deployment of tactical nuclear weapons might have significant international political costs.[25]

Chinese assessments of the international strategic environment in the 1950s and 1960s also reduced the perceived military value of tactical nuclear weapons. Mao's focus on the inevitability of war between communist and imperialist countries meant that nuclear weapons had little chance of preventing war. Indeed, the official Chinese assessment of the strategic environment from the late 1960s through the 1980s predicted "early war, major war, and nuclear war." In such a setting, tactical nuclear weapons offered little hope of preventing escalation in the face of the vastly superior nuclear capabilities of the United States and the Soviet Union. Instead, China must "dig tunnels deep and pile grain high" to prepare itself to survive a likely nuclear war. This belief manifested itself in an emphasis on large nuclear weapons to compensate for inaccurate strategic delivery systems, efforts to build civil defenses, and a massive effort to build a defense infrastructure in China's interior that would be less vulnerable to nuclear attack.[26]

A shift in the official Chinese assessment occurred in 1985. Deng Xiaoping believed that rapprochement with the United States and changes in the Soviet Union made a large-scale global war unlikely for a long time, permitting China to reduce the priority of defense modernization in order to focus on economic modernization. As a result, the Central Military Commission ordered the PLA to make a strategic transition from preparing for an "early war, major war, and nuclear war" to "peacetime army building." The shift in emphasis from inevitable global war to preventable local wars suggested the need "to build a deterrence force to postpone war and to contain it [if it breaks out]."[27] Ironically, the assessment of a more benign international strategic environment suggested a potentially larger role for nuclear weapons in general and tactical nuclear weapons in particular.

Deng Xiaoping's new assessment of the international strategic environment prompted a corresponding shift in PLA doctrine and modernization efforts. Instead of focusing on mobilizing the population for a "people's war" that could defeat a major invasion by a superior force, the PLA now focused on preparing for "local wars" on China's borders. Because local wars would be limited in both scope and objectives, the new strategy suggested the need for more modern military forces that could be rapidly deployed to the site of a conflict. (After observing the success of U.S. forces in the 1991 Gulf War, PLA doctrine shifted again to a focus on preparing for a "local war under high-tech conditions."[28]) The expectation of limited local wars (albeit ones that might involve the United States or the Soviet Union) placed a premium on controlling escalation in order to ensure victory. The new assessment of a more benign strategic environment (and the resulting shifts in PLA doctrine) thus reduced the overall priority of defense modernization while simultaneously increasing the theoretical utility of tactical nuclear weapons in controlling escalation.

These shifts also corresponded with a theoretical debate about nuclear deterrence and the role of nuclear weapons that may indicate a significant shift in China's thinking. During the late 1980s, a number of mid-level PLA military officers and strategists began exploring the concept of limited nuclear deterrence.[29] Limited deterrence lies between China's de facto doctrine of minimum deterrence and the maximum deterrence policies of the superpowers. Minimum deterrence is established when a state has a small, survivable, second-strike strategic nuclear force that can impose unacceptable damage on an adversary (i.e., countervalue targeting). Maximum deterrence involves extensive strategic nuclear forces that could be configured for a first-strike posture against an adversary's nuclear forces (i.e., counterforce targeting) as well as substantial tactical nuclear weapons to provide escalation control during a nuclear war.

Although Chinese analysts rejected the maximal posture of the superpowers, the writings of some Chinese analysts reflected a new interest in the possible need to prepare to fight a more limited nuclear war. Limited deterrence, in the view of many Chinese strategists, could provide a way for China to bolster its minimum deterrent and to fill in the missing rungs on an escalation ladder. These strategists envision scenarios in which China would want to prevent use of strategic nuclear forces, but would want to have tactical nuclear weapons as an option if it was being defeated in a conventional war.[30] Using tactical nuclear weapons in such a conflict would signal China's resolve and might force an adversary with superior conventional forces but limited interests to settle the conflict rather than risk a Chinese strategic nuclear strike.

It is unclear whether this debate about limited deterrence is influencing China's strategic nuclear modernization and decisions about force structure. As Alastair Iain Johnston has stated, there is insufficient evidence to draw a clear connection between this theoretical debate about deterrence and China's strategic R&D and modernization programs. It is possible that the ongoing Chinese doctrinal debate might result in increased interest in tactical nuclear weapons and in developing a nuclear war-fighting capability. However, significant technological and financial barriers stand in the way of developing the intelligence, command and control, and weapons capabilities necessary to support a limited deterrence doctrine. China's current strategic modernization efforts appear to be focused primarily on building a more survivable nuclear deterrent. This goal is being pursued by the development of a second-generation ballistic missile submarine and by efforts to build a new generation of ballistic missiles that are solid fueled, mobile, and more capable of penetrating missile defenses.[31] Some of these shorter-range ballistic missiles (such as the DF-21 and DF-15) are nuclear capable and might be considered to be tactical in nature. No similar effort appears to be under way to upgrade China's obsolete strategic bomber force or to adopt China's Russian fighters to a nuclear delivery role. Although China's emphasis on defending its land and maritime borders suggests a possible role for naval tactical nuclear weapons, the authors have found no mention of Chinese interest in these weapons in either Western or Chinese sources.

China's Changing Strategic Environment and TNW Scenarios

The preceding analysis has focused on China's assessment of the international strategic environment and how this has shaped China's military doctrine and thinking about the potential value of tactical nuclear weapons. This approach can be applied at a more concrete level in analyzing the potential utility of tactical nuclear weapons in specific scenarios and against specific adversaries. Here the interesting point is the apparent divergence between trends in Chinese debates about deterrence and the overall improvements in

China's security environment in the late 1980s and 1990s. At the same time that some Chinese strategists began to discuss the theoretical value of tactical nuclear weapons in nuclear war fighting, China's security environment was changing in ways that reduced their applicability to the actual military scenarios confronting China.

In the 1970s and 1980s, persistent Sino-Soviet border disputes and the Soviet Union's conventional military superiority gave China incentives to develop and deploy tactical nuclear weapons.[32] However, the dramatic warming in China's relations with Russia and the overall improvement in China's post–Cold War external security environment have greatly reduced the scenarios in which tactical nuclear weapons would have significant military utility. Although the possibility of a future military clash with Russia cannot be entirely ruled out, China currently enjoys a close "strategic partnership" with Russia. Moreover, Russian force reductions and the low operational readiness of Russian conventional forces make it highly unlikely that Russia could mount a large-scale invasion of Chinese territory—the principal scenario in which the military advantages of tactical nuclear weapons might outweigh the heavy political disadvantages of being the first to use nuclear weapons. However, if Sino-Russian relations deteriorated significantly, Russia's increased reliance on tactical nuclear weapons to compensate for its conventional military weakness might force Chinese strategists to plan for a conflict in which tactical nuclear weapons could be used.

A review of China's other neighbors reveals no plausible scenarios where the use of tactical nuclear weapons would be militarily desirable or necessary. Although China has an active border dispute with India, the terrain in the disputed sectors makes conventional operations difficult. Given Chinese conventional forces advantages along the disputed border, India is unlikely to penetrate far enough into Chinese territory to force Chinese leaders to contemplate the use of tactical nuclear weapons. Although China had territorial disputes with a number of other countries in Northeast and Southeast Asia, it is difficult to imagine these disputes escalating into a conflict big enough to use nuclear weapons.

The one potential exception is Taiwan. This is the one sovereignty issue where the perceived stakes for Chinese leaders might be high enough to outweigh the political costs of using nuclear weapons. This issue has spawned a whole industry of analysis probing various military scenarios, including invasions, blockades, missile attacks, and strikes against Taiwanese islands, such as Quemoy and Matsu. It is beyond the scope of this chapter to reexamine conventional armed conflict scenarios in the Taiwan Strait, but it is appropriate to examine the potential consequences of tactical nuclear weapons. Most Chinese discussions of the potential value of nuclear weapons in a Taiwan crisis have focused on how China's strategic nuclear deterrent will force the United States to think twice before intervening on Taiwan's behalf.[33] However, if the threat of the use of nuclear weapons against the U.S. homeland did not deter U.S. intervention, tactical nuclear weapons might provide Chinese leaders with additional military options besides publicly backing down from its nuclear threats or launching a suicidal nuclear attack on the United States.

It should be emphasized that the tactical nuclear weapons scenarios discussed here are speculative and based on logical analysis of possible scenarios rather than any evidence of specific Chinese thinking or operational planning. In addition to its general no-first-use pledge, China has made specific commitments not to use nuclear weapons against Taiwan (which were reaffirmed in 1996 and 1999).[34] Moreover, the economic, political, and military consequences of using nuclear weapons against Taiwan or against U.S. forces defending Taiwan would be extremely high. China, which has been very conscious of its international image, would likely become an international pariah and its considerable economic achievements of the last twenty years would be put at risk. China would also risk U.S. nuclear retaliation against its military forces or territory.

With these important caveats in mind, there are four speculative scenarios for tactical nuclear weapons use in a Taiwan scenario: explosion of a tactical nuclear weapon to demonstrate China's resolve to prevent Taiwan independence or to compel reunification; use of a tactical nuclear weapon designed to emit an electromagnetic pulse to damage Taiwan's communications and military forces; a nuclear attack on a U.S. aircraft carrier; and the possible use of tactical nuclear weapons against U.S. bases in Japan or on Guam.

Demonstration of resolve: China could use a tactical nuclear weapon to demonstrate its resolve to prevent Taiwan independence or to compel reunification. The most likely targets would be an uninhabited island off Taiwan's coast or an island defended by Taiwan military forces. The goal would be to compel Taiwan to withdraw a declaration of independence or to accept forced reunification while minimizing civilian casualties and the international political costs of violating China's no-first-use pledge. However, such a demonstration of resolve might not be credible enough to force Taiwan to capitulate. It would also likely prompt an explicit U.S. threat to use nuclear weapons against China if an actual nuclear attack was carried out.

Use of an electromagnetic pulse (EMP) weapon: China could explode a nuclear weapon to produce a large EMP pulse that would destroy Taiwan's communications systems. The goal would be to damage Taiwan's command and control systems to create a window of vulnerability that Chinese military forces could exploit in order to win a victory before U.S. forces could intervene.[35] There are significant technical restrictions that make this scenario difficult and unpredictable, even if China has developed a suitable EMP weapon.[36] Does China have nuclear weapons devoted to an EMP role or operational plans for generating an EMP? No one has published definitive information, but some have asserted that China may develop such weapons. For example, Chien Chung, a Taiwanese nuclear scientist, believes that China has developed the capability to confine the effects of EMP to a limited area enveloping Taiwan and has emphasized that Taiwanese electrical and electronic equipment are not well protected against EMP effects.[37] However, even if an EMP weapon successfully destroyed or degraded much of the Taiwan military's communications system, the PLA would still need to be able to use missiles, air power, and amphibious forces to compel Taiwan to surrender. The political costs of this scenario would also be high, especially if an EMP explosion intended for a high altitude inadvertently burst near the ground and caused significant civilian casualties.

Attack on a U.S. aircraft carrier: China could launch an attack on a U.S. aircraft carrier and its battle group intervening in a Taiwan crisis. The goal would be not only to destroy a military target, but also to inflict sufficient casualties and shock to cause the United States to break off its military intervention. China would have significant difficulty in penetrating a carrier battle group's air defenses to deliver a tactical nuclear weapon. The most effective delivery system would likely be a cruise missile.[38] This would be an extremely risky option. Regardless of whether the attack failed or succeeded, China would open itself up to U.S. nuclear retaliation. Moreover, a nuclear attack might stimulate a "Pearl Harbor effect" that would increase U.S. commitments rather than dissuade U.S. intervention. The long-term consequences for U.S.-China relations (and for China's future economic development) would be devastating.

Attacks on U.S. bases in Asia: China could launch nuclear attacks on U.S. bases in Okinawa and on Guam. The goal would be to damage U.S. military forces and bases that might be used in an intervention in the Taiwan Strait and to dissuade the United States from continuing its military efforts on Taiwan's behalf. Given the proximity of civilian housing to U.S. bases in Okinawa and Guam, such an attack would cause significant civilian casualties in addition to the possible adverse results in scenario three. The United States would be highly likely to retaliate with nuclear weapons to fulfill its treaty commitments to Japan or to avenge the deaths of U.S. citizens on Guam.

None of these scenarios offer a high probability of success, even if China possesses the necessary tactical nuclear weapons and effective delivery systems. All would constitute a reversal of China's declared nuclear policy and expose China to tremendous international pressure. Moreover, the long-term consequences for China's economy and relations with other countries would be extremely high. Thus, even in the one situation where the perceived stakes for China's leaders are sufficiently high to consider the use of tactical nuclear weapons, it is difficult to find a scenario where tactical nuclear weapons could promise a military victory at an acceptable level of risk. Indeed, the most worrisome scenario would be one where China was losing a conventional conflict in the Taiwan Strait and used tactical nuclear weapons in a desperate effort to win (or to find a face-saving defeat that would allow the regime to survive). Fortunately, the risk-averse nature of the Chinese political leadership suggests that any of these tactical nuclear scenarios are extremely unlikely.

Arms Control Considerations

Arms control for its own sake can lead to disastrous results.[39] Nations should pursue arms control only if their security would be enhanced, and they should expect potential adversaries to also participate.[40] An essential prerequisite before undertaking arms control is to understand how particular weapons systems either contribute to or detract from a nation's security. Assessments of weapons systems are embedded in a complex dynamical process. Security requirements change over time and interact with many factors, such as other nations' security needs and domestic political considerations, quite often in complicated feedback loops, where "effects" are not just endpoints but can also act as drivers of "causes."

Two main components of security dynamics relevant to Chinese tactical nuclear weapons are the evolving structure of China's nuclear doctrine, which may be moving away from a purely minimal deterrent posture, and the real or perceived threats to China's sovereignty and integrity. In the early stages of China's nuclear weapons program in the late 1950s and early 1960s, the objective was to free China from the threat of nuclear blackmail. Tactical nuclear weapons likely played little or no role in nuclear weapons development. However, as the Soviet threat on China's borders increased in the late 1960s and 1970s, some evidence suggests that China may have sought to counter this threat in part by producing or developing the capability to produce tactical nuclear weapons. As this threat receded in the mid-1980s, China lost a major rationale for tactical nuclear weapons. Other reasons may have convinced Beijing to develop, maintain, modify, or expand its tactical nuclear weapons arsenal, if such an arsenal exists.

Once weapons systems are built and outlive their original security objective, political and military forces frequently conspire to resist dismantlement of the weapons. Military planners try to find other apparently compelling threats for holding on to these weapons, or they may anticipate a future contingency, such as an armed conflict over Taiwan. Alternatively, political leaders may be reluctant to relinquish certain weapons, especially nuclear weapons, for reasons of prestige, leverage over other nations, and resistance to coercion by other nations. If China has developed tactical nuclear weapons based on a certain set of threats that no longer exist, it may be unwilling to give them up for the reasons discussed above.

Arms control abhors a vacuum. It cannot survive without verifiable information about quantities and capabilities of armaments. As discussed elsewhere in this book, the United States and Russia continue to be guarded about their tactical nuclear weapons arsenals. Nevertheless, the 1991–92 presidential nuclear initiatives took a major step toward increasing transparency about American and Russian tactical nuclear weapons capabilities and bringing them into an arms control regime. China remains far from this position because it has not even acknowledged possession of tactical nuclear weapons. Thus, any discussion of Chinese tactical nuclear weapons arms control remains hypothetical. However, a more concrete basis for an examination of tactical nuclear weapons arms control for China could rest on the greater certainty of China's capability to develop tactical nuclear weapons. A possible tactical nuclear weapons arms control regime would have to give appropriate weight to this latent capability. Nevertheless, a better understanding of how nuclear weapons fit into China's security considerations is necessary before bringing China into either strategic or tactical nuclear arms control negotiations.

This analysis paints a pessimistic picture of the likelihood of engaging China in tactical nuclear weapons arms control. However, other methods such as confidence-building measures could strengthen the security of China and the nations that interact with it and eventually lay a foundation for mutually beneficial arms control measures. Like effective arms control, confidence-building measures should aim to reduce the likelihood of war. They can achieve this goal in a number of ways, including keeping open lines of communication, demonstrating the absence of specific weapons systems in deployed forces, and establishing zones free of particular weapons. The United States and China should investigate confidence-building measures that would reduce the likelihood of nuclear weapons being used in a conflict over Taiwan, including the possibility of a Taiwan Strait nuclear-weapons free zone (NWFZ) and measures that would allow the U.S. and Chinese navies to demonstrate that they do not have tactical nuclear weapons deployed on their ships.

Conclusion

Substantial evidence has been presented here to demonstrate that China has the capability to develop tactical nuclear weapons. In contrast, little hard evidence exists to substantiate claims that China has weaponized or deployed usable tactical nuclear weapons. Moreover, official Chinese government statements have not acknowledged China's possession of these weapons.

The preceding assessment of changes in Chinese nuclear doctrine and possible applications of tactical nuclear weapons does not resolve key questions about China's possible possession of them. There are two diverging trends. Beginning in the mid-1980s, there was increasing discussion among PLA strategists about the potential role of tactical nuclear weapons in the context of a broader debate over the desirability of a doctrinal shift from credible minimal deterrence to limited deterrence. However, it is far from clear whether this thinking has resulted or will result in deployed tactical nuclear weapons. Ironically, the turn toward a more benign international security environment for China in the mid-1980s may have provided a more prominent theoretical justification for tactical nuclear weapons deployment. At the same time, the actual military scenarios confronting Chinese defense planners have changed in ways that greatly reduce the potential utility of tactical nuclear weapons. The collapse of Russian conventional military capabilities and the warming in Sino-Russian relations have virtually eliminated the most prominent scenario under which China would have contemplated using tactical nuclear weapons.

Including China in a tactical nuclear weapons arms control regime would be very difficult because of the lack of transparency about China's nuclear capabilities and intentions. The tension between China's no-first-use pledges and the war-fighting nature of tactical nuclear weapons would probably make Chinese leaders reluctant to pay the political costs of acknowledging TNW possession, if China does indeed have these weapons in its arsenal. China would also be reluctant to join a regime that allowed the United States and Russia to maintain significant portions of their much larger tactical nuclear weapons arsenals. Nevertheless, one possible basis for including China in tactical nuclear weapons arms control discussions could be through the examination of the latent capability to produce such weapons. Although formal Chinese participation in tactical nuclear weapons arms control is unlikely in the foreseeable future, confidence-building measures could offer fruitful first steps on the road to arms control.

Part III

Arms Control, Nuclear Dangers, and Tactical Nuclear Weapons

Incentives for Nuclear Restraint

The Role of Inducement Strategies in Controlling Russian Tactical Nuclear Weapons

David Cortright and Andrea Gabbitas

Various means for controlling and reducing nuclear dangers are available to states. These approaches can be divided into three types: denial, coercive, and persuasive strategies. Denial strategies employ export-control regimes, the imposition of sanctions, and the use of military force. Coercive strategies, such as threats to cancel or block foreign aid or to use military force, work by increasing the costs of pursuing unsavory nuclear policies. Persuasive strategies can also be used effectively in nuclear arms control—often in combination with the first—by offering positive inducements to the target states. In this chapter we examine the role of incentives as instruments of bargaining leverage for nonproliferation and disarmament purposes. We develop a bargaining model that emphasizes the merits of positive inducements as means of encouraging nuclear restraint. Our goal is to identify strategies that the United States could employ in reducing the danger of uncontrolled tactical nuclear weapons (TNW) in Russia.

This chapter begins with an overview of the theory of incentives as instruments of international statecraft. We emphasize the importance of combining sanctions with incentives and the need for positive inducements to create effective bargaining dynamics. We review the role of incentives in disarmament diplomacy and identify factors that account for success or failure, highlighting the cases of Ukraine and North Korea as precedents for incentives-based bargaining to prevent weapons proliferation. We conclude with an examination of political bargaining dynamics between the United States and Russia and the options available for policymakers to reduce the dangers posed by uncontrolled tactical nuclear weapons.

The United States and Russia both face conflicting national interests that affect their policies on tactical nuclear weapons. While both states have an interest in reducing the threat posed by these weapons, each has revised its security doctrine in recent years to give increased importance to the role of tactical nuclear weapons—as an active element of counterproliferation policy in the United States, and as compensation for reduced conventional military capability in Russia. While Russia has expressed greater interest in strategic nuclear reductions, in part because its nuclear capabilities are shrinking through obsolescence, it has not adequately reined in or secured its vast arsenal of tactical nuclear weapons. The United States has been reluctant to accept deeper cuts in strategic nuclear forces or to eliminate its remaining tactical weapons, especially the 1,350 nuclear weapons that remain in Europe as part of NATO.[1] Nonetheless, even in the absence of a strong political commitment to reduce the number of tactical nuclear weapons, it is important to develop strategies that can advance these objectives. These weapons present a significant danger, and in the wake of 11 September, there is a new urgency in both the United States and Russia to keep nuclear materials out of the hands of terrorists. However, negotiations have not yet touched on the specific problem of tactical nuclear weapons. We believe that the demonstrated availability of effective strategies can improve the feasibility and political viability of arms reduction policies and help to mitigate this danger.

Expanding the Tools of Statecraft
in International Relations

In both diplomatic history and international relations theory, coercion has concentrated on threats of force. Although sanctions and incentives have always been a part of international policy, their prominence and frequency of use have increased in recent years. Sanctions have recently come into vogue as one of the most popular international foreign policy tools. Before 1990, when East-West cooperation was rare, UN sanctions were imposed only twice, against Rhodesia (1965) and South Africa (1979). However, following the end of the Cold War, multilateral sanctions were imposed by the Security Council fourteen times.[2] The United States and the European Union also applied sanctions with increasing frequency. By one count, the 1990s witnessed fifty new cases of economic sanctions—multilateral, unilateral, and regional.[3]

The use of inducement strategies has also become more prevalent in international affairs. In 1996–97 a task force of the Carnegie Commission on the Prevention of Deadly Conflict examined the use of incentives and reviewed fifteen cases in which inducement strategies figured prominently in attempts to resolve international conflict.[4] The European Union, the Organization for Security and Cooperation in Europe, and other multilateral institutions have frequently offered inducements to resolve conflict in their regions and beyond. The World Bank and other international financial institutions have applied conditionality and "good governance" criteria in their aid programs to advance human rights and other policy norms.[5] The United States and other major powers have applied inducement strategies to advance foreign policy objectives.

There have been a number of important successes in recent years that point toward the value of incentives-based bargaining. The European Union and NATO have used the offer of membership in these institutions to encourage postcommunist states in Central and Eastern Europe to institute democratic reforms, resolve border disputes, and guarantee the rights of ethnic minorities. The World Bank offered economic support for the peace process in Mozambique, funding the demobilization of combatants to facilitate demilitarization and prevent the resumption of armed conflict. The United States supported the UN-brokered peace process in El Salvador by increasing financial assistance but also by threatening to reduce its aid as a means of bringing the contending parties to the negotiating table. The United States and other governments provided economic, diplomatic, and security inducements to encourage denuclearization in North Korea and Ukraine, as we examine in more detail below.

Understanding Incentives

The use of military and other forms of coercion is widely studied in international relations, while much less attention has been devoted to defining and analyzing the role of incentives. Although scholars frequently refer to "carrots and sticks" as tools of international diplomacy, most of their attention is devoted to the latter. The role of carrots—political and economic inducements for cooperation—is often a neglected stepchild and is thus undertheorized.

Alexander George and others have argued that conventional political theory places too much emphasis on the threatened or actual use of military force, while largely ignoring approaches that reduce tensions or encourage agreement.[6] Roger Fisher observed that during the Cold War the United States created elaborate means for delivering threats but developed "no comparable sophistication regarding the making of offers." Providing rewards as a means of exerting influence is a strategy that, according to Fisher, has received "far too little organized consideration."[7] An "inducement theory" is needed to supplement traditional deterrence theory and provide a more complete understanding of international affairs.[8]

The definition of what constitutes an incentive is subject to varying interpretations. Most analysts agree that the inducement process involves the offer of a reward or benefit by the sender in exchange for a particular action or response by the recipient. Incentives are offered as a means of encouraging a desired policy or behavior. For instance, the European Union (EU) offers the carrot of membership only for states that accept and implement specified policies and standards. Often, incentives are directly related to the desired policy outcome, as when the World Bank assisted the peace process in Mozambique by funding the demobilization of combatants. Incentives are most successful when they substitute for the benefits that the target state expects to derive from the undesirable policy. However, incentives may also be offered in other issue areas and linked to the dispute. In either case, incentives must offer the target sufficient benefits to make a change in behavior attractive.

Mixing Carrots and Sticks

Sanctions and incentives are spoken of separately, but in practice they are closely linked. In his classic *Economic Statecraft*, David Baldwin combined the definition of the two terms by describing sanctions as both positive and negative, referring to incentives as "positive sanctions."[9] We prefer to separate the two terms, as most analysts do, but we acknowledge their close connection. Ending a negative sanction can be considered a positive incentive, while removing an incentive can be seen as a sanction. The art of diplomacy lies in creatively blending positive and negative influences. Sanctions are imposed or threatened to persuade the target to change an objectionable policy. Incentives are offered to reward the change in policy. What the stick cannot accomplish by itself, George noted, may be achieved by combining it with the carrot.[10] The use of negative sanctions can lay the groundwork for the offer of positive inducements, and the provision of incentives can increase the attractiveness of changes sought through sanctions.

Recent empirical studies confirm the benefits of inducement policies and the special advantages of combining incentives with sanctions. Reports from the Center of International Relations at the University of California, Los

Angeles, and from the Department of Sociology and Political Science at the Norwegian University of Science and Technology provide important evidence that the combined use of sanctions and incentives is superior to the application of either approach alone. In the California study, "A Larger Role for Positive Sanctions in Cases of Compellance?" Gitty Amini examined twenty-two cases of compellance that featured the use of sanctions and incentives either alone or in combination.[11] The study found that positive measures are more successful than negative sanctions, and that the combination of incentives and sanctions is more effective than the use of incentives alone. According to the study, "as one moves from the exclusive use of threats and punishments to the use of rewards and promises, the likelihood for success in a compellance situation increases by 34 percent. Additionally, if one opts to use both carrots and sticks, over the use of carrots alone, one is again 34 percent more likely to succeed. . . . There is a definite correlation between success and inclusion of positive sanctions, either alone or in conjunction with negative ones."[12]

In the Norwegian study, "Sanctions and Incentives," Han Dorussen and Jongryn Mo analyzed the specific role of incentives in the 116 sanctions cases examined in the landmark study of the Institute for International Economics in Washington, D.C., *Economic Sanctions Reconsidered*. By reexamining the cases in which positive inducements were applied along with sanctions, and then cross-correlating the use of incentives with the likelihood of success, Dorussen and Mo were able to document the benefits of inducement strategies. The authors declared, "Incentives increase the effectiveness of sanctions." They concluded that "the simultaneous use of incentives and sanctions is more effective than the use of sanctions or incentives separately."[13]

One of the reasons that a combination of sanctions and incentives works better than either approach alone is that the mixing of the two helps to overcome the problems associated with each. Policies that are either too coercive or too conciliatory have drawbacks. Sanctions scholars have noted the tendency of targeted regimes to adopt strategies of resistance, and to redirect coercive pressures onto vulnerable populations or opposition groups. Leaders who are targeted by sanctions often attempt to generate a rally-'round-the-flag effect as a defense against external coercion. In contrast, the addition of positive inducements helps to encourage a state to bend to the coercer's demands. Not only do inducements increase the tangible benefits of compliance, but they also help to lower the adversary's political costs by allowing a face-saving alternative that purely threat-based strategies do not provide. Paul Gordon Lauren points out that incentives play a psychological role by reducing "the opponent's disinclination to comply with the demands" and helping to deescalate the conflict.[14] Thus, a strategy that uses a mixture of threats and inducements may increase the likelihood of coercive success.

Pure inducement policies can also have negative side effects. Incentives may be perceived by a target or recipient regime as a sign of weakness or appeasement. Critics worry that incentives may be seen as a reward for wrongdoing, and that others will be motivated to engage in similar transgressions in the hope of obtaining like rewards. The moral hazards associated with incentives can be addressed by retaining the capacity and will to apply sanctions if necessary. According to Martin Patchen, inducement strategies work best when they flow from strength and are accompanied by a latent threat capacity.[15] When carrots are mixed with sticks, or at least the threat of sticks, the dangers of appeasement or appearing to encourage wrongdoing can be diminished.

Positive Reciprocity

Attempting to understand the circumstances that facilitate cooperation is crucial to international security policy, and to the goal of reducing nuclear dangers. In explaining how and why cooperation flourishes, cooperation theorists have emphasized what might be termed the power of positive reciprocity. Robert Axelrod's pioneering work in game theory demonstrated that the simple tit-for-tat process, in which one party responds in kind to the gestures of the other, is a highly stable form of cooperation.[16] Axelrod's research tested which strategy would be most successful in solving the familiar prisoner's dilemma puzzle. He found that tit-for-tat was the consistent winner. Responding in kind to the other player proved to be the most effective strategy. Positive responses to conciliatory gestures offer the best prospect for mutually beneficial cooperation.

The history of the Cold War confirms the ability of cooperative gestures to induce reciprocal behavior. In relations between the United States and the Soviet Union, conciliatory gestures often led to reduced tensions, while hardline policies usually produced a mirror response of heightened animosity. Lloyd Jensen found in his review of U.S.-Soviet arms talks that concessions by one side tended to be reciprocated by the other.[17] William Gamson and André Modigliani examined eight episodes in which Western nations made conciliatory gestures to the Soviet Union from 1946 to 1963. In seven out of the eight cases, the Soviet Union responded with cooperative behavior. By contrast, there was a tendency toward "refractory" actions and increased belligerence when one side was confronted by hostile actions from the other.[18] Patchen's review of the literature on this subject found that "the usual tendency is for one side in a dispute to reciprocate the [conciliatory] moves of the other, to match incentives if offered with return incentives."[19]

A dramatic example of the power of positive reciprocity occurred in September 1991 when President George H. W. Bush announced the unilateral demobilization of U.S. tactical nuclear weapons from ships and submarines and the removal and dismantlement of nuclear artillery and short-range missiles in Europe.[20] This bold initiative was promptly reciprocated by Soviet President Mikhail Gorbachev, who announced a similar and even more sweeping withdrawal and dismantlement of tactical nuclear weapons from Soviet forces. These unilateral initiatives resulted in significant reductions, removing some 13,000 nuclear weapons from active deployment. The 1991 experience shows the ability of positive incentives to control and reduce nuclear weapons and their dangers.

Charles Osgood pioneered the consideration of risk reduction initiatives with his concept of graduated and reciprocated initiatives (GRIT) in tension reduction.[21] The GRIT strategy was designed to go beyond simple tit-for-tat reciprocity, and called for employing a series of conciliatory measures to reduce tensions and distrust.[22] The initiating side announces a series of accommodating steps and continues even in the absence of a reciprocal response. If the other side exploits the situation or acts in a hostile manner, the initiating side responds in kind, although only to the limited extent necessary to restore the status quo. If the other side reciprocates positively, the pace of conciliatory action is accelerated. The Bush-Gorbachev nuclear reductions and other mutual concessions at the end of the Cold War partially followed the GRIT strategy and helped to dispel the decades-long clouds of fear and mistrust that obstructed East-West cooperation. These examples corroborate the wisdom of offering concessions as a strategy for achieving mutual benefit. As Alexander Wendt observed, "positive reciprocation can foster a sense of common identification and help to create mutual interests between former adversaries."[23] Deborah Welch Larson similarly emphasized the importance of conciliatory action as a way of reducing distrust and establishing the foundations for cooperative behavior.[24]

A potential consequence of positive reciprocity is that in some cases the use of negative sanctions may be counterproductive. Sanctions could compromise the cooperative relationship that exists between certain states. In such circumstances states must rely on what P. Terrence Hopmann calls "soft" bargaining strategies, those in which the bargaining strategy focuses on "positive movements in which one actor behaves in order to increase the potential gains relative to no agreement for another actor."[25] In these cases, inducement strategies can be very successful by offering the target large enough benefits that cooperation becomes the most attractive option.

Making Incentives Work

The Carnegie Commission working group on incentives examined the variables that account for the success or failure of inducement strategies. Among the factors identified by the working group were the nature of the objectives sought, the value of the incentives package, the credibility of the sender, and political dynamics within the sender and recipient regimes. In his recent study on appeasement in international affairs, Stephen Rock identified three determining factors: the nature of the adversary, the adversary's perception of the inducements, and the presence or absence of exogenous incentives. We briefly examine each factor below.

As with sanctions or any other attempt to exert external influence, incentives are more likely to succeed in pursuit of limited change rather than sweeping political transformation. Incentives are more effective, according to Arnold Wolfers, in the area of "low politics" than in matters that affect national sovereignty or territorial integrity.[26] Inducement policies are not likely to be successful by themselves in persuading a recipient to alter policies that affect its basic security interests. If the goal is a change of regime or a major shift in political alignment, incentives alone are not likely to be effective. For the more limited purpose of facilitating a negotiated agreement, however, incentive policies can be highly successful.

Some states are more difficult to appease than others, as Rock notes. A war-seeking state that is bent on aggression cannot be appeased and is best met with deterrence strategies rather than conciliatory policies. If the adversary state pursues more-limited instrumental objectives, or if it pursues non-security goals, it is more likely to respond to inducements. According to Rock, "The less extensive the needs/demands of an adversary whose hostile behavior is instrumental, the more likely appeasement is to succeed."[27]

The most effective incentive strategies are those that are focused on a single objective and consistently sustained over time. When there are multiple or conflicting objectives, attempts to influence policy are likely to be confused and ineffective. Mixed signals create problems of misperception and lessen the prospects of success.[28] Competing interests and cross-cutting agendas are often a problem in international affairs. In the case of U.S.-Russian relations, for example, the concern to reduce nuclear dangers has had to compete with antiterrorism priorities, trade policy, and other political interests.

The perception of value is one of the most important variables in the success of incentives. In economic theory, an incentive is calibrated to increase the value of the option preferred by the sender over what the recipient would otherwise choose. An incentive offer seeks to change a recipient's calculation of cost and benefit regarding the policy objectives in question. The scale of the incentive depends on the magnitude of the desired change in policy. The greater the change, the larger the required inducements package. The value of the incentives offered must match or exceed the value the recipient attaches to the policy being challenged. According to Rock, the inducements must address the needs and demands of the recipient.[29]

The effectiveness of sanctions depends on the credibility of the sender. A reputation for fulfilling pledges and a demonstrated ability to deliver the promised rewards are crucial to success.[30] Promptness in delivering rewards is especially important. The swift fulfillment of a pledge increases the influence of the offer and raises the likelihood of positive reciprocation. Delays in the implementation of an incentive tend to impede cooperation. According to Axelrod, the quicker the response to a conciliatory gesture, the more predictable and enduring the ensuing cooperation.[31]

Exogenous factors outside the control of the sending state often influence the effectiveness of inducement policies. These factors may be at the international level, such as the recipient's loss or gain of an ally, or they may be internal, such as a sudden change in domestic political alignments. These international or domestic factors are often unpredictable and may significantly determine whether a conflict is "ripe" for resolution through incentives-based bargaining. A keen sensitivity to the political opportunities for change, both international and internal, is important in determining whether an attempt at external influence is likely to succeed.

Political dynamics within the recipient and sender significantly affect the impact of inducement strategies. As Denis Goulet observed, "an incentive system can only sway a subject who is disposed to respond."[32] The impact of an incentive depends on the perceptions and preferences of political actors within the recipient regime. The intended beneficiaries of an incentive offer will always be the final judges of its effectiveness. Inducement policies are most effective when they appeal to a recipient's subjective perception of value and when they are targeted to particular stakeholders and political actors within the recipient regime. Inducements should be designed to strengthen the position of reform constituencies within the recipient regime.[33] Understanding and shaping the likely internal consequences of an incentives offer is crucial to the prospects for success.

Political dynamics within the sender are also important. If a multilateral effort is involved, competing interests and messages among the senders make it more difficult to remain focused on the objective and deliver the promised rewards. A single state may be better able to focus on implementing a coherent incentive policy, but competing political interests within that state can impede effectiveness. U.S. incentive policies toward North Korea have suffered from domestic political opposition to the 1994 Agreed Framework, as noted below. Unity of purpose and coherence of message are crucial to success.

Incentives for Nuclear Nonproliferation

In recent decades, incentive tools have been used frequently by the United States to persuade states not to develop nuclear weapons. U.S. security assurances through the NATO alliance and commitments to Japan and other East

Asian states helped to prevent some of these alliance partners from considering the development of an autonomous nuclear weapons capability. The U.S. Atoms for Peace program initiated in 1953 and the 1968 Nuclear Nonproliferation Treaty offered the promise of civilian nuclear technology in exchange for a commitment by recipients to refrain from the development of nuclear weapons. These generic incentive policies, combined with specific benefits for individual states, were successful in persuading a number of nuclear-capable countries not to develop nuclear weapons.

Virginia Foran and Leonard Spector examined the use of incentives for nonproliferation on behalf of the Carnegie Commission and distilled a number of lessons that are summarized below.[34] Foran and Spector found in their examination of cases that incentives are usually offered as part of a package of both positive and negative measures. The carrot-and-stick policy of combining sanctions and incentives has been a key part of U.S. nonproliferation policy.

The stronger the potential proliferator's motivation to develop nuclear weapons, the more difficult it is to influence that state's decision making, and the larger the incentives package needed to prevent proliferation.[35] When incentives can provide the benefits that the state expected to receive from proliferation, it is more likely that proliferation can be avoided. Thus, the stronger the security motivation for developing nuclear weapons, the greater the nonproliferation challenge. It is much more difficult to provide for another state's security than for other needs or desires. When security concerns are a dominant consideration, as opposed to the desire for prestige or economic advantage, financial or economic measures are usually insufficient to change a country's policy preferences. In these instances political assurances and security guarantees must be added to economic offers to increase the potential effectiveness of nonproliferation policy. When the United States has been willing to provide for the potential proliferator's security, as in the cases of Japan, South Korea, and Germany, proliferation has been halted.

The political relationship between the sender and the potential proliferator significantly influences the prospects for success. When the sender and the potential proliferator are on friendly terms, they are better able to communicate and negotiate a bargain to achieve mutual satisfaction. The value of the relationship itself may be an important incentive for reaching agreement.[36]

Foran and Spector developed the concept of a state's "reservation price." This is the lowest price a state will accept for what it is being asked to give up. For the potential proliferator, the reservation price is commensurate in value to the benefits the state seeks to derive from developing nuclear weapons. For the sender, the reservation price is the value of the incentives package needed to match the recipient's perception of the benefits of nuclear development. The incentives a sender offers must equal or exceed the potential proliferator's reservation price.[37] The greater the sunk costs, that is, the investment the potential proliferator has already made in its nuclear program, the larger the value of the incentive needed to match or exceed those costs.

Foran and Spector summarized their hypotheses by identifying three significant variables that may influence the success or failure of an inducement strategy: 1) the degree of enmity or friendliness between the states; 2) the strength of the motive to proliferate; and 3) the magnitude of the political and financial investment in the nuclear program.[38] The success of an incentive policy is more likely when the states involved have friendly relations, when a nuclear program is not essential to the national security of the recipient state, and when the level of investment in the nuclear program is relatively low or of diminishing value to the recipient state.

Encouraging Denuclearization in Ukraine

The effort to persuade Ukraine to denuclearize in the early 1990s illustrates the successful use of incentives to reduce nuclear dangers. When the Soviet Union dissolved in December 1991, Ukraine—along with Belarus and Kazakhstan—found itself an independent state with nuclear weapons on its soil. Approximately 1,800 strategic nuclear warheads from the Soviet nuclear arsenal remained in Ukraine, although Russian authorities had control over these forces. Ukraine initially indicated its readiness to give up these weapons, but nationalist voices in the parliament soon began to argue for retaining the nuclear weapons as a means of guarding Ukrainian independence against Russian domination. The United States became concerned about the prospect of a nuclear-armed Ukraine and began to work with Russia, the United Kingdom, and other countries to persuade Ukraine to follow through on its initial pledges in the 1992 Lisbon Protocol to join the Non-Proliferation Treaty (NPT) as a nonnuclear state. Through the provision of economic assistance and political and security assurances, the United States and other nations were successful in convincing Ukraine to fulfill its initial commitments.

The United States provided $175 million in economic assistance in July 1993, in exchange for Ukraine agreeing to begin transferring its nuclear warheads to Russia. Without this and future U.S. assistance, Ukraine's economy was likely to falter, thus providing a significant incentive for Ukraine to cooperate. The offer of aid was intended as a gesture of U.S. support for Ukrainian independence and a sign of Washington's interest in developing a cooperative relationship with the newly independent country.[39] The provision of economic assistance opened the way for a series of negotiations among the United States, Ukraine, and Russia that led to the January 1994 Trilateral Statement signed by Presidents Bill Clinton, Leonid Kravchuk, and Boris Yeltsin. Under the terms of the Trilateral Statement, Ukraine agreed to transfer all the nuclear warheads on its territory to Russia in exchange for shipment of uranium fuel rods for use in nuclear power reactors and as compensation for relinquishing the weapons-grade uranium and the warheads.[40] The United States agreed to provide Ukraine continuing economic assistance and technical support for the secure dismantlement of the nuclear weapons on its soil. The United States, Russia, the United Kingdom, and France also promised to provide explicit security guarantees upon Ukraine's ratification of the NPT, which was pushed through parliament in November 1994. These four countries pledged not to use nuclear weapons against Ukraine and to respect the integrity of its borders.

The success of inducement strategies in denuclearizing Ukraine can be attributed to several factors. The United States and Ukraine, although having no formal relationship previously, had many reasons for wanting to establish friendly ties. Each had historic suspicions of Russia and saw the other as an important potential ally. Newly independent, postcommunist Russia also hoped for friendly relations with the United States and certainly did not wish to see the emergence of a rival nuclear weapons state on its southern border. Ukraine's interest in becoming a nuclear weapons state was uncertain at best, notwithstanding the pronuclear appeals of some members of parliament, and the country's leaders were willing to trade away the weapons for the right price. The United States and Russia were able to pay that price by providing economic, political, and security assurances to meet Ukraine's needs. Thanks to a set of targeted incentives, Ukraine's security was enhanced by giving up its nuclear weapons rather than by keeping them.

Preventing Proliferation in North Korea: An Incentives Success Story

Positive incentives were a key part of exacting North Korean concessions in its nuclear and ballistic missile programs. North Korea invested a vast amount of scarce resources in its nuclear and ballistic missile programs, placing considerable importance on the potential role of these weapons as bargaining chips and a guarantee of its security. Many of the conditions Foran and Spector identified as conducive to incentives-based bargaining were not present. Nonetheless, the United States and its partners, South Korea and Japan, were able to successfully negotiate the 1994 Agreed Framework, resulting in a verified freeze of nuclear production activities. The North Korea case shows that even in challenging circumstances, inducement strategies can be effective in achieving denuclearization objectives.

The crisis was precipitated when Pyongyang announced in March 1993 its intention to withdraw from the NPT. The specter of a nuclear North Korea, armed with ballistic missiles, posed an unacceptable threat to the United States and its East Asian allies. Some in the United States argued for a coercive response to North Korea's announcement, including the threat or use of military force and the imposition of further economic sanctions. But this strategy risked significant costs to the United States and its allies. War on the heavily armed Korean Peninsula would result in serious casualties, and additional sanctions could cause complete economic collapse in a country that was already one of the most isolated in the world. To avoid these disagreeable outcomes, Washington and its partners turned to the use of incentives-based diplomacy to negotiate a settlement. The result was the October 1994 Agreed Framework that successfully defused the crisis in Korea and contained Pyongyang's nuclear production program.[41]

Under the Agreed Framework, North Korea agreed to halt its nuclear production activities and to refrain from the reprocessing of spent fuel rods. Pyongyang withdrew its threat to pull out of the NPT and accepted full-scope safeguards and inspections of designated facilities. It also pledged to shut down its proliferation-prone graphite-moderated nuclear reactors. In return, the United States, Japan, and South Korea agreed to finance the construction of two 1,000-megawatt light-water reactors in North Korea. Washington also agreed to supply the North with approximately five hundred thousand tons of heavy oil per year as compensation for the loss of energy supplies resulting from the shutdown of the graphite-moderated reactors. The United States also agreed to take steps toward improving bilateral diplomatic relations, through the exchange of liaison offices and subsequent negotiations to begin normalizing political relations.

Despite criticisms of the agreement in the United States, the Agreed Framework was partly successful in shutting down the North Korean nuclear production program. According to Leon Sigal, the North was "punctilious in observing the letter" of the agreement.[42] North Korea complied with its pledges to halt plutonium production activities and permit international monitoring. U.S. officials subsequently learned in 2002, however, and North Korean officials admitted, that Pyongyang violated the spirit of the Agreed Framework by acquiring highly enriched uranium for nuclear purposes. This disclosure jeopardized the continuation of the previously negotiated agreement and has resulted in a new crisis.

In 1998 another proliferation crisis developed on the Korean Peninsula when Pyongyang tested a Taepo Dong 1 multistage ballistic missile over Japanese territory. Although the missile test failed, the prospect of North Korea developing ballistic missiles capable of delivering nuclear weapons raised new security concerns in the region and beyond. In the United States critics argued that the earlier incentives policy had only emboldened North Korea to embark on additional weapons development in the hope of gaining new rewards. Supporters of engagement countered that coercive policies would only push North Korea toward more provocative policies and that engagement had worked previously and was necessary again now to contain the weapons threat from North Korea.[43]

The United States was aware of the North Korean predisposition to accept inducements. On several occasions in earlier years North Korean officials signaled a willingness to trade their ballistic missile program for economic compensation and a lifting of U.S. sanctions. In 1992 and 1993 North Korea held talks with Israel on a proposed bargain in which Pyongyang agreed to suspend ballistic missile sales to Iran and other Middle East states in exchange for the establishment of diplomatic relations and hundreds of millions of dollars worth of investment and technical assistance.[44] Washington later began its own round of missile negotiations with North Korea. In June 1998 North Korea offered to negotiate an end to its missile sales in exchange for U.S. concessions. A North Korean statement declared, "If the United States really wants to prevent our missile export, it should lift the economic embargo as early as possible, and make a compensation for the losses to be caused by discontinued missile export."[45] In May 1999 Washington responded positively to the North Korean declaration and dispatched former defense secretary William Perry to Pyongyang with a historic offer to lift U.S. sanctions in exchange for the cancellation of the North's ballistic missile program.[46] However, the Bush administration turned its back on the proposed deal and raised new demands for more intrusive and wide-ranging U.S. inspections in North Korea that effectively scuttled the prospects for completing the agreement. Incentives-based bargaining produced an agreement to halt ballistic missile development, but a lack of political will in the United States prevented fulfillment of the accord.

The Challenge of Russian
Tactical Nuclear Weapons

The case of Russian tactical nuclear weapons presents a new challenge for U.S. arms control strategies. As in the cases of Ukraine and North Korea, Russia's nuclear arsenal poses a large threat to the United States and its interests, which Washington should take steps to mitigate.[47] However, unlike the nonproliferation cases addressed above, the implementation of additional sanctions is not an attractive option or a credible threat against Russia. Neither does the threat of military action give the United States any coercive leverage. Therefore, the United States will be forced to rely on soft bargaining strategies. The best option available to U.S. policymakers is the implementation of an inducement strategy that gives Russia sufficient incentive to comply with U.S. desires to control its tactical nuclear weapons. However, creating an appropriate and acceptable set of inducements remains difficult. Although the post–11 September security environment provides a window of opportunity to cooperate with Russia in a variety of areas, there are still some impediments to tactical nuclear weapons reductions.

Currently, the main impediment to reductions in tactical nuclear weapons is the perceived utility of tactical nuclear weapons on both sides. After the end of the Cold War, as the Soviet empire collapsed, so did the effectiveness of its military. In addition to losing large numbers of its soldiers, the weakness of the Russian economy resulted in an inability to adequately pay or train those soldiers who remained. Russia quickly realized it had become conventionally inferior to both NATO and China, the two powers that remained on its borders. Unable to deter these powers, Russia turned to tactical nuclear weapons to make up for its conventional inferiority, a strategy that the United States used to deter a Soviet attack on NATO members during the Cold War when Washington feared the Soviets might dominate a conventional conflict. As long as Russia believes that tactical nuclear weapons are crucial to deterring a major war, it will be difficult to convince Moscow to dismantle these weapons.

The United States also finds continued utility in its tactical nuclear weapons. There are 1,350 tactical nuclear bombs still deployed to Europe as part of NATO's extended deterrent. Since these weapons make up a critical part of the U.S. nuclear commitment to Europe, many European and U.S. government officials object to their withdrawal.[48] The United States is also pursuing new types of tactical nuclear weapons and new roles for those that already exist. Leaks about the content of the 2002 Nuclear Posture Review revealed that the Pentagon believes that there is a need for low-yield nuclear weapons with the capability to destroy underground targets and that nuclear weapons could be used in retaliation for attacks by all forms of weapons of mass destruction, not just in response to nuclear attacks.[49] Expanding the role for U.S. tactical nuclear weapons will make it much more difficult to achieve agreements on the reduction of Russian weapons.

The Applicability of Incentives to the Russian Case

The theory and case studies outlined above provide several important insights into what kinds of inducements might be most successful in convincing Russia to reduce its tactical nuclear weapons arsenal. Using the lessons learned through prior inducement strategies in the nuclear arena helps to create a set of potential inducements that could induce Russian cooperation in controlling the threat from its tactical nuclear weapons. Four main factors affect the role and utility of inducements in the case of Russia.

First, inducements are most successful when they address the goals pursued by the target state. The fact that Russia maintains its tactical nuclear weapons to preserve its security makes the application of inducements more difficult, because, as noted above, states are more likely to respond positively to inducements when the change sought is in the *nonsecurity* arena. Since Russia's tactical nuclear weapons fulfill a security need, inducements that are targeted to improve Russia's security situation are likely to be most successful. Several potential inducements in the security arena do exist and will be discussed below. However, it is difficult for one state to credibly provide security for another. Given that Russia still claims a need for tactical nuclear weapons to mitigate its conventional inferiority to other regional powers, the United States will have to make Russian reductions in these weapons seem attractive to Moscow by offering Russia significant enough inducements to change its decision calculus. Political assurances and an improvement in Russian security will be a key part of any inducement strategy.

Positive inducements that address Russia's economic weakness could also be offered. Strengthening its economy is another of Russia's top priorities, and thus significant benefits could be offered in this area. Although this is not the main reason Russia seeks to keep its tactical nuclear weapons, economic constraints have limited the resources that Russia is able to devote to the dismantlement of nuclear weapons, thus providing some incentive to keep even weapons that are outdated or unnecessary. Russia also is likely to have trouble paying its external debt in the coming years, which will affect the nation's economic stability and its ability to accept foreign investment. Inducement strategies that address these economic needs could offer significant enough benefits to Russia to make cooperation on tactical nuclear weapons attractive. However, if the relationship with the United States were to sour, it is unlikely that economic inducements alone would induce Russian cooperation.

Additionally, an inducement strategy must take into account Russia's desire to maintain its great-power status. One of the main impediments to an agreement on tactical nuclear weapons is the seemingly incompatible demands of the United States and Russia. Given that Russia has between two and thirteen times the number of tactical nuclear weapons as the United States has, Washington feels that Russia should take steps to reduce its tactical nuclear weapons unilaterally in order to bring them down to numbers that approximate those held by the United States. However, Russia has often been unwilling to reduce its tactical nuclear arsenal without U.S. concessions, because it fears looking weak.

The second factor that will affect the success of inducement strategies is the positive relationship that has grown out of U.S.-Russian cooperation after the attacks of 11 September. This event has had a significant effect on the type of instruments that are available in persuading Russia to give up its tactical nuclear weapons. Before 11 September, the relationship between Washington and Moscow was rocky. The United States was engaged in a series of policies that Russia saw as negatively affecting its security, including NATO enlargement and the potential U.S. withdrawal from the ABM treaty. Additionally, the United States was highly critical of Russia's war in Chechnya, while Moscow opposed U.S. military action and stringent sanctions against Iraq. However, the World Trade Center and Pentagon attacks created an unanticipated alignment of U.S. and Russian interests. Issues that had been bones of contention before September faded from the foreground. The United States withdrew from the ABM treaty with only minor Russian grumbling, and it is taken as a given that that the next round of NATO expansion will include the Baltic states. The United States responded to Russian help in the war on terrorism by encouraging a closer relationship between Russia and NATO and offering U.S. strategic nuclear reductions. Each state is responding to the other's cooperative efforts with concessions of its own.

This evidence of positive reciprocity in the current U.S.-Russian relationship indicates that inducements are likely to be the most useful tool for persuading Russia to reach agreement on tactical nuclear weapons reductions. Additionally, the history of U.S.-Soviet relations during the Cold War further suggests that Russia will react positively to an inducement strategy.[50] Therefore, the United States should offer Russia targeted incentives that will encourage Moscow to respond in kind in order to maintain the benefits of the new cooperative relationship. Furthermore, a more positive relationship should increase Russia's security, perhaps allowing Russia to concentrate its forces on greater threats and reducing its need for tactical nuclear weapons to counter the West's military potential.

However, the lessons of positive reciprocity should also be a caution to the United States. Although cooperation immediately following 11 September appeared to be reciprocal, since December the United States has pursued a more unilateralist strategy that has ignored many of Russia's concerns. This has caused domestic opposition to Putin's pro-American stance to spread. Many in the Russian elite are beginning to argue that the United States is responding to Russian cooperation with aggressive policies that pursue U.S. interests at Russia's expense.[51] Despite U.S. actions, Putin has continued to respond with cooperation. His actions follow (though perhaps not deliberately) the GRIT strategy, aimed at encouraging the United States to break from its Cold War adversarial posture and foster an enduring cooperative relationship. However, if the United States does not begin to respond more positively to Russian concessions, Putin's position in Russia will become untenable and he will be forced to backtrack from cooperation with the United States. This situation would make an agreement on tactical nuclear weapons much more difficult to accomplish.

Third, since 11 September, the United States and Russia have begun to perceive a common terrorist threat to their national security. Fearing that terrorist groups could become armed with weapons of mass destruction, the two states have agreed to cooperate in the area of nuclear materials security. Bush and Putin plan ''to enhance bilateral and multilateral action to stem the export and proliferation of nuclear, chemical and biological materials, related technologies, and delivery systems as a critical component of the battle to defeat international terrorism.''[52] Both leaders acknowledge the dangers that stem from the Russian nuclear complex and are working together to mitigate these dangers. Increased cooperation on nuclear issues will increase the interaction and trust between the states. This could potentially reduce some of the barriers to prior cooperation, such as secrecy about facilities and components, and make verification of the proper allocation of U.S. disarmament funding or arms agreements increasingly possible. A more cooperative relationship in this area could spill over into strategic or tactical nuclear weapons reductions.

Fourth, the potential for inducement strategies to work is benefited by Russia's current desire to strengthen its relationship with the United States. As noted by Foran and Spector, the value of the political relationship alone may be a sufficient incentive for cooperation.[53] Although Russia is unlikely to reduce its tactical nuclear weapons only to improve its relationship with the United States, it is clear that Putin highly values a more positive relationship. The numerous concessions that Russia has made in the aftermath of 11 September (especially given the failure of a partnership to develop out of Russia's prior concessions) show that a U.S.-Russian partnership is more highly valued than nearly all other nonvital Russian interests. Thus, there currently is a window of opportunity for U.S.-Russian cooperation. If an inducement package of sufficient value were offered to Russia, a deal might be struck. The ability of the United States to offer this package may be limited by political will (discussed below) rather than by opportunity.

Potential Inducement Strategies for Reductions in Tactical Nuclear Weapons

This section will outline five potential inducement strategies that are available for dealing with Russian tactical nuclear weapons, including each strategy's pros and cons.[54] Three types of targeted inducements will increase the chances of attaining Russian cooperation on tactical nuclear weapons. As mentioned above, inducements that address the security concerns that Russia's tactical nuclear weapons are held to counter will likely be the most effective in gaining Russian cooperation. However, economic inducements may also have a significant amount of power given Russia's economic instability. Finally, Russia wants to maintain its great-power status. Thus, inducements that cement Russia as a key international player will likely be well received in Moscow. Additionally, it would certainly be possible to combine two or more of the following inducements. This would increase the benefits to Russia from controlling its tactical nuclear weapons and improve the likelihood of cooperation.

Removal of U.S. Tactical Nuclear Weapons from Europe

Nuclear arms control between the United States and Russia has had a long history of bilateral agreements, reductions, and limitations. Asking Russia to dismantle large numbers of tactical nuclear weapons unilaterally, especially at a time when Russia is struggling to retain global perceptions of it as a world power, is unlikely to meet with much success. Although economic constraints will force Russia to reduce its strategic nuclear weapons regardless of the U.S. decision on storage, Russia has pressed for a formal agreement to cement compatible U.S. reductions.[55] Given that Russia does not see these U.S. strategic weapons as a threat to its security, companion reductions seem more like an attempt to remain politically on par with the United States, because possession of nuclear weapons is one way Russia claims great-power status.

It is therefore likely that in the area of tactical nuclear weapons, Russia would also prefer bilateral reductions to unilateral disarmament, even though Russia currently has many more tactical nuclear weapons than the United States does.[56] Offering to remove and dismantle U.S. tactical bombs in Europe would be the most potent inducement within the immediate TNW issue area. Not only are these weapons within reach of Russia, but they also are a vestige of the Cold War, deployed to make the U.S. nuclear commitment to Europe more credible and originally to deter a Soviet invasion. Without a new threat for these weapons to counter, they remind the United States and Russia of a more adversarial period in history, rather than reinforcing the positive relationship that the two nations are trying to forge. Giving up the tactical bombs in Europe would be an important symbol that they no longer serve any purpose. This would be the first step in persuading Russia that its tactical nuclear weapons are also irrelevant or unusable. As long as the United States keeps tactical nuclear weapons in Europe as a deterrent, Russia will feel justified in maintaining its own deterrent.

U.S.-Russian tactical reductions have a second benefit; they would allow Russia to save face. Instead of having to dismantle its tactical nuclear weapons out of weakness—either political or economic—a parallel disarmament would codify Russia's place as a key global player by putting it on par with the United States. Additionally, Russia prefers making cuts to its nuclear forces by bilateral agreement rather than through purely unilateral actions. Withdrawing tactical nuclear weapons from Europe would be a U.S. concession to Russian interests, an important change from U.S. unilateralist policies that reinforce ideas of Russia's irrelevance in the current international system.

Despite the benefits of this inducement strategy, it may not be of sufficient value to induce Russian cooperation. Russia does not perceive a significant threat from U.S. tactical nuclear weapons in Europe.[57] Therefore, eliminating these weapons does not improve Russia's security situation. Since NATO's conventional forces would remain superior to Russian forces, the Russian need for tactical nuclear weapons would not be eliminated and Moscow would be unlikely to get rid of them. However, if the United States were to offer other inducements that improved Russian security, the elimination of U.S. tactical nuclear weapons in Europe would be a useful inducement to add to an overall incentive strategy. The withdrawal of these weapons would be a valuable symbol of a U.S. departure from Cold War thinking.

Forming a Single Cap on Tactical and Strategic Nuclear Weapons

Russia has already expressed interest in strategic nuclear reductions, pledging in November 2001 to reduce its strategic arsenal to approximately 1,500 warheads.[58] In fact, Russia may proceed with these reductions regardless of the fact that the United States will store some of the weapons that it pledged to eliminate. Many of Russia's weapons—both strategic and tactical—are reaching the end of their service life, and Moscow needs to decide whether to destroy these weapons or to implement life extension programs.[59] However, Russia lacks the money necessary to extend the life of all of its weapons, making it desirable to reduce its strategic arsenal to cut costs.[60]

Creating a joint cap for both strategic and tactical weapons could prove highly beneficial for Russia, especially if relations with the West continue to improve, reducing or even eliminating the need for tactical nuclear weapons to counter a threat from NATO. Under this strategy, Russia and the United States could determine the mix of the tactical and strategic weapons in their own arsenals under a signed treaty that delineated a clear limit on warheads. A formal arms limitation treaty based on warheads has been a key pursuit of Moscow, which does not believe in differentiating between "deployed" warheads and those in "strategic reserve."[61] A signed treaty with the United States would allow Russia to save face, especially in the wake of several concessions on arms reductions after 11 September. The formalization of arms reductions would reinforce a relationship of equal standing between the United States and Russia, strengthening Russia's status as a great power.

A joint cap would also allow Russia to save the costs of life-extension problems. However, this inducement would be even more attractive to Russia if it were coupled with additional Cooperative Threat Reduction (CTR) funding to store and dismantle these weapons. Not only would this give Russia the much-needed funding to deal with the dismantlement costs, but it also would improve the safety of Russia's tactical nuclear weapons and the nuclear material they hold.

Finally, this inducement would allow Russia to keep a limited number of its tactical nuclear weapons if it truly believed that these weapons were integral to its security. Therefore, this strategy would meet many U.S. concerns over tactical nuclear weapons and maintain a certain amount of security for Russia while it is still rebuilding its conventional forces.

The problem with a formal arms control treaty is that it would be difficult to verify. In fact, verification is a major impediment to signing a formal agreement on the reduction of strategic weapons.[62] However, Russia still prefers a signed agreement with verification measures to unilateral declarations. If a joint cap were put into place, verification of TNW reductions would likely be even more difficult than verification of strategic weapons given that Russia might want to keep some of these weapons deployed if it felt that they were necessary for deterring conventional war.

Additionally, some might argue that creating a limit that is higher than the current declared number for strategic weapons might invite the United States to keep more strategic weapons than it has declared it will maintain in the current set of reductions, thus reversing arms control measures already in place. However, a joint cap could be instituted that would reduce the total arsenals of both states. The result of a cap would likely be that the United States would keep greater numbers of strategic weapons than Russia does (as it already plans to do), while Russia would most likely keep more tactical nuclear weapons than the United States does.

Finally, U.S. plans to store weapons that are "eliminated" through arms control measures might present a problem for a negotiated joint cap.[63] First of all, there may not be any political will for Washington to sign another arms control treaty given its reluctance to do so following the November 2001 summit. As we learned in the case of North Korea, political will is necessary for the success of inducement strategies. Without significant backing of the strategy, it may not carry any credibility. If the target state does not believe that the United States will follow through with its promises, it will be reluctant to cooperate for fear that a U.S. withdrawal of its incentives will result in a significant loss of face. Second, Russia might follow the U.S. lead and keep many of its tactical nuclear weapons in storage rather than actually eliminate them. As well as presenting a problem for the negotiation of an agreement, this would fail to eliminate many of the problems that exist with tactical nuclear weapons. Rather, significant numbers might remain and could be vulnerable to theft. In this case, there would be little benefit to either the United States or Russia in creating a joint cap.

Guarantees on Nondeployment to New NATO Members

At the time of the last round of NATO expansion, Russia pushed the United States to sign an agreement to not deploy nuclear weapons to the soil of its new members. Washington declared that it saw no need to deploy weapons to these states, though it refused to sign a formal treaty. Since the addition of Poland, Hungary, and the Czech Republic brought NATO significantly closer to Russia's western border, it is not surprising that Russia felt that its security was threatened by the expansion of a military alliance that was built to counter it. Although Putin does not consider NATO to be a direct threat to Russian security, Russia remains prepared to counter the massive military force to the West. A signed agreement by the United States that it will not deploy nuclear weapons on the territory of the Visegrad states—or new member states that will be added in the next round of expansion—would be a very positive sign that NATO has moved past Cold War, anti-Russia thinking. NATO could also take further confidence-building measures to reassure Russia. If NATO would agree to limit conventional deployments in the new NATO states (by either type of weaponry or troop numbers) without prior notification of Russia, the need for Russian deployment of tactical nuclear weapons to counter an expanding NATO would be reduced and agreement on these weapons might be reached. Certainly, if NATO continues to deploy weapons that threaten Russia, Moscow will not feel particularly pressured to limit weaponry that concerns the NATO states.

This inducement directly addresses Russia's desire for greater security, especially vis-à-vis NATO. As both the theory and the case studies show, security inducements are likely to be the most persuasive. Although this inducement would not reduce NATO's conventional or nuclear force structure, it would help to persuade those in Russia who fear NATO expansion that NATO is not posturing to contain Russia. This would also be an important concession that would allow Russia to save face and open the door to better relations between Russia and NATO. However, the biggest problem with offering limits on future NATO deployments is the lack of political will in the United States to do so. Washington refused to formally limit NATO deployments in 1999 and may continue to do so. The Bush administration has proven reluctant to sign treaties that limit its freedom of action and would likely see limits on NATO deployments in the same light. Without some willingness in Washington to forgo its unilateralist policy choices, this inducement will not be politically viable.

Giving Russia a Lead Role in the NATO-Russia Partnership

Although Russian membership in NATO is still unlikely in the short term, it would be possible to improve Russian security by further upgrading its status within existing NATO structures. The creation of the NATO-Russia Council in the fall of 2001 is a good first step toward alleviating some of Russia's security concerns, however more needs to be done to ensure that this relationship does not end in failure as did the 1997 NATO-Russia Permanent Joint Council in Russian eyes.[64] If serious steps are not taken to make Russia a lasting part of the alliance, especially given Russia's current nonveto status,

Moscow may not see much advantage in this partnership and may see cooperation as ephemeral. Giving Russia a lead role in the alliance's fight against terrorism could both cement the partnership and offer Russia the international prestige and leadership role it desires. Such a role seems logical given that there is "broad acceptance for proposals that Russia should work closely with NATO."[65] It is generally agreed that NATO-Russia cooperation on terrorism and nuclear materials protection is necessary. Furthermore, using the joint council for the discussion of matters critical to the security of both NATO and Russia would help to both integrate Russia into the West and to reduce the threat that NATO poses to Russia. As positive reciprocity suggests, allowing Russia a say in the deliberations of the alliance could create a basis for further cooperation between Russia and the West in other areas.

This inducement strategy has two main benefits. First, it addresses Russian security needs, thus affording some of the security that Russian tactical nuclear weapons are intended to provide and making Russian compliance more likely. A credible and lasting improvement in Russia's relations with Europe and the United States would allow Russia to concentrate its military forces on deterring or quelling conflicts on its other borders, including providing a better defense against a potential Chinese threat. Even if Russia felt that tactical nuclear weapons were still necessary to deter or halt an invasion of Russian territory by a superior force, many fewer weapons would be necessary to concentrate only on China. Second, this strategy allows Russia to save face by giving it a carrot that recognizes Russia as a major European power that should take a lead in security discussions. This is a status that Russia has long argued for as it fights to maintain its great-power status.

Expediting Russian WTO Membership on Favorable Terms

President Putin has listed membership in the World Trade Organization (WTO) as one of his top priorities for Russia. Russia believes that WTO membership will increase the flow of foreign direct investment into Russia and strengthen its economy. Thus, both Putin and Russian Prime Minister Mikhail Kasyanov have called for the United States and the European Union to support Russia's candidacy.[66] After 11 September, Russia's aid in the campaign against terrorism was rewarded with U.S. backing for Russian membership, mirrored by EU endorsement. Furthermore, the pace of Russian accession sped up in 2002, leading some to believe that membership in 2004 might be possible. However, debate over whether Russia could meet the requirements for WTO membership in the near term and whether WTO membership would have a positive effect on the Russian economy have kept skepticism about Russian membership high.[67] Furthermore, the Bush administration has pledged that it will not lower the bar for Russian membership, and Putin has refused to accept unreasonable standards, increasing the possibility that a deal on the terms of WTO accession will be difficult to strike.

Despite the declared stringency of the requirements, China was allowed to join the WTO while still pursuing several reforms over a transitional period because of its status as a developing country.[68] Russia, too, could be made eligible for exceptions to the stringent standards for WTO membership given the fact that it is still in the process of building a stable market economy. Allowing Russia to protect certain sectors such as agriculture or textiles for a fixed period would be an important concession to Russian interests, while still bringing Russia closer toward the economic integration with the West that it craves.

This inducement strategy has several benefits. First, it addresses Russia's economic concerns, allowing further stability to the country and perhaps allowing for an increased investment into Russian conventional forces, eventually alleviating the need for tactical nuclear weapons. Additionally, increased Western direct investment in Russia and greater economic integration with the West could help to further ease Russian security concerns, making Russian compliance more likely. An improvement of Russia's relations with Europe and the United States would allow Russia to concentrate its military forces on deterring or quelling conflicts on its other borders, including providing a better defense against a potential Chinese threat. Even if Russia felt that tactical nuclear weapons were still necessary to deter or halt an invasion of Russian territory by a superior force, many fewer weapons would be necessary to counter China. Finally, this strategy allows Russia to save face by giving it concessions that recognize Russian concerns rather than dictating terms from a position of strength. Early entry to the WTO on favorable terms would paint Russia as a strong economy that should not be excluded from international economic organizations, thus reinforcing Russia's self-perception as a great power.

Debt Forgiveness and/or Debt Swap

Another potential inducement that could be used to persuade Russia to give up many of its tactical nuclear weapons would be Western debt forgiveness. Waiving some of Russia's debt—or even restructuring it—would be a significant inducement. Russia's foreign debt totals $147 billion, which will continue to be a significant burden on the Russian economy despite projections that Russia will be able to meet these obligations.[69] Russia has recently resumed its arms trade with Iran in the face of significant U.S. pressure, largely because of the economic boost that these sales will give to the ailing Russian defense industry.[70] This is one sign that Russia is desperate for hard currency to stabilize important sectors of its economy. Similar "debt for security" swaps have been advocated by policy analysts, politicians, and academics and aim to reduce the debt held by Russia while improving the international security environment. In the TNW arena, this type of program would allow Russia to pay off its debt (or part of its debt) into a fund that could then pay for the dismantlement of Russian tactical nuclear weapons (and potentially other nonproliferation programs). The advantage of this program for Russia is that they could pay off their debt while reinvesting in the Russian economy. Given the continued burden of paying off its debt obligations,[71] a debt swap would enable Russia to pay its debt without dipping into its hard currency and foreign reserves. This, in turn, could help to stabilize the Russian economy and attract foreign investment, two things Moscow is anxious to see happen. Given the importance of stabilizing the Russian economy for several of Russia's other goals (e.g., closer cooperation with Europe; membership in the WTO; or, over the longer term, membership in the European Union), reducing Russia's debt would be a powerful inducement.

Any of these debt forgiveness projects would require multilateral cooperation, because most of Russia's debt is held by Germany and Italy.[72] The U.S. Senate has already proposed a bill that would institute a swap of debt for nonproliferation initiatives.[73] Other nations will have to follow suit for debt forgiveness to succeed as a nonproliferation strategy. Although this means that more states would have to be involved in the negotiations, multilateral inducement strategies have proven successful in both the cases of Ukraine and North Korea. In the Ukrainian case, financial inducements from several prominent states in the region helped to tie Ukraine to the West, further stabilizing its economy and helping to guarantee its security. Multilateral economic inducements offered to Russia would likely have the same effect.

Incentive theory suggests that the value of the inducements offered must equal the value of Russia's tactical nuclear weapons. There are many opportunities for U.S. and European investment that are currently held back by the weakness of the Russian economy. Especially given the fact that many of Russia's tactical nuclear weapons are reaching the end of their service life, financial inducements could approach the sunk costs in the TNW program and provide sufficient benefits to make cooperation in this area seem attractive. Russia will incur significant costs if it chooses to extend the life of these weapons, and Putin has already decided that these costs are too great in the area of strategic weapons. A thoughtful inducement package that offers sufficient benefits could persuade Russia to choose tactical nuclear weapons dismantlement.

Conclusion

Inducement strategies have proven to be an important part of preventing the spread of nuclear weapons. Inducement theory and past cases where incentives were employed offer lessons that can be applied to the challenge of controlling tactical nuclear weapons. In fact, history suggests that incentive strategies could play a positive role in the case of Russian tactical nuclear weapons. The cases of Ukraine and North Korea demonstrate that a combination of economic assistance and political assurances can be effective in encouraging nonproliferation. Additionally, Foran and Spector argue that incentives for nuclear restraint are more likely to succeed under several conditions—when the sender and recipient are on friendly terms, when nuclear capability is not vital to a recipient's national security, and when the benefits offered by a sender match the perceived value of nuclear capability and the recipient's prior investment in the nuclear program. Many of these conditions are present in the case of controlling Russia's tactical nuclear weapons. Furthermore, Russia's current interest in a cooperative relationship with the United States appears to follow a GRIT strategy centered around positive responses to U.S. policy moves, making it more likely that U.S. carrots could produce further Russian cooperation, even in different issue areas. Among the incentives that might be successful in persuading Russia to limit tactical nuclear weapons are the removal of U.S. tactical nuclear weapons from Europe, a single cap on tactical and strategic nuclear weapons, guarantees of nondeployment of nuclear weapons in new NATO member states, giving Russia a lead in the Russia-NATO partnership, early and favorable accession into the WTO, and a debt for disarmament swap. By taking into account Russia's main concerns—security, economic stability, and international prestige—the proposed incentives could be successful in persuading Russia to cooperate further in the arena of arms control for tactical nuclear weapons.

Tactical Nuclear Weapons and the Promise of Arms Control

Jonathan Dean

In the spectrum of nuclear weapons, tactical weapons—smaller, more portable warheads, bombs, and mines—may present the highest danger of theft, forcible seizure, and actual use. According to recent intelligence reports, these are the types of weapons that present or future bin Ladens are seeking to acquire. As the specter of nuclear terrorism looms larger than ever, tactical nuclear weapons (TNWs) represent a unique menace to 21st-century security. Despite this fact, this most dangerous category of weapons is not constrained by any treaty. Unlike strategic nuclear weapons, there is no U.S.-Russian data exchange, no clear understanding as to their number, and no agreement to restrict the level of their deployment. The threat of terrorism, however, may prompt the United States and Russia to develop a strategy for controlling tactical nuclear weapons.

What Can Be Done?

When it comes to tactical nuclear weapons, the world of "what is being done" is vastly different from "what can be done" and "what should be done." In an ideal world, a world in which nuclear weapons were reduced to verified levels on their way to elimination under the Non-Proliferation Treaty, tactical nuclear weapons would be controlled in the same manner as strategic nuclear weapons. Information on their number and location would be exchanged among the nuclear weapon states and their level would fall under the same low, negotiated limits as strategic nuclear weapons—perhaps 200 warheads of both types for each weapon state. Surplus weapons, both strategic and tactical, would be destroyed under bilateral or international monitoring, and their fissile material would be turned over to the International Atomic Energy Agency (IAEA) for safe storage. Storage sites for the small number of remaining permitted weapons would be dispersed in deep bunkers protected by site defense missile defenses and would also be bilaterally or multilaterally monitored. The weapons could be withdrawn from storage by owner states but not without alerting monitors. The path would be cleared for the complete elimination of nuclear weapons.

Under these circumstances, the possibility of the theft, illegal sale, or unauthorized or accidental use of tactical nuclear weapons—and the greater temptation to deliberately use them—would be greatly reduced and the world would be a much safer place.[1] Unfortunately, these ideal circumstances do not exist. To limit the risks posed by tactical nuclear weapons, the U.S. and Russian governments must make a major shift in arms control policy. A look back at international efforts to control tactical nuclear weapons sheds light on the challenges ahead.

What Has Been Done—The Existing Regime

The current arms control regime for tactical nuclear weapons is based on three unilateral statements: a public statement by President George H. W. Bush on 27 September 1991; a public statement by Soviet President Mikhail Gorbachev on 5 October 1991; and a public statement by Russian Federation President Boris Yeltsin on 29 January 1992. The U.S. declaration provided for the *elimination* of all ground-launched U.S. tactical nuclear warheads, nuclear artillery shells, and nuclear depth charges, and for the *withdrawal* of tactical nuclear weapons from U.S. surface ships and attack submarines and from land-based naval aircraft. Mikhail Gorbachev, for the Soviet Union, and then Boris Yeltsin, for Russia, its nuclear weapon successor state, pledged to *eliminate* nuclear warheads from land-based tactical-range missiles, artillery, and mines and to *withdraw* nuclear warheads from air defense weapons, surface ships, attack submarines, and land-based naval aviation.[2]

As many commentators have pointed out, including those in this book, this was a promising beginning for arms control of tactical nuclear weapons, but these unilateral statements were not legally binding and are subject to change. There was no data exchange and no provision for verification. Aside from Russian naval aviation, nuclear weapons for land-based combat aircraft were not affected. Nor were submarine-launched ballistic missiles. Only ground-launched tactical-range missile warheads, artillery shells, and mines were to be completely eliminated; other weapons could be stored or eliminated on the decision of the owner government. Subsequent statements about warhead elimination have been mainly in percentage terms without specification of the base amount. Much of the ensuing U.S.-Russian discussion of tactical nuclear weapons has been directed, vainly, to overcoming these shortcomings.

How Many Tactical Nuclear Weapons Are There?

There have been no serious charges of outright violation as concerns withdrawal of tactical weapons from their delivery platforms, like naval vessels or artillery pieces. But storage and dismantling of these weapons has been questioned by both sides. In particular, Western governments have wondered aloud how many tactical weapons Russia had at the outset, and how many it has now. In chapter 2 of this book Joshua Handler provides one of the most recent and thorough accountings of the Russian TNW arsenal, placing it at 3,380 warheads as of 2002. However, even Handler notes that uncertainties underlie estimates of the Russian arsenal, "because of the lack of reliable information about the size of the Russian stockpile and the rate of Russian warhead dismantlements."[3] Other unofficial estimates of remaining Russian tactical nuclear weapons range from a low of 2,000 to a high of 20,000. Meanwhile, Russian Duma member Alexei Arbatov has forecast that nearly all existing Russian tactical nuclear weapons (as well as many strategic ones) would reach the end of their service life by 2003.[4] The Russian Federation has taken steps toward resuming production of tactical nuclear warheads. Some Russian experts say that the current level of Russian tactical weapons is about 2,000 and that only enough new warheads are being manufactured to maintain and not exceed this level.[5] However, there is no independent information on the rate of production of new warheads or on total numbers.[6] Two rounds of discussions in the NATO-Russia Permanent Joint Council, intended by NATO to lead to exchange of warhead numbers, resulted in unsatisfactory Russian statements about elimination of tactical warheads expressed in terms of percentage of unstated base figures. Such vagueness and contradictions regarding the character of some of the world's most dangerous weapons makes it impossible to achieve a sense of security regarding the Russian arsenal.

The United States is estimated to have 1,120 tactical nuclear weapons;[7] Most of these are gravity bombs, of which about 150 are stored in Europe for possible use by aircraft of seven NATO countries. The remainder consists of 320 Tomahawk cruise missiles with nuclear warheads. As regards other nuclear weapon states, France has a few types of tactical air-to-ground nuclear weapons, and China has several types of tactical weapons. Using the U.S.-Russian criterion of substrategic range, Israeli, Indian, and Pakistani nuclear weapons would also be considered tactical.

Tactical Weapons Concerns Are Not New

Over the years, Russia has complained about continuing deployment of U.S. tactical nuclear weapons in Europe. On several occasions, it has suggested that they be withdrawn to the United States. Russia has also complained about U.S. submarine-launched nuclear cruise missiles. Total destruction of these weapons by both sides was urged by President Yeltsin as early as 1992, in his speech reaffirming the Gorbachev statement on Russian tactical nuclear weapons. Russia's concerns about submarine-launched cruise missiles are apparently twofold: One is the possibility of an accurate surprise attack with conventional cruise missiles that could destroy much of Russia's nuclear strike force in Western Russia. Second, some Russians have also pointed out that conventional cruise missiles could be covertly converted to nuclear-armed missiles using warheads from Pershing-22 ground-launched cruise missiles (which the United States stored after destruction of the Pershing launchers required by the Intermediate-Range Nuclear Forces [INF] Treaty). There are visual differences between conventional and nuclear warheads for Tomahawks, but they are perceptible only at close range. The Russian concern here is apparently the very rapid upload capabilities of long-range submarine-launched nuclear-tipped missiles with a range of up to 2,500 kilometers. The United States has many hundreds of conventional cruise missiles for ships and submarines. These weapons were used in Kosovo, against Iraq, against the Al-Qaeda network in Sudan and Afghanistan after the embassy bombings in Kenya and Tanzania, and in Afghanistan after the 11 September attacks.

For their part, the United States and its European allies were worried about Russian tactical nuclear weapons. Their total number was unknown, but it is believed by some experts to approach 20,000. In the mid-1990s, tactical nuclear weapons were still scattered in numerous, poorly guarded storage sites and appeared to be dangerously exposed to theft, illegal sale, or forcible seizure. These were the "loose nukes" about which there were so many stories in the Western media. There was also another danger: Many of these weapons could be launched on the same missiles now used for strategic warheads, or by shorter-range missiles not covered in the Strategic Arms Reduction Treaty (START) or INF Treaty, undermining the value of the deployment limits for strategic warheads in the START treaties and placing Western Europe under potential threat. Speaking for the European Union, European representatives took the initiative to call for reduction of tactical nuclear weapons in the March 2000 Review Conference of the Nuclear Non-Proliferation Treaty. In short, tactical nuclear warheads are still considered the most dangerous component of the Russian nuclear arsenal and remain unconstrained.

The Helsinki Accords

To cope with these dangers, the ideal world outcome described at the beginning of this chapter appeared within reach when President Bill Clinton and President Yeltsin met in 1997 in Helsinki to discuss the outlines of a possible START III Treaty. The two leaders then agreed that strategic weapons would be cut to a level of about 2,000 on each side. Reductions would be made "irreversible," with full and verified information exchange about the weapons of the other side—numbers, types, and where stored—monitored destruction of warheads withdrawn from operational deployment, and agreed disposal of their fissile material so it could not be reused for weapons. This approach was intended to replace the START I-START II approach of simply withdrawing warheads from operational deployment by offloading them from delivery vehicles and storing them intact for relatively rapid uploading. Backed by the prospect of an international agreement to end production of fissile material for weapons, the new approach would have been the beginning of real nuclear disarmament, a process that could be reversed only by lengthy and highly visible resumption of production of fissile material.

The Helsinki agreement also took account of the concerns of both governments over tactical nuclear weapons, stating, "The Presidents also agreed that, in the context of START III negotiations, their experts will explore as separate issues possible measures relating to nuclear long-range sea-launched cruise missiles and tactical nuclear systems, to include appropriate confidence-building and transparency measures."[8]

The two governments agreed that tactical nuclear weapons would be the subject of negotiation during the START III talks. But the content and form of these negotiations was not further developed at the Helsinki meeting. Under favorable conditions, tactical nuclear weapons would have been included in the same count as strategic warheads and given the same treatment; subsequently, this possibility was discussed on several occasions by the two governments. At least *something* would be done about these uncounted, uncontrolled, uncovered nuclear weapons. Unfortunately, this promising agreement was not carried out in the ensuing four years, because of the weak government in Russia and controversy over U.S. plans for nationwide missile defense.

Current Bush Administration Policy

The advent of the Bush administration in January 2001 brought the apparent end of these hard-won possibilities. The new administration opposed negotiated arms control agreements as clumsy, time-consuming, and inflexible. It declared its belief in reduction of nuclear weapons through parallel unilateral action by Russia and the United States—without formal agreement or verification. Presumably, if the United States became convinced that the Russians were cheating, it could compensate by increasing the number of its own deployed strategic-range nuclear weapons, drawing on its hedge reserve to do so. Moreover, administration officials said, since the United States and Russia were no longer Cold War opponents, they should not be expected to act in lockstep. Each could decide on its own what it would do and inform the other.

In November 2001 President Bush and President Putin informally agreed that each country would reduce its deployed strategic nuclear warheads to 2,000 or fewer. The Bush administration wanted to leave the agreement at that, but Russia insisted on a written agreement, preferably a ratified treaty, to include specific verification measures. Reluctantly, the Bush administration agreed to explore the possibility of a written agreement. Finally, in May 2002 the United States and Russia signed the Moscow Treaty on Strategic Offensive Reductions (SOR). The SOR reduces operationally deployed strategic warheads from the November 2001 levels of 5,000–6,000 on each side to no more than 2,200 for each side by 2012. The treaty provides that each party will remove warheads from missiles, bombers, and submarines, but each party will be permitted to retain delivery systems for such warheads. The SOR is not clear on what should be done with warheads removed from service, provides no new verification measures, and allows three-month notification for unilateral withdrawal. The SOR makes no reference to tactical nuclear weapons.

This chapter will return to the U.S.-Russian talks on strategic reductions, but first, a review of related arms control issues.

Other Arms Control Issues

Under the current Bush administration, U.S. commitments to international arms control agreements seem less certain than in the past. Within the first year, the Bush administration was unwilling to support the reintroduction of the Comprehensive Test Ban Treaty to a new vote in the U.S. Senate. It withdrew from the negotiations on a verification protocol for the 1972 Biological Weapons Convention, arguing that the draft protocol would create an illusory sense of security while tying the hands of the United States and preventing it from acting flexibly in its own interests. It did not pursue the Clinton administration's approach of seeking amendment of the ABM Treaty to cover its program for nationwide missile defense. Instead, it announced withdrawal from the ABM Treaty to pursue missile defense more freely. The administration restored some cuts made by its Office of the Budget in "Nunn-Lugar" funds used to safeguard Russian weapons of mass destruction—the benefits of this program for U.S. security were evident, and this program did not involve any treaty obligations for the United States.

After the 11 September terrorist attacks in New York and Washington, the administration understandably gave priority to destruction of the Al-Qaeda network, but in some respects, this emphasis also pushed negotiated arms control further into the background. For example, in the interest of strengthening the antiterrorist coalition, the administration lifted sanctions against Pakistan and India that had been imposed after their May 1998 nuclear weapons tests and, focusing on the Al-Qaeda and Kashmir issues, tactfully avoided pressing either government on nuclear issues.

The administration's long-awaited Nuclear Posture Review (NPR) was presented to Congress on 8 January 2002, and portions of the report were made public on 9 January. Bush administration spokespersons said the United States would reduce the level of its operationally deployed strategic warheads to between 2,200 and 1,700 over a 10-year period. An unspecified portion of the warheads withdrawn from field deployment would be stored intact in an active reserve, ready for uploading. Neither the number of these active reserve warheads, nor their relationship to the approximately 2,500 warheads stored by the Clinton administration as a "hedge" against possible Russian misconduct, was specified. Moreover, the unclassified version of the Nuclear Posture Review made no mention of existing tactical nuclear weapons but left open the possibility for developing a new class of tactical nuclear weapons. The NPR initiates a joint Department of Defense-Department of Energy study to be conducted over three years, which will explore the feasibility of a low-yield nuclear weapon for use against hardened and deeply buried targets (HDBT)—so-called nuclear "bunker busters."

Russian leaders publicly objected to the absence of measures in the NPR that could make the projected reduction of strategic warheads "irreversible" in the sense of the 1997 Helsinki agreement. The real Russian objection was that the Bush administration considered it necessary to retain a large "hedge" of rapidly uploadable strategic nuclear weapons in circumstances where the United States had declared a new partnership with Russia of common action against terrorism. Russian officials also repeatedly declared their concerns about U.S. cruise missiles on submarines. They pointed out that the provision in the NPR to convert four Trident ballistic missile submarines to cruise missiles increased the risk both of preemptive conventional attack and of rapid covert upload of nuclear cruise missiles.

Lack of Interest in Tactical Nuclear Weapons Reductions

There are many uncertainties about the Bush administration's approach to strategic nuclear reductions, with its focus on parallel unilateral actions with a minimum of written agreement. As noted, U.S. and Russian officials did not include tactical nuclear weapons in the SOR. However, despite their continuing concerns about tactical nuclear weapons, U.S. and Russian officials have not indicated that the issue of tactical nuclear weapons would be included on the agenda of foreseeable reduction talks, if any. In the case of the SOR, both sides apparently believed there were enough problems without complicating the issue with tactical nuclear weapons. These weapons remained in the limbo in which they had rested since the Bush-Gorbachev-Yeltsin agreements of 1991.

In short, in spite of the many obvious defects of the 1991–92 agreements on tactical nuclear weapons and numerous expressions of concern by both the United States and Russia in the ensuing decade, neither side appeared concerned enough to insist that they be tackled soon in the effort to find a solution. Given that, in addition to their risk of theft or illegal sale, tactical nuclear weapons could in many cases be substituted for withdrawn "strategic" warheads on both sides, the uncertainties connected with these nuclear weapons are far-reaching. In ten years, instead of only 2,000 deployed long-range Russian nuclear warheads under the Bush-Putin understanding, there could be 1,000 more tactical warheads on their own launchers and 300 or more nuclear Tomahawk missiles ready to be loaded on U.S. submarines. This degree of uncertainty seriously devalues the reassurance from reductions of strategic nuclear weapons and poses its own separate dangers. It also shifts the focus of efforts to decrease the threat from nuclear weapons back to control of delivery systems—missiles and aircraft.

Possible Solutions

Against this background, a return to the Clinton-Yeltsin approach of the 1990s will probably have to await either a change in the U.S. administration or a nuclear weapons catastrophe. Greater support of both houses of Congress would be useful, but it might not bring decisive change.

Despite apparent disinterest on both sides, it would have been desirable to bring the tactical nuclear weapons issue back into the U.S.-Russian dialogue while the debate over the nature of strategic arms reduction commitments was still going on. Given that the strategic weapons issue is at least partially resolved, the United States and Russia should now resume their interrupted discussion over some mutually acceptable trade-offs for tactical nuclear weapons. A special problem with restrictions on Russian tactical nuclear weapons is that control might be related to the number of warheads rather than launchers, in contrast to the strategic talks, where the number of warheads deployed was estimated mainly by estimating launcher capacity. Setting an absolute level of warheads, rather than merely a deployed level, requires that the base level be known (e.g., how many tactical nuclear warheads Russia has produced, how many it has destroyed, how many it now has, of what type, and where they are stored). This is a very difficult objective, particularly with regards to storage sites. Knowledge of their location makes them a desirable target.

In these circumstances, it is difficult to propose attractive negotiating possibilities for the future. We can assume at the outset that, given the relative weakness of its conventional forces and its first-use doctrine, Russia will not be willing to eliminate its entire stockpile of tactical nuclear weapons. We can also assume that the United States will also wish to retain some of these versatile weapons. Consequently, the area of negotiation on tactical nuclear weapons would be restricted even if a low level of interest on both sides can be surmounted.

Over the years, experts have made many proposals for trade-offs between U.S. tactical nuclear weapons deployed in Europe and Russian tactical nuclear weapons. For example, it has been proposed that these weapons be frozen in level and location and that there be data exchange on the number stored at each site in NATO countries and in a large segment of Russia (for example, Russia west of the Urals). Sensors could help to count the number of warheads without revealing warhead design information, which is very carefully guarded by each side. This proposal is problematic in that it informs targeters on each side of the storage location of weapons, although warheads could be moved relatively rapidly in a crisis situation. Nonetheless, this proposal has the benefit that it can be developed further to a reduction scheme and that its implementation would not require knowledge of the total Russian stockpile of tactical nuclear weapons or its storage sites.

In another approach, all U.S. and Russian tactical warheads could be withdrawn from an area of Western and central Europe, which would exclude storage sites for French and U.K. nuclear weapons, and from a large area of western Russia. Also, a nuclear weapon-free zone would be established, as has been proposed for central Europe alone. The absence of nuclear weapons could be verified by air and ground sensors. This approach does not have enduring benefits, because weapons could be brought into the weapon-free zone with relative rapidity from each side.[9]

Former START I and START II negotiator Linton Brooks has made the practical suggestion that effort should be made to gain Russian agreement to bring tactical weapons under coverage of the Cooperative Threat Program (Nunn-Lugar) for protection and dismantlement.[10] In practice this would involve payment of U.S. funds to improve the storage security and rate of dismantlement of Russian tactical weapons. Presumably, U.S. officials have raised this idea with their Russian counterparts. However, Russian experts state that Russia has already consolidated previously scattered storage sites and improved their security, and that dismantlement of Russian tactical weapons is on schedule.

Russian military leaders have repeatedly expressed concerns about the possibility of a devastating surprise attack on nuclear weapon sites in western Russia by conventionally armed U.S. cruise missiles and technically superior NATO combat aircraft armed with conventional weapons. These Russian concerns may point to the possibility of some trade-off between these Western weapons and Russian tactical nuclear weapons. NATO aircraft come under the Conventional Forces in Europe (CFE) Treaty, so, if it were desired, some reduction here might be feasible. However, controlling U.S. conventionally armed cruise missiles on both submarines and surface ships would probably require keepout zones that U.S. missile-equipped vessels could not enter (a concept that the U.S. Navy has already rejected) and perhaps controls on the entire U.S. stockpile of these weapons, as well as controls (e.g., data exchange, ceilings, and verification) on the entire Russian stockpile of tactical nuclear weapons.

Another possibility would be an agreement combining these approaches and covering reductions or withdrawals of U.S. submarine-launched cruise missiles, NATO air forces, and U.S. tactical nuclear weapons in Europe in return for reduction of Russian nuclear weapons.

Finally, a solution could arise from the fact that, in connection with the 2002 Nuclear Posture Review, Bush administration officials have indicated a willingness to occasionally review the level of warheads in the active stockpile of strategic warheads contemplated under the NPR. If there is flexibility here, the United States could reduce the level of its active stockpile in return for some move with regard to Russian tactical nuclear weapons. Once again, verification would be a problem.

Most of these possible solutions have been canvassed over the years, but none have been energetically supported by either the U.S. or the Russian government. Nor has either side taken the initiative to propose a well-founded solution of the problem of tactical nuclear weapons. This suggests that up to now, for both governments, accepting a dangerous status quo is preferable to the probable cost of most solutions yet proposed.

A Logical Conclusion

It is improbable that an agreement to restrict or reduce tactical nuclear weapons will be reached in the foreseeable future. The total elimination of these weapons is even less probable; both sides are likely to want to retain a few for the sake of reassurance and their presumed capacity to deal with a wide range of contingencies. Alexei Arbatov forecasts that only 1,000 tactical Russian warheads will remain in 2003.[11] Other Russian warheads will have exceeded their service life and their nuclear "pits" will have to be remade or the warhead discarded. Other Russian experts speak of a Russian stockpile of 2,000 tactical warheads. If accurate, these figures are far less alarming than the 20,000 figure often given as the total of Russian tactical nuclear weapons. If these lower figures represent the dimensions of the tactical weapons problem in four to five years, and they can be verified, it may be possible to address the problem more productively than at present. The easiest solution in that case may be to include tactical weapons under strategic weapon ceilings and permit each government "freedom to mix," that is, to have the number of each type it wishes as long as the agreed overall ceiling is respected. Verification would still be a problem, however.

Terrorism: A New Precipitating Factor?

A new challenge with regard to tactical nuclear weapons has arisen. The 11 September terrorist attacks in New York and Washington revealed that the Al-Qaeda network was larger and better organized than previously thought and had devoted considerable effort to acquiring nuclear weapons. Concerns that terrorists could lay their hands on Russian nuclear weapons, which were poorly guarded by low-paid soldiers, increased already existing U.S. worries about Russia's tactical nuclear arsenal. But the September attacks also increased Russian worries about possible terrorist use of nuclear weapons.

In his State of the Union message of 29 January 2002, President Bush linked support of terrorism by Iraq, Iran, and North Korea with efforts of the same governments to develop nuclear weapons. The inference was clear that these governments could be capable of supplying the terrorist groups they were supporting—or other terrorist groups—with nuclear weapons. Al-Qaeda's organizational capability and the capabilities of these potential suppliers are considerable. Both Iraq and North Korea appeared close to producing operational nuclear weapons when their efforts were interrupted. Consequently, the prospect that a terrorist group could gain access to portable nuclear weapons, frequently discussed over the past decade, now appears considerably more real.

The 2002 Nuclear Posture Review made clear the Bush administration's position that nuclear weapons are here to stay. There is no mention in the unclassified version of the report of a goal, however distant, or even a possibility of ultimate elimination of nuclear weapons. Instead, the report points even more clearly than the Clinton policy of deliberate ambiguity to the potential use of U.S. nuclear weapons for retaliation against attack by biological or chemical weapons. This point stands even though the administration will also try to develop conventional weapon capabilities to give the president a choice of responsive weapons.

Conclusion

Unless there is a major shift in U.S. or Russian policy, tactical nuclear weapons will continue to exist and pose a serious threat to U.S. and world security. However, both the U.S. and Russian governments now apparently consider the possibility of terrorist use of nuclear weapons in some form to have greatly increased. Therefore, it is possible that increased concern over terrorist seizure or use of nuclear weapons from Russian, Iraqi, North Korean, or Iranian sources may ultimately provide the motivation necessary to trigger negotiations on tactical nuclear weapons. In its March 2003 report on its resolution of advice and consent on the Moscow Treaty of May 24, 2002, the U.S. Senate urged the president to engage the Russian government in a discussion of cooperative measures to improve accurate accounting and security of non-strategic weapons on both sides and to provide U.S. or other international assistance to improve accounting and security of Russian TNWs. However, the Senate resolution does not ask for negotiation or other steps to reduce the stockpiles of these weapons.

The possibility of terrorist use of nuclear weapons cannot be fully blocked by the threat of use of U.S. weapons, nuclear or conventional, or by future missile defenses, whatever their capability may be. Consequently, negotiation to better control tactical nuclear weapons drawing on approaches illustrated here remains a necessity, first with Russia, but also with North Korea, Iran, and other potential proliferators.

Appendix A
The 1991–1992 Presidential
Nuclear Initiatives

PRESIDENT GEORGE H. W. BUSH

Address to the Nation on Reducing United States
and Soviet Nuclear Weapons

September 27, 1991

Good evening. Tonight I'd like to speak with you about our future and the future of the generations to come.

The world has changed at a fantastic pace, with each day writing a fresh page of history before yesterday's ink has even dried. And most recently, we've seen the peoples of the Soviet Union turn to democracy and freedom, and discard a system of government based on oppression and fear.

Like the East Europeans before them, they face the daunting challenge of building fresh political structures, based on human rights, democratic principles, and market economies. Their task is far from easy and far from over. They will need our help, and they will get it.

But these dramatic changes challenge our nation as well. Our country has always stood for freedom and democracy. And when the newly elected leaders of Eastern Europe grappled with forming their new governments, they looked to the United States. They looked to American democratic principles in building their own free societies. Even the leaders of the USSR Republics are reading *The Federalist Papers,* written by America's founders, to find new ideas and inspiration.

Today, America must lead again, as it always has, as only it can. And we will. We must also provide the inspiration for lasting peace. And we will do that, too. We can now take steps in response to these dramatic developments, steps that can help the Soviet peoples in their quest for peace and prosperity.

More importantly, we can now take steps to make the world a less dangerous place than ever before in the nuclear age.

A year ago, I described a new strategy for American defenses, reflecting the world's changing security environment. That strategy shifted our focus away from the fear that preoccupied us for 40 years, the prospect of a global confrontation. Instead, it concentrated more on regional conflicts, such as the one we just faced in the Persian Gulf.

I spelled out a strategic concept, guided by the need to maintain the forces required to exercise forward presence in key areas, to respond effectively in crises, to maintain a credible nuclear deterrent, and to retain the national capacity to rebuild our forces should that be needed.

We are now moving to reshape the U.S. military to reflect that concept. The new base force will be smaller by half a million than today's military, with fewer Army divisions, Air Force wings, Navy ships, and strategic nuclear forces. This new force will be versatile, able to respond around the world to challenges, old and new.

As I just mentioned, the changes that allowed us to adjust our security strategy a year ago have greatly accelerated. The prospect of a Soviet invasion into Western Europe, launched with little or no warning, is no longer a realistic threat. The Warsaw Pact has crumbled. In the Soviet Union, the advocates of democracy triumphed over a coup that would have restored the old system of repression. The reformers are now starting to fashion their own futures, moving even faster toward democracy's horizon.

New leaders in the Kremlin and the Republics are now questioning the need for their huge nuclear arsenal. The Soviet nuclear stockpile now seems less an instrument of national security, and more of a burden. As a result, we now have an unparalleled opportunity to change the nuclear posture of both the United States and the Soviet Union.

If we and the Soviet leaders take the right steps—some on our own, some on their own, some together—we can dramatically shrink the arsenal of the world's nuclear weapons. We can more effectively discourage the spread of nuclear weapons. We can rely more on defensive measures in our strategic relationship. We can enhance stability and actually reduce the risk of nuclear war. Now is the time to seize this opportunity.

After careful study and consultations with my senior advisers and after considering valuable counsel from Prime Minister Major, President Mitterrand, Chancellor Kohl, and other allied leaders, I am announcing today a series of sweeping initiatives affecting every aspect of our nuclear forces on land, on ships, and on aircraft. I met again today with our Joint Chiefs of Staff, and I can tell you they wholeheartedly endorse each of these steps.

I will begin with the category in which we will make the most fundamental change in nuclear forces in over 40 years, nonstrategic or theater weapons.

Last year, I canceled U.S. plans to modernize our ground-launched theater nuclear weapons. Later, our NATO allies joined us in announcing that the alliance would propose the mutual elimination of all nuclear artillery shells from Europe, as soon as short-range nuclear force negotiations began with the Soviets. But starting these talks now would only perpetuate these systems, while we engage in lengthy negotiations. Last month's events not only permit, but indeed demand swifter, bolder action.

I am therefore directing that the United States eliminate its entire worldwide inventory of ground-launched short-range, that is, theater nuclear weapons. We will bring home and destroy all of our nuclear artillery shells and short-range ballistic missile warheads. We will, of course, ensure that we preserve an effective air-delivered nuclear capability in Europe. That is essential to NATO's security.

In turn, I have asked the Soviets to go down this road with us, to destroy their entire inventory of ground-launched theater nuclear weapons: not only their nuclear artillery, and nuclear warheads for short-range ballistic missiles, but also the theater systems the U.S. no longer has, systems like nuclear warheads for air-defense missiles, and nuclear land mines.

Recognizing further the major changes in the international military landscape, the United States will withdraw all tactical nuclear weapons from its surface ships and attack submarines, as well as those nuclear weapons associated with our land-based naval aircraft. This means removing all nuclear Tomahawk cruise missiles from U.S. ships and submarines, as well as nuclear bombs aboard aircraft carriers. The bottom line is that under normal circumstances, our ships will not carry tactical nuclear weapons.

Many of these land- and sea-based warheads will be dismantled and destroyed. Those remaining will be secured in central areas where they would be available if necessary in a future crisis.

Again, there is every reason for the Soviet Union to match our actions: by removing all tactical nuclear weapons from its ships and attack submarines; by withdrawing nuclear weapons for land-based naval aircraft; and by destroying many of them and consolidating what remains at central locations. I urge them to do so.

No category of nuclear weapons has received more attention than those in our strategic arsenals. The Strategic Arms Reduction Treaty, START, which President Gorbachev and I signed last July, was the culmination of almost a decade's work. It calls for substantial stabilizing reductions and effective verification. Prompt ratification by both parties is essential.

But I also believe the time is right to use START as a springboard to achieve additional stabilizing changes.

First, to further reduce tensions, I am directing that all United States strategic bombers immediately stand down from their alert posture. As a comparable gesture, I call upon the Soviet Union to confine its mobile missiles to their garrisons, where they will be safer and more secure.

Second, the United States will immediately stand down from alert all intercontinental ballistic missiles scheduled for deactivation under START. Rather than waiting for the treaty's reduction plan to run its full seven-year course, we will accelerate elimination of these systems, once START is ratified. I call upon the Soviet Union to do the same.

Third, I am terminating the development of the mobile Peacekeeper ICBM as well as the mobile portions of the small ICBM program. The small single-warhead ICBM will be our only remaining ICBM modernization program. And I call upon the Soviets to terminate any and all programs for future ICBMs with more than one warhead, and to limit ICBM modernization to one type of single warhead missile, just as we have done.

Fourth, I am canceling the current program to build a replacement for the nuclear short-range attack missile for our strategic bombers.

Fifth, as a result of the strategic nuclear weapons adjustments that I've just outlined, the United States will streamline its command and control procedures, allowing us to more effectively manage our strategic nuclear forces.

As the system works now, the Navy commands the submarine part of our strategic deterrent, while the Air Force commands the bomber and land-based elements. But as we reduce our strategic forces, the operational command structure must be as direct as possible. And I have therefore approved the recommendation of Secretary Cheney and the Joint Chiefs to consolidate operational command of these forces into a U.S. strategic command under one commander with participation from both services.

Since the 1970s, the most vulnerable and unstable part of the U.S. and Soviet nuclear forces has been intercontinental missiles with more than one warhead. Both sides have these ICBMs in fixed silos in the ground where they are more vulnerable than missiles on submarines.

I propose that the U.S. and the Soviet Union seek early agreement to eliminate from their inventories all ICBMs with multiple warheads. After developing a timetable acceptable to both sides, we could rapidly move to modify or eliminate these systems under procedures already established in the START agreement. In short, such an action would take away the single most unstable part of our nuclear arsenals.

But there is more to do. The United States and the Soviet Union are not the only nations with ballistic missiles. Some 15 nations have them now, and in less than a decade that number could grow to 20. The recent conflict in the Persian Gulf demonstrates in no uncertain terms that the time has come for strong action on this growing threat to world peace.

Accordingly, I am calling on the Soviet leadership to join us in taking immediate concrete steps to permit the limited deployment of nonnuclear defenses to protect against limited ballistic missile strikes, whatever their source, without undermining the credibility of existing deterrent forces. And we will intensify our effort to curb nuclear and missile proliferation. These two efforts will be mutually reinforcing. To foster cooperation, the United States soon will propose additional initiatives in the area of ballistic missile early warning.

Finally, let me discuss yet another opportunity for cooperation that can make our world safer.

During last month's attempted coup in Moscow, many Americans asked me if I thought Soviet nuclear weapons were under adequate control. I do not believe that America was at increased risk of nuclear attack during those tense days. But I do believe more can be done to ensure the safe handling and dismantling of Soviet nuclear weapons.

Therefore, I propose that we begin discussions with the Soviet Union to explore cooperation in three areas: First, we should explore joint technical cooperation on the safe and environmentally responsible storage, transportation, dismantling, and destruction of nuclear warheads. Second, we should discuss existing arrangements for the physical security and safety of nuclear weapons and how these might be enhanced. And third, we should discuss nuclear command and control arrangements, and how these might be improved to provide more protection against the unauthorized or accidental use of nuclear weapons.

My friend, French President Mitterrand, offered a similar idea a short while ago. After further consultations with the alliance and when the leadership in the USSR is ready, we will begin this effort.

The initiatives that I'm announcing build on the new defense strategy that I set out a year ago, one that shifted our focus away from the prospect of global confrontation. We're consulting with our allies on the implementation of many of these steps which fit well with the new post–Cold War strategy and force posture that we've developed in NATO.

As we implement these initiatives we will closely watch how the new Soviet leadership responds. We expect our bold initiatives to meet with equally bold steps on the Soviet side. If this happens, further cooperation is inevitable. If it does not, then an historic opportunity will have been lost. Regardless, let no one doubt we will still retain the necessary strength to protect our security and that of our allies and to respond as necessary.

In addition, regional instabilities, the spread of weapons of mass destruction, and as we saw during the conflict in the Gulf, territorial ambitions of power-hungry tyrants, still require us to maintain a strong military to protect our national interests and to honor commitments to our allies.

Therefore, we must implement a coherent plan for a significantly smaller but fully capable military, one that enhances stability but is still sufficient to convince any potential adversary that the cost of aggression would exceed any possible gain.

We can safely afford to take the steps I've announced today, steps that are designed to reduce the dangers of miscalculation in a crisis. But to do so, we must also pursue vigorously those elements of our strategic modernization program that serve the same purpose. We must fully fund the B-2 and SDI program. We can make radical changes in the nuclear postures of both sides to make them smaller, safer, and more stable. But the United States must maintain modern nuclear forces, including the strategic triad, and thus ensure the credibility of our deterrent.

Some will say that these initiatives call for a budget windfall for domestic programs. But the peace dividend I seek is not measured in dollars but in greater security. In the near term, some of these steps may even cost money. Given the ambitious plan I have already proposed to reduce U.S. defense spending by 25 percent, we cannot afforded to make any unwise or unwarranted cuts in the defense budget that I have submitted to Congress. I am counting on congressional support to ensure we have the funds necessary to restructure our forces prudently and implement the decisions that I have outlined tonight.

Twenty years ago when I had the opportunity to serve this country as Ambassador to the United Nations. I once talked about the vision that was in the minds of the UN's founders, how they dreamed of a new age when the great powers of the world would cooperate in peace as they had as allies in war.

Today I consulted with President Gorbachev. And while he hasn't had time to absorb the details, I believe the Soviet response will clearly be positive. I also spoke with President Yeltsin, and he had a similar reaction, positive, hopeful.

Now, the Soviet people and their leaders can shed the heavy burden of a dangerous and costly nuclear arsenal which has threatened world peace for the past five decades. They can join us in these dramatic moves toward a new world of peace and security.

Tonight, as I see the drama of democracy unfolding around the globe, perhaps we are closer to that new world then every before. The future is ours to influence, to shape, to mold. While we must not gamble that future, neither can we forfeit the historic opportunity now before us.

It has been said, "Destiny is not a matter of chance. It is a matter of choice. It is not a thing to be waited for. It's a thing to be achieved." The United States has always stood where duty required us to stand. Now let them say that we led where destiny required us to lead, to a more peaceful, hopeful future. We cannot give a more precious gift to the children of the world.

Thank you, good night, and God bless the United States of America.

Note: The president spoke at 8:02 P.M. in the Oval Office at the White House. In his remarks, he referred to Prime Minister John Major of the United Kingdom; President Francois Mitterrand of France; Chancellor Helmut Kohl of Germany; Secretary of Defense Dick Cheney; President Mikhail Gorbachev of the Soviet Union; and President Boris Yeltsin of the Republic of Russia.[1]

SOVIET PRESIDENT MIKHAIL GORBACHEV

Address to the Nation on Reducing and Eliminating Soviet
and United States Nuclear Weapons

October 5, 1991

Dear Compatriots,

A week ago, the President of the United States, George Bush, put forward an important initiative on nuclear weapons.

We see in this initiative the confirmation that new thinking has received wide support in the international community. George Bush's proposals are a fitting continuation of the work begun at Rekjavik. That is my basic assessment. I know that Boris Yeltsin and the leaders of the other republics share this opinion.

In this statement I shall announce the steps we are taking and the proposals we are making in response.

First. The following actions will be taken with regard to tactical nuclear weapons :

- ◆ All nuclear artillery ammunition and nuclear warheads for tactical missiles will be destroyed;
- ◆ Nuclear warheads of anti-aircraft missiles will be removed from the army and stored in central bases. Part of them will be destroyed. All nuclear mines will be destroyed;
- ◆ All tactical nuclear weapons will be removed from surface ships and multipurpose submarines. These weapons, as well as weapons from ground-based naval aviation, will be placed in central storage areas. Part of them will be destroyed.

Thus, the Soviet Union and the United States are taking radical measures on a reciprocal basis leading to the elimination of tactical nuclear weapons.

Moreover, we propose that the United States should on a reciprocal basis completely eliminate all tactical nuclear weapons from its naval forces. Also on a reciprocal basis, we could remove from active duty units of forward-based (tactical) aviation all nuclear ammunition (bombs and aircraft missiles) and store them in centralised bases.

The USSR calls on the other nuclear powers to join in these far-reaching Soviet-United States measures with regard to tactical nuclear weapons.

Second. Like the United States president, I am in favour of the earliest possible ratification of the Treaty on Strategic Offensive Weapons. This issue will be discussed at the first session of the reconstituted Supreme Soviet of the USSR.

Taking into account the unilateral steps on strategic offensive weapons announced by George Bush, we shall take the following measures :

◆ Our heavy bombers, like those of the United States, will be taken off alert and their nuclear weapons will be stored;

◆ Work will be halted on the new modified short-range missile for Soviet heavy bombers;

◆ The Soviet Union will halt work on a mobile small international ballistic missile;

◆ Plans to build new launchers for intercontinental ballistic missiles on railway cars and to modernize those missiles will be abandoned. Thus, the number of our mobile intercontinental ballistic missiles with multiple individually targeted warheads will not increase;

◆ All our intercontinental ballistic missiles on railway cars will be returned to their permanent storage sites;

◆ As a step in response, we shall remove from day-to-day alert status 503 intercontinental ballistic missiles, including 134 ballistic missiles with multiple individually targeted warheads;

◆ We have already removed from active service three nuclear missile submarines with 44 launchers for submarine-based ballistic missiles, and three more submarines with 48 launchers are now being removed.

Third. We have decided to make deeper cuts in our strategic offensive weapons than are envisaged in the Treaty on Strategic Offensive Weapons. As a result, at the end of the seven-year period, the remaining number of nuclear warheads in our possession will be 5,000 instead of the 6,000 envisaged under the Treaty. We would, of course, welcome reciprocal steps by the United States.

We propose to the United States that immediately after the ratification of the Treaty, intensive negotiations should be begun on further radical reductions in strategic offensive weapons by approximately half.

We are ready to discuss United States proposals on nonnuclear anti-aircraft systems.

We propose that we examine with the United States the possibility of creating joint systems with ground- and space-based elements to avert nuclear missiles attacks.

Fourth. We declare an immediate one-year unilateral moratorium on nuclear weapons tests. We hope other nuclear powers will follow our example. This will open the way to the earliest possible and complete cessation of nuclear testing.

We are in favour of reaching an agreement with the Unted States on a controlled cessation of the production of all fissionable materials for weapons.

Fifth. We are ready to begin a detailed dialogue with the Untied States on the development of safe and ecologically clean technologies to store and transport nuclear warheads and methods of utilizing nuclear explosive devices and increasing nuclear safety.

To increase the reliability of nuclear-arms control we are placing all strategic nuclear weapons under single control and including all strategic defense systems in a single arm of the armed services.

Sixth. We hope that eventually the other nuclear powers will actively join in the efforts of the USSR and the United States.

I believe the time has come for a joint statement by all nuclear powers renouncing a first nuclear strike. The USSR has long firmly adhered to this principle.

I am convinced that a similar step by the American side would have an enourmous impact.

Seventh. We welcome the plans by the United States administration to reduce its armed forced by 500,000 in the immediate future. On our side we intend to reduce our armed forces by 700,000.

In conclusion, I wish to stress the following: by acting in this way—unilaterally, bilaterally, and through negotiations—we are decisively advancing the disarmament process and approaching the goal proclaimed at the beginning of 1986—a nuclear-free, safer, and more stable world.

The governments, experts, and departments will have much to do. The question is one of a new stage in one of the main trends of international development.

The question of a new Soviet-U.S. summit meeting has naturally arisen. I have just had a conversation with the United States President, George Bush, and told him about the steps we are taking in response to his initiative. We had a good discussion. The President of the United States made a positive assessment of our principles and expressed satisfaction with our approach to solving key problems of world politics.[2]

RUSSIAN PRESIDENT BORIS YELTSIN

Address to the Nation on Russia's Policy in the Field
of Arms Limitation and Reduction

January 29, 1992

Citizens of Russia,

My address today is devoted to a problem of vital importance. It is about Russia's practical steps in the field of arms limitation and reduction.

Our position of principle consists in the following: nuclear weapons and other means of mass annihilation in the world must be liquidated.

Of course, this must be done gradually on a parity basis.

In this vitally important matter we are open for cooperation with all states and international organisations, including within the framework of the United Nations.

The steps I am going to speak about today have been prepared on the basis of constant interaction with the commonwealth member states and are consistent with agreements reached at the meetings of their leaders in Minsk, Alma-Ata, and Moscow.

Russia regards itself as the legal successor to the USSR in the field of responsibility for fulfilling international obligations.

We confirm all obligations under bilateral and multilateral agreements in the field of arms limitations and disarmament which were signed by the Soviet Union and are in effect at present.

The leadership of Russia confirms its commitment to the policy of radical cuts in nuclear arms, ensuring maximum safety of nuclear arms and all installations related to their development, production, and exploitation.

Russia is coming up with the initiative to create an international agency for ensuring nuclear arms reduction.

On the following stages the agency could gradually cover by its control the whole nuclear cycle, from the production of uranium, deuterium, and tritium to the dumping of nuclear waste.

Measures which we are taking in the sphere of disarmament are not undermining in any way the defence potential of Russia and member states of the Commonwealth. We are seeking to achieve the reasonable minimum sufficiency of the nuclear and conventional weapons.

This is our main principle in the creation of the armed forces. The sticking to this principle will make it possible to save considerable resources. They will be channeled to meeting civilian needs and implementing the reform.

Conditions are now ripe which permit to take new major steps aimed at arms reduction. We are taking some of them unilaterally, and others—on the terms of reciprocity.

These are the steps we have taken and intend to take on a priority basis:

First. In the sphere of strategic offensive armaments. The Treaty on Strategic Offensive Armaments has been submitted for ratification to the Parliament of the Russian Federation. The process of the ratification of the Treaty has been started in the United States as well. In my opinion, this key document should be put into effect as soon as possible, including its approval by Belarus, Kazakhstan, and Ukraine.

Before the coming into force of the Treaty on Strategic Offensive Armaments, Russia has taken a number of major steps, aimed at reducing the strategic arsenal:

- ◆ some 600 ground-based and sea-based strategic ballistic missiles, or nearly 1,250 nuclear charges, have been removed from stand-by alert,

130 silo launchers for intercontinental ballistic missiles have been liquidated or are being prepared for liquidation.

◆ six nuclear submarines have been prepared for dismantling missile launchers.

◆ several strategic weapons development and modernisation programmes have been canceled.

Strategic nuclear weapons, stationed on Ukrainian territory, will be dismantled earlier than planned. Corresponding agreements about this have already been reached.

I want to emphasize that we are not pursuing unilateral disarmament. The United States is taking parallel steps in a gesture of good will.

It is now possible and necessary to move further along this road.

The following decisions have been reached recently:

◆ the production of heavy tu-160 and tu-95ms bombers will be stopped.

◆ the production of existing types of long-distance air-borne cruise missiles will be stopped. On a mutual basis with the United States, we are prepared to give up the development of new types of such missiles.

◆ the production of existing types of long-distance sea-based nuclear missiles will be stopped. New types of such missiles will not be developed. In addition, we are prepared—on a bilateral basis—to scrap all existing long-distance sea-based nuclear cruise missiles.

◆ we will not hold exercises involving large numbers of heavy bombers. This means that no more than 30 (such bombers) can take part in an exercise.

◆ the number of nuclear submarines on combat patrol, carrying ballistic missiles, has been halved and will be further reduced. We are prepared, on a bilateral basis, to stop using such submarines for combat duty.

◆ within a three-year period, instead of the planned seven years, Russia will reduce the number of strategic offensive weapons on combat duty, to agreed levels.

We will reach the level that is envisaged in a corresponding treaty four years earlier.

If there is mutual understanding with the United States, we could achieve this even faster.

We believe that strategic offensive weapons that will be left in Russia and the United States after the reductions should not be aimed at American and Russian targets respectively.

Important talks with Western leaders will be held in the next few days. Proposals on new, deep reductions in strategic offensive weapons, to the level of 2,000–2,500 strategic nuclear warheads on each side, have been prepared.

We hope that other nuclear powers—China, Britain, and France—will join the process of all-out nuclear disarmament.

Secondly, tactical nuclear arms. Major steps to reduce these weapons have already been taken, simultaneously with the United States.

We stopped recently the production of nuclear warheads for ground-based tactical missiles, as well as the manufacturing of nuclear artillery shells and nuclear mines. The stockpiles of such nuclear charges will be eliminated.

Russia is eliminating one third of sea-based tactical nuclear weapons and half of nuclear warheads for anti-aircraft missiles. Measures in this direction have been taken already.

We also intend to reduce by half the stockpiles of tactical nuclear ammunition for the air force. The remaining tactical nuclear weapons for the air force could be removed from frontline (tactical) air force units, on the basis of reciprocity with the United States, and deployed on bases for centralised stockpiling.

Third. Anti-missile defence and space. Russia reiterated its allegiance to the Anti-Ballistic Missile Treaty. It is an important factor of maintaining strategic stability in the world.

We are ready to continue impartial discussion of the U.S. proposal on the limitation of nonnuclear anti-ballistic missile systems. Our principle is well-known. We shall support this approach, if this consolidates world strategic stability and Russia's security.

I am also voicing Russia's readiness to eliminate, on the basis of reciprocity with the United States, the existing anti-satellite systems and work out an agreement on fully banning the armaments, specially designed for destroying satellites.

We are ready to develop, then create and jointly operate a global defence system, instead of the SDI system.

Fourth. Nuclear weapons tests and the production of fissionable materials for military purposes. Russia emphatically favours the banning of all nuclear weapons tests.

We abide by the year-long moratorium on nuclear explosions, declared in October 1991, and hope that other nuclear powers will also refrain from conducting nuclear tests. The atmosphere of reciprocal restraint would help attain an agreement on renouncing such tests altogether. Reduction of the number of tests in stages is quite possible.

In the interests of eventually attaining that goal, we propose to the United States to resume bilateral talks on further cuts in nuclear weapons tests.

Russia plans to carry on the programme for the termination of production of weapons-grade plutonium. Industrial reactors to manufacture weapons-grade plutonium will be shut down by the year 2000, and some of them even as early as 1993. We confirm the proposal to the U.S. to come to agreement on controlled termination of the production of fissionable materials for weapons.

Five. Nonproliferation of weapons of mass destruction and their delivery vehicles. Russia confirms its obligations under the Nuclear Non-Proliferation Treaty, including as its depositary. We count on the earliest accession to the Treaty of Belarus, Kazakhstan, and Ukraine, as well as other member countries of the Commonwealth of Independent States as nonnuclear states.

Russia declares its full support for the activity of the International Atomic Energy Agency (IAEA) and comes out in favour of enhancing the efficiency of its safeguards.

We are taking additional steps to prevent our exports from spreading weapons of mass destruction.

Work is currently under way to make Russia embrace the full-scale IAEA safeguards as a condition for our peaceful nuclear exports.

Russia intends in principle to accede to the international regime of nonproliferation of missiles and missile technology as its equal participant.

We support efforts of the so-called Australian Group on monitoring chemical exports.

The Russian Federation plans to adopt domestic legislation to regulate exports from Russia of materials, equipment, and technologies with "dual applications" that can be used to create nuclear, chemical, and biological weapons, as well as combat missiles.

A state system to monitor these exports is being created. We will work to establish the closest cooperation and coordination between all member countries of the Commonwealth of Independent States on these issues.

Russia supports the guiding principles of arms trade, approved in London in October 1991.

Six. Conventional weapons. The Treaty on Conventional Armed Forces in Europe was submitted for ratification by the Russian parliament. Other member states of the Commonwealth of Independent States, whose territory comes under this treaty, also attach significance to its ratification.

Russia confirms its intention to reduce along with other commonwealth countries the armed forces of the former USSR by 700,000 people in terms of actual strength.

Russia attaches great significance to the current talks in Vienna on reduction of personnel and confidence-building measures, as well as to new talks on security and cooperation in Europe.

The latter might become a permanent all-European forum for the quest for ways to creating a collective all-European security system.

Russia in cooperation with Kazakhstan, Kyrgyzstan, and Tajikistan will work for reaching agreement at the talks with China on the reduction of armed forces and armaments in the border area.

It was decided not to hold in 1992 major military exercises with the participation of more than 13,000 people, and not only on the European, but also on the Asian part of the Commonwealth of Independent States.

We also hope that there is a possibility to sign a treaty on the "open sky" regime in the near future.

Seven. Chemical weapons.

We favour the early concluding (in 1992) of a global convention on a chemical weapons ban. It is needed for safely blocking the way to acquiring chemical weapons, without infringing upon the lawful economic interests of its signatories.

Russia sticks to the 1990 agreement, reached with the United States, on nonproduction and elimination of chemical weapons. However, the schedule of the elimination of such weapons, envisaged by the agreement, calls for some corrections.

All chemical weapons of the former USSR are deployed on the territory of Russia, and it is taking upon itself the responsibility for its elimination. We are preparing a corresponding state programme.

We are open to cooperation on this issue with the U.S. and other parties concerned.

Eight. Biological weapons.

Russia is for strict implementation of the 1972 biological weapons convention, for the creation on a multilateral basis of a relevant verification mechanism, for the implementation of confidence-building and openness measures.

Considering that implementation of the convention lags behind, I declare that Russia abandons its reservations concerning the possibility of using biological weapons in response. They were made by the USSR to the 1925 Geneva Protocol on the Prohibition of the Use in War of Chemical and Bacteriological Weapons.

Nine. Defense budget.

Russia will continue to make drastic cuts in its defense budget, orienting it towards meeting social goals.

Between 1990–1991 defense spending in comparable prices was already reduced by 20 percent, including purchases of weapons and technology by 30 percent.

In 1992 we plan to reduce military spending by another 10 percent (in 1991 prices). The volume of arms purchases will be nearly halved this year as compared with 1991.

Ten. Conversion. Russia welcomes and favours extending international cooperation in the field of military conversion.

For our part, we will encourage such cooperation by giving priority to and providing tax breaks for relevant joint projects.

Esteemed citizens of Russia,

I have just set out the action plan of the Russian federation on matters of arms reduction and disarmament. I hope that it will receive your support and will be appreciated by all peoples of the Commonwealth of Independent States.

I am convinced that it fully meets the interests of our country and other countries of the world. If it is fulfilled, our life will become not only calm and safe but also more prosperous.

Several hours ago U.S. President George Bush addressed the American people proposing radical cuts in the nuclear potentials and stronger stability measures in relations between our countries.

We held preliminary consultations on these matters with each other and are currently engaged in dialogue on the practical implementation of this policy, the proposed initiatives. Note is taken of the proximity of positions of both sides.

This is the guarantee of success on the road of reduction of offensive nuclear weapons.

Thank you for your attention.[3]

Appendix B
Suggested Reading on
Tactical Nuclear Weapons

Cotta-Ramusino, Paolo. "Forgotten Nukes: American Nuclear Weapons in Europe." Italian Union of Scientists for Disarmament (USPID, Unione Scienziati per il Disarmo), proceedings of the VII International Castiglioncello Conference, "Nuclear and Conventional Disarmament: Progress or Stalemate?" Castiglioncello (Italy) 25–28 September 1997.

Feiveson, Harold A., ed. *The Nuclear Turning Point: A Blueprint for Deep Cuts and De-Alerting of Nuclear Weapons*. Washington, D.C.: Brookings Institution, 1999.

Handler, Josh. "The September 1991 Presidential Nuclear Initiatives (PNIs) and the Elimination, Storing and Security Aspects of Tactical Nuclear Weapons (TNWs)." Presentation for Time to Control Tactical Nuclear Weapons, seminar hosted by United Nations Institute for Disarmament Research (UNIDIR), Center for Nonproliferation Studies (CNS), Monterey, California, The Peace Research Institute Frankfurt (PRIF), United Nations, New York, 24 September 2001.

Kanwal, Gurmeet. "Does India Need Tactical Nuclear Weapons?" Occasional Paper, Institute for Defence Studies and Analyses, New Delhi, India, 2001.

Konovalov, Alexander. "Forgotten Nukes: Tactical Nuclear Weapons." Italian Union of Scientists for Disarmament (USPID, Unione Scienziati per il Disarmo), Proceedings of the VII International Castiglioncello Conference, "Nuclear and Conventional Disarmament: Progress or Stalemate?" Castiglioncello (Italy) 25–28 September 1997.

Lambert, Stephen P., and David A. Miller. *Russia's Crumbling Tactical Nuclear Weapons Complex: An Opportunity for Arms Control*. Occasional Paper 12, Institute for National Security Studies, April 1997.

Lewis, George, and Andrea Gabbitas. *What Should Be Done about Tactical Nuclear Weapons?* Occasional Paper, The Atlantic Council of the United States, March 1999.

Mello, Greg. "Beware the Nuclear Warrior." Los Alamos Study Group, 4 April 2001.

Müller, Harald, and Annette Schaper. "Definitions, Types, Missions, Risks and Options for Control: A European Perspective." In *Tactical Nuclear Weapons: Options for Control,* edited by William C. Potter et al. Geneva: United Nations Institute for Disarmament Research (UNIDIR), Publication UNIDIR/2000/20, 2000.

Nelson, Robert W. "Low-Yield Earth-Penetrating Nuclear Weapons." F.A.S. Public Interest Report, *Journal of the Federation of American Scientists* 54, No. 1 (January/February 2001).

Potter, William C., and Nikolai Sokov. "The Nature of the Problem." In *Tactical Nuclear Weapons: Options for Control,* edited by William C. Potter et al. Geneva: United Nations Institute for Disarmament Research (UNIDIR), Publication UNIDIR/2000/20, 2000.

Robinson, C. Paul. "A White Paper: Pursuing a New Nuclear Weapons Policy for the 21st Century." Los Alamos Study Group. March 2001.

Safranchuk, Ivan. "Strategic and Tactical Nuclear Weapons: An Attempt of Classification." PIR Center for Policy Studies in Russia, report no. 20, June 2000.

———. "Tactical Nuclear Weapons in the Modern World and Russia's Sub-Strategic Nuclear Forces." PIR Center for Policy Studies in Russia, report no. 16, March 2000.

Shevtsov, A., et al. *Tactical Nuclear Weapons: A Perspective from Ukraine.* Geneva: United Nations Institute for Disarmament Research (UNIDIR), Publication: UNIDIR/2000/21, 2000.

Sokov, Nikolai. "Tactical Nuclear Weapons Elimination: Next Step for Arms Control." *The Nonproliferation Review* 4, No. 2 (Winter 1997).

———. "The Advantages and Pitfalls of Non-Negotiated Arms Reductions: The Case of Tactical Nuclear Weapons." *Disarmament Diplomacy* 21 (1998).

Notes

Alexander and Millar, Chapter 1

1. Note that illicit acquisition of tactical or other nuclear warheads or bombs is distinct from illicit acquisition of nuclear materials for use in either development of warheads or bombs and use of nuclear material in so-called "dirty bombs." In dirty bombs, nuclear material is dispersed by a conventional explosion, with the intent of contaminating territory and exposing humans. However, the need for control of nuclear materials may be linked to the control of nuclear weapons.

2. For a perspective on Cold War tactical nuclear weapons deployment, see: "Appendix 1: Nuclear Weapon Delivery Systems Distribution in NATO," in *Tactical Nuclear Weapons: European Perspectives* (London: Taylor & Francis, Ltd., for Stockholm International Peace Research Institute, 1978), 109–129; and, "Appendix 2: General Tables—U.S.A. and USSR," in *Tactical Nuclear Weapons: European Perspectives* (London: Taylor & Francis, Ltd., for Stockholm International Peace Research Institute, 1978), 130–36.

3. Tactical nuclear weapons receive periodic mention in international nonproliferation discourse. For example, the 2000 Nonproliferation Treaty RevCon calls for "the further reduction of non-strategic nuclear weapons, based on unilateral initiatives and as an integral part of the arms-control process." For more information on this, see Tariq Rauf, "Towards NPT 2005: An Action Plan for the '13-steps' towards Nuclear Disarmament Agreed at NPT 2000," Monterey Institute for International Studies, 2001. However, concrete steps or actual implementation of measures to reduce or control TNWs have not occurred, other than the 1991–92 presidential nuclear initiatives.

4. See Joshua Handler's chapter for a thorough review of the current U.S. tactical nuclear arsenal.

5. In any event, the Russian TNW arsenal would appear to be contracting. This is not only because of the 1991–92 PNIs, but also because of the aging of the force itself. For example, Dr. Alexei G. Arbatov, deputy chairman of the Defence Committee of the Russian Duma, has suggested that existing Russian TNWs are bound for technical obsolescence. Many Russian TNWs slated for elimination under the PNIs "were to be eliminated anyway by 2003 because their design lives will have expired." (Alexei Arbatov, "Appendix A: Deep Cuts and De-alerting: A Russian Perspective," in Harold A. Feiveson, ed., *The Nuclear Turning Point: A Blueprint for Deep Cuts and De-Alerting of Nuclear Weapons* [Washington, D.C.: Brookings Institution Press, 1999], 320.) Arbatov also raises doubt regarding whether Russia's stymied economy could allow for these retired warheads to be replaced. He argues that "[I]t is unlikely that after 2003 there will be more than a few hundred or at most 1,000 tactical nuclear weapons in the Russian armed forces." (Ibid.) Nonetheless, without verification mechanisms or greater

international effort to address Russia's TNW, Arbatov's assertions remain unknowable.

6. For example, in testimony before the U.S. Congress, Admiral Richard W. Meis, commander in chief, U.S. Strategic Command, indicated support for a National Institute for Public Policy report in which the development of new low-yield nuclear weapons is advocated (testimony before the Strategic Subcommittee, Senate Armed Services Committee, U.S. Senate, 107th Cong., 1st session, Washington, D.C., 11 July 2001). The admiral noted that he believes "the approach outlined by the National Institute for Public Policy study, *Rationale and Requirements for U.S. Nuclear Forces and Arms Control,* is a good blueprint to adopt." The National Institute for Public Policy.

7. For an overview of world TNW munitions and delivery systems, see "Appendix: Types, Delivery Systems and Locations of TNWs," in William Potter et al., *Tactical Nuclear Weapons: Options for Control,* United Nations Institute for Disarmament Research, Geneva, 2000.

8. See Sydney J. Freedberg Jr., "Beyond Duck and Cover," *National Journal* Nos. 50–52 (15 December 2001): 38–45.

9. Ibid.

10. For a review of effects of low-yield and other nuclear weapons, see, for example, Charles S. Grace, *Nuclear Weapons: Principles, Effects and Survivability* (New York: Brassey's [UK], 1994); Robert Nelson's chapter in this book for the effect of so-called "bunker buster" tactical nuclear weapons; also, Ira Helfan, M.D., "Effects of a Nuclear Explosion," *Physicians for Social Responsibility (PSR)* 6 August 2001.

11. For broader treatment of the definitional issue, see Andrea Gabbitas, "Nonstrategic Nuclear Weapons: Problems of Definition" in *Controlling Non-Strategic Nuclear Weapons: Obstacles and Opportunities.* Jeffrey A. Larsen and Kurt J. Klingenberger, eds. USAF Institute for National Security Studies: U.S. Air Force Academy, Colorado Springs, Colorado, 2001, chapter 2.

12. An overview of issues complicating the definition of TNW is provided by George Lewis and Andrea Gabbitas in "What Should Be Done about Tactical Nuclear Weapons?" occasional paper, The Atlantic Council, March 1999, 1–4. The authors conclude that, "it appears that this default definition of TNWs is the most practical," 3.

13. Lewis and Gabbitas, "What Should Be Done about Tactical Nuclear Weapons?" 8.

14. Stephen M. Younger, "Nuclear Weapons in the Twenty-First Century," Los Alamos National Laboratory, LAUR-00–2850, Los Alamos, New Mexico, 27 June 2000, 1.

15. Senators John Warner (R-Va.) and Wayne Allard (R-Colo.) added a provision to the 2001 Defense Authorization Bill requiring this study to the Floyd D. Spence National Defense Authorization Act for Fiscal Year 2001, PL 106–398 (2000). Specifically, the report notes that Section 1044 of PL 106–398 calls for a review of requirements; an assessment of plans to meet those requirements; identification of potential future targets, research and development efforts, and options to defeat these future targets; and an estimate of cost to accomplish the various options.

16. The Hon. Elizabeth Furse and the Hon. John Spratt, Jr., "Prohibition on Research and Development of Low-Yield Nuclear Weapons," National Defense Authorization Act for Fiscal Year 1994, PL 103–160, U.S. Congress, 103d Cong., 1st Session, Washington, D.C., 1993, §3136.

17. The Hon. Mike Thompson, Statement on Mininukes, in Support of HR 4205: "The Defense Authorization Bill for FY 2000 (22 May 2000)," U.S. House of Representatives, 106th Cong., 2d session, 11 October 2000.

18. Final congressional approval of this request was pending at time of publication.

19. For an assessment of Russia's nuclear dependency in the context of conventional warfare contingencies, see Stephen P. Lampert and David A. Miller, "Russia's Crumbling Tactical Nuclear Weapons Complex: An Opportunity for Arms Control," occasional paper, Institute for National Security Studies, U.S. Air Force Academy, Colorado, 12 April 1997, 10.

20. See Mark Kramer, "What Is Driving Russia's New Strategic Concept?" brief, Program on New Approaches to Russian Security (PONARS), Davis Center for Russian Studies, Harvard University, January 2000.

21. See Fritz W. Ermarth, "Alternatives to Genocide: Missile Defense and the Future of Nuclear Weapons," remarks offered at the Hanns Seidel Stiftung Conference on Ballistic Missile Defence in Munich, Germany, May 2001.

22. See, for example, Sam Nunn, William Perry, and Eugene Habiger, "Still Missing: A Nuclear Strategy" (*Washington Post,* 21 May 2002, p. A17), in which the authors write, "tactical nuclear weapons . . . are the nuclear weapons most attractive to terrorists—even more valuable to them than fissile material and much more portable than strategic warheads." An article in *Time* magazine by Bruce W. Nelan stated that Russian tactical nuclear weapons "often have external KBUs [the Russian equivalent of PALs] that can be removed, and many have none at all . . . some older [tactical nuclear] weapons in the Russian arsenal do not have KBUs and many others have broken down and have not been repaired" (see "Present Danger: Russia's Nuclear Forces Are Sliding into Disrepair and even Moscow Is Worried about What Might Happen," *Time* magazine 149, No. 14 [7 April 1997]).

23. For greater discussion of the risks of illicit or accidental use, see Harald Müller and Annette Schaper, "Definitions, Types, Missions, Risks and Options for Control: A European Perspective," in William Potter, Nikolai Sokov, Harald Müller, and Annette Schaper, *Tactical Nuclear Weapons: Options for Control* (Geneva: United Nations Institute for Disarmament Research, 2000), 38–39.

24. See "Threats, Countermeasures, Technical Barriers, and Accomplishments," U.S. Department of Defense, in *Chemical and Biological Defense Program: Annual Report to Congress,* March 2000.

25. See Peter Barnes, "Tiny Nukes Pose Big Threat: Could Terrorists Have Cold War–Era Portable Nuclear Weapons?" (commentary, ABC News, New York, 9 October 2001).

26. See U.S. Commission on National Security/21st Century, "Road Map for National Security: Imperative for Change" (phase III report, Washington, D.C., 15 February 2001).

27. To date, U.S. officials have not publicly advocated the use of TNWs. However, media reports have included numerous references to those speculating on the use (or usefulness) of TNWs. See, for example, Paul de la Garza, "U.S. Ramps Up the Rhetoric, Weighs Options," *St. Petersburg Times,* 13 September 2001 (late Tampa edition), 27A; William Neikirk and Steve Hedges, "Talk of Retaliation Includes War; Bin Laden Is Suspected as Perpetrator," *Sun-Sentinel* (Fort Lauderdale, Fla., national edition, 12 September 2001), 20A; Tim Luckhurst, "Fear Turns to Fury as War Cries Grow," *Herald* (Glasgow), 11; "Zhirinovsky Thinks U.S. May Use Nuclear Weapons to Take Vengeance," *Interfax News Agency,* News Bulletin, 12 September 2001; Dana Milbank, "U.S. Pressed on Nuclear Response," *Washington Post,* 4 October 2001.

28. See C. Paul Robinson, "A White Paper: Pursuing a New Nuclear Weapons Policy for the 21st Century," March 2001, Sandia National Laboratories; reproduced by Los Alamos Study Group.

29. For an interesting analysis of this question from the Cold War era, which concludes that TNWs "have no conceivable role in future ground warfare" and examines

numerous strategic and battlefield scenarios, including the Korean War, see Philip W. Dyer, "Will Tactical Nuclear Weapons Ever Be Used?" *Political Science Quarterly* 88, No. 2 (June 1973): 214–29.

30. See Greg Mello, "Beware the Nuclear Warrior," *Albuquerque Tribune*, 12 April 2001.

31. For a discussion of the "intentions" versus "capabilities" issue, framed in the context of offense-defense balance, see Robert Jervis's classic essay, "Cooperation under the Security Dilemma," *World Politics* 30, No. 2 (January 1978): 167–214.

32. See Ivan Safranchuk, "Tactical Nuclear Weapons in the Modern World and Russia's Sub-Strategic Nuclear Forces," PIR Center for Policy Studies in Russia, report no. 16, March 2000.

33. Ibid.

34. See United States, Joint Chiefs of Staff, "Doctrine for Joint Theater Nuclear Operations," 3–12.1.

35. Ibid.

36. Ibid.

37. See William Arkin, Robert S. Norris, and Josh Handler, "Taking Stock: Worldwide Nuclear Deployments 1998," Washington, D.C., National Resources Defense Council, Inc., March 1998, Footnote 75.

38. See William Potter and Nikolai Sokov, "Tactical Nuclear Weapons: The Nature of the Problem," CNS Reports, Center for Nonproliferation Studies, Monterey Institute of International Studies, 4 January 2001, 6, 11.

Handler, Chapter 2

1. See President George Bush, "New Initiatives to Reduce U.S. Nuclear Forces," *U.S. Department of State Dispatch*, 30 September 1991, Vol. 2, No. 39; M. S. Gorbachev, "Gorbachev Proposals on Nuclear Arms Control," *Central Television, First All Union Programme*, 5 October 1991; President Yeltsin's Disarmament Statement, 29 January 1992, *Moscow Teleradiokompaniya Ostankino Television, First Program Network*, 29 January 1992; "Boris Yeltsin's Statement on Arms Control," ITAR-TASS, 29 January 1992.

2. See Agence France Presse, "France Hails U.S. Arms Moves as 'Real Turning-Point,'" 28 September 1991; Agence France Presse, "Major Hails Bush Move," 28 September 1991; Kyodo News, "Prime Minister Kaifu Welcomes Bush Proposal," 28 September 1991; Agence France Presse, "Genscher Welcomes Bush Disarmament Initiative," 4 October 1991.

3. See U.S. Department of Defense, "DOD Review Recommends Reduction in Nuclear Forces," press release and accompanying "Nuclear Posture Review" briefing, 22 September 1994.

4. In terms of choosing which tactical nuclear weapons (TNWs) to include in the U.S. PNI, the historical context was important. Brent Scowcroft, National Security adviser to President George Bush, wrote in their joint memoir that the reunification of Germany made short range TNW "undesirable"; South Korea was suggesting the removal of U.S. TNW; "a number of countries," including Japan and New Zealand, had problems with the U.S. Navy carrying nuclear weapons into their ports, and the United States neither confirms nor denies policy; and, finally, nuclear antisubmarine warfare (ASW) weapons were no longer the "preferred" way to attack submarines. As a result, he then recommended to Bush that the United States get rid of all TNW except air-delivered ones. George Bush and Brent Scowcroft, *A World Transformed* (New York: Knopf, 1998), 536–47.

In regards to naval TNW, this is an interesting frank admission by a high policy-maker that public protests (of which there were many in the 1980s against U.S. nuclear-capable and armed vessels) and foreign concerns led directly to their withdrawal and the elimination of most. For more on the genesis of President Bush's 27 September proposals, see John E. Yang, "Bush Plan Emerged after Failed Coup: White House Wanted to Take Advantage of Timing, Officials Say," *Washington Post*, 28 September 1991; Andrew Rosenthal, "Bush's Arms Plan: Arms Plan Germinated in Back-Porch Session," *New York Times*, 29 September 1991; Doyle McManus, "Bush Acted to Help Gorbachev Control A-Arms," *Los Angeles Times*, 29 September 1991; Michael Beschloss and Strobe Talbott, *At the Highest Levels* (Boston: Little, Brown, and Co. 1993); Colin L. Powell, *My American Journey* (New York: Random House, 1995); James Baker, *The Politics of Diplomacy: Revolution, War and Peace* (New York: Putnam and Sons, 1995).

For Gorbachev's reaction, see interview with Gorbachev, "Gorbachev-Bush Proposals 'A Serious Advance towards a Nonnuclear World,'" *Central Television, First All Union Programme*, 28 September 1991. For background on Gorbachev's reaction, see Pavel Palazchenko's description of the initial response of Gorbachev and his advisers, Pavel Palazchenko, *My Years with Gorbachev and Shevardnadze* (University Park: Pennsylvania State University Press, 1997). Also, one of Gorbachev's key advisers, Anatoly Chernyaev, mentions the Kremlin's positive reaction briefly in regard to strategic nuclear weapons, saying Gorbachev's response to Bush did not meet with the "usual resistance and delays on the part of the military." Anatoly Chernyaev, *My Six Years with Gorbachev*. Translated and edited by Robert D. English and Elizabeth Tucker (University Park: Pennsylvania State University Press, 1997).

5. See Defense Secretary Dick Cheney and Chairman of the Joint Chiefs of Staff Gen. Colin Powell, "Defense Department Briefing: Details of President Bush's Arms Proposal," 27 September 1991; Pete Williams, "Defense Department Briefing," 1 October 1991. For background on U.S. weapons systems, see Cochran et al., *U.S. Nuclear Forces and Capabilities, Nuclear Weapons Databook, Volume I* (Cambridge, Mass.: Ballinger Press, 1984); Natural Resources Defense Council (NRDC) Nuclear Notebook, "U.S. Nuclear Weapons Stockpile," *Bulletin of the Atomic Scientists*, June 1991 and June 1992.

6. Because of the controversy over deployment of enhanced radiation (ER) or "neutron bombs" in Europe in the late 1970s and 1980s, the ER warhead versions of Lance missiles and the W-79 8-in artillery shell were not deployed overseas but kept in the United States. This controversy began when reporter Walter Pincus exposed the program in a June 1977 *Washington Post* story. Walter Pincus, "Carter Is Weighing Radiation Warhead," *Washington Post*, 7 June 1977.

7. The United States had deployed many different types of TNW, but these other systems—such as Army Atomic Demolition Munitions (ADM), Ground-launched Cruise Missile (GLCM), Honest John and Pershing 1a and 2 missiles and Navy AAW missiles, ASROC and SUBROC antisubmarine warfare (ASW) rockets—were retired before the September–October 1991 PNIs and thus were not included in the PNIs. Their warheads were dismantled during 1980s and 1990s, except for the GLCM W-84 warhead, which is retained in the inactive stockpile. In addition to sources cited in elimination section below, see Andrew Weston-Dawkes, U.S. DOE, Office of Declassification, "Enduring Stockpile—1998," 2 October 1998 FAX, released under the Freedom of Information Act (FOIA) to Princeton University's Program on Science and Global Security (PSGS).

8. South Korean President Roh Tae Woo announced on national television that no nuclear weapons were in South Korea as of mid-December 1991; James Sterngold, "Seoul Says It Now Has No Nuclear Arms," *New York Times*, 19 December 1991.

In terms of Army weapons in Europe and naval TNW: "Today I can tell you that all of the planned withdrawals are complete. All ground-launched tactical nuclear weapons have been returned to U.S. territory, as have all naval tactical nuclear weapons. Those weapons designated to be destroyed are being retired and scheduled for destruction." President George Bush, "Statement on the United States Nuclear Weapons Initiative," 2 July 1992. According to the U.S. Air Force's 6th Airlift Squadron history, the removal of U.S. nuclear weapons from Europe during 1991–92, was "the largest nuclear weapons movement in United States' history." The 6th Airlift Squadron conducted Prime Nuclear Airlift Force (PNAF) missions, i.e., it had the main responsibility for airlifting U.S. nuclear weapons to and from Europe, while based at McGuire AFB, N.J. Over 1,600 PNAF missions were conducted between 1971 and 1993; McGuire AFB website, accessed 8 November 2000. http://www.mcguire.af.mil.

9. "No nuclear weapons remain in the custody of US ground forces"; U.S. Department of Defense, "DOD Review Recommends Reduction in Nuclear Forces," press release and accompanying "Nuclear Posture Review" briefing, 22 September 1994.

10. "On the basis of President Bush's 1991 Nuclear Initiative, NATO took the decision to reduce the number of nuclear weapons available for its substrategic forces in Europe by over 85 percent. These reductions were completed in 1993." Press release M-DPC/NPG-1(2001)87, "Final Communiqué: Ministerial Meeting of the Defense Planning Committee and the Nuclear Planning Group," 7 June 2001.

11. See C. Bruce Tarter, director, University of California, Lawrence Livermore National Laboratory, "The Department of Energy's Budget Request for FY 1998," Hearing of the Subcommittee on Strategic Forces Committee on Armed Services U.S. Senate, 19 March 1997; H. Waugh and W. White, Pantex Site representatives, Defense Nuclear Facilities Safety Board, "Pantex Plant Activity Report for Week Ending February 8, 2002," memorandum, 8 February 2002. U.S. Department of Energy, "Nuclear Weapons Disassembly (by Weapons Program) at Pantex Plant," "Pantex Plant Nuclear Weapons Disassembly History by Weapons System," "Nuclear Warhead Dismantlement 1997–1999 and 2000," and "Retired/Cancelled Weapons," all released under FOIA or from DOE Public Affairs to Princeton University's PSGS.

12. See *U.S. Defense Nuclear Facilities Safety Board, Tenth Annual Report to Congress,* February 2000. According to this report, there were "many difficulties encountered by DOE while readying the W79 for dismantlement." Also see John Gordon, Undersecretary for Nuclear Security, and administrator, National Nuclear Security Administration, U.S. Energy Department, "Statement Before the Senate Appropriations Subcommittee on Energy and Water Development," 26 April 2001.

13. See "DOD Review Recommends Reduction in Nuclear Forces," press release and accompanying "Nuclear Posture Review" briefing, U.S. Department of Defense, 22 September 1994.

14. See Naval Surface Warfare Center, Indian Head Division, Detachment McAlester, "War Reserve Weapons Maintenance and Logistics: Nuclear Weapons Consolidation," *Navy Nuclear Weapons Digest* (Third/Fourth Quarters 1997); released under the FOIA to Princeton University's PSGS.

15. See Director, Strategic Systems Programs, "Completion Inspection at Strategic Weapons Facility Pacific," letter 5 March 1998 to the Chief of Naval Operations (N41); released under the FOIA to Princeton University's PSGS.

16. Both tables from William Arkin and Richard Fieldhouse, *Nuclear Battlefields: Global Links in the Arms Race* (Cambridge, Mass.: Ballinger Press, 1985); Greenpeace/NRDC, *Taking Stock: U.S. Nuclear Deployments at the End of the Cold War,* (1992); William Arkin, Robert Norris, Joshua Handler, *Taking Stock: Worldwide Nuclear Deployments, 1998* (Washington, D.C.: Natural Resources Defense Council, March 1998); Hans Kristensen and Joshua Handler, "Appendix 6A. Tables of Nuclear Forces," *SIPRI Yearbook*

2001; Electronic Systems Center, Hanscom AFB, "WS3 (Weapons Storage and Security System) Sustainment Program," Program Management Review Briefing for USAFE LG, 3 March 2000, released under the FOIA to Princeton University's PSGS.

17. Information obtained under the FOIA from DSWA and from U.S. Defense Department's Defense Threat Reduction Agency Public Affairs by Princeton University's PSGS.

18. See Vladimir Lobov, General of the Army, "The Motherland's Armed Forces Today and Tomorrow," *Krasnaya Zvezda,* 29 November 1991; Gen. Vitally Yakovlev, "Realization of Reduction and Limitation Programs for Nuclear Weapons and the Opportunity of an Information Exchange on Amount of Produced Fissile Materials and Their Localization," talk prepared for the U.S.-Russian Workshop on CTB, Fissile Material Cutoff and Plutonium Disposal," 15–17 December 1993, Washington, D.C., Natural Resources Defense Council, Federation of American Scientists, Moscow Physical-Technical Institute.

19. Ibid.

20. See *Proliferation: Threat and Response*, U.S. Department of Defense, November 1997, 44.

21. In addition to sources cited below, for a lengthier review of Soviet TNW removals from Eastern Europe and former Soviet Union republics, see Joshua Handler, *Russian Nuclear Warhead Dismantlement Rates and Storage Site Capacity: Implications for the Implementation of START II and De-Alerting Initiatives*, 1999, CEES Report No. AC-99–01. It remains unclear if Soviet TNW were deployed in Bulgaria.

22. From 1990 to 1991, all TNWs were removed from the former Warsaw Pact countries with the last train "loaded by tactical warheads" leaving Germany during the summer of 1991; Gen. Vitally Yakovlev, U.S.-Russian Workshop on CTB, Fissile Material Cutoff and Plutonium Disposal," 15–17 December 1993. Lt. Gen. Vladimir Korotkov, deputy chief of the Main Department of the CIS Armed Forces, said all nuclear weapons were removed from the Transcaucasian republics in the summer of 1990; "General: No Nuclear Arms in Caucasus," *Interfax,* 12 March 1992.

23. In 1992 General Zelentsov of the 12th Main Directorate of the Russian MOD said there were "no tactical nuclear weapons in the Central Asian republics or in Kazakhstan. The last warhead had been withdrawn from their territories last year"; Victor Litovkin, "Generals in Moscow Categorically Deny Sales of Nuclear Weapons," *Izvestia,* 17 March 1992; General Zelentsov said that "The process of the transfer of tactical nuclear weapons from other CIS states began as early as last year [1991]. Gradually their numbers were reduced and they were evacuated first from the states which are the farthest from Russia. Their number has gradually decreased as they were withdrawn first from the countries that are geographically most distant from Russia, and then from the countries that are closer to it." "Press Conference on Withdrawal of Tactical Nuclear Weapons from the Ukraine by Members of CIS and Ukraine Military," official Kremlin international news broadcast, 6 May 1992, (Federal News Service). Gen. Gely Batenin, an adviser to the Russian Foreign Ministry, said that all tactical nuclear weapons had been removed from the Baltic States, Transcaucasia, and Central Asia; Alexander Rahr, "Batenin on Nuclear Weapons," *RFE/RL*, No. 236, 13 December 1991.

24. General Zelentsov said, "They [tactical nuclear weapons] were withdrawn from Belarus some time ago, and from Ukrainian territory they were pulled out, in fact, yesterday. To be more exact, it happened last night." General Yakovlev added that in the "course of the last transfer, some 1,000 nuclear units have been evacuated—tactical nuclear weapons." These were mostly air defense weapons, tactical aviation bombs, and naval tactical weapons. "Press Conference on Withdrawal of Tactical Nuclear

Weapons from the Ukraine by Members of CIS and Ukraine Military," official Kremlin international news broadcast, 6 May 1992.

25. See Mikhail Shimansky, "First Interview with First Defense Minister of Byelarus," *Izvestia*, 24 April 1992.

26. "All tactical nuclear weapons have been removed from vessels, multipurpose submarines, and aircraft of the naval forces, and placed in centralized storage." Information from the Russian Ministry of Defense reported in Vadim Byrkin, "Tactical Nuclear Weapons Removed from Vessels," ITAR-TASS World Service, 4 February 1993.

27. Foreign Ministry spokesman Mikhail Demurin reportedly said that "The nuclear warheads of anti-aircraft missiles have been withdrawn." "Disarmament Initiatives to be Fulfilled by Year 2000," *Interfax*, 26 September 1996.

28. "All the warheads of the ground forces, artillery shells and tactical nuclear warheads, have been removed and the units which maintained nuclear warheads have been disbanded." Press conference with Lt. Gen. Igor Valynkin, chief of the 12th Main Directorate of the Russian Ministry of Defense, regarding the nuclear security in Russian Federation armed forces, Russian Ministry of Defense, official Kremlin international news broadcast, 25 September 1997 (Federal News Service).

29. See Hans Kristensen and Joshua Handler, "Appendix 10A. World Nuclear Forces," *SIPRI Yearbook 2002*.

30. See "Statement of the Delegation of the Russian Federation at the First Session of the Preparatory Committee for the 2005 NPT Review Conference under Article VI of the Treaty," New York, 11 April 2002.

31. See "Disarmament Initiatives to Be Fulfilled by Year 2000," *Interfax*, 26 September 1996.

32. By December 1997, General Valynkin said that 60 percent of the TNW removed from Ukraine, Byelorussia, and Kazakhstan had been destroyed. Moreover, mines would be destroyed by the year 2000. Vladimir Georgiev and Igor Frolov, "A Storm in a Bottle," *Nezavisimaya Gazeta*, 12 December 1997.

33. See Mikhail Shevtsov, "Russia Strictly Fulfilling Nuclear Test Ban Treaty," ITAR-TASS, 9 October 1998. General Valynkin in an interview noted that the elimination of "expired nuclear weapons" was ongoing, and that nuclear mines and shells were also being dismantled. Vladimir Karpenko, "Emergency Situations Will Never Occur at Nuclear Facilities Thanks to Special Security Regime," *Rossiiskiye Vesti*, 28 October 1998.

34. "[Interviewer] Do the Missile and Artillery Troops remain a means of employing tactical nuclear weapons?"

"[Mukhin] The Missile and Artillery Troops still remain a means of employing them. But in today's conditions, when there is a gradual elimination of tactical nuclear weapons going on, we no longer have them in storage." Sergey Sokut, interview with Lt. Gen. Nikolay Mukhin, deputy chief of the Missile and Artillery Troops of the RF Armed Forces, "The Primary Weapon to Defeat the Enemy: That Is How Lt-Gen Nikolay Mukhin, deputy chief of the Missile and Artillery Troops of the RF Armed Forces, Characterizes the Role of the 'God of War,'" *Nezavisimoye Voyennoye Obozreniye*, 13–19 November 1998.

35. "Russia also continues to consistently implement its unilateral initiatives related to tactical nuclear weapons. Such weapons have been completely removed from surface ships and multipurpose submarines, as well as from the land-based naval aircraft, and are stored at centralized storage facilities. One third of all nuclear munitions for the sea-based tactical missiles and naval aircraft has been eliminated We are about to complete the destruction of nuclear warheads from tactical missiles, artillery shells and nuclear mines We have destroyed half of the nuclear warheads for anti-aircraft missiles

and for nuclear gravity bombs." Igor S. Ivanov, Minister of Foreign Affairs of the Russian Federation, "Statement at the Review Conference of the Parties to the Treaty on the Non-Proliferation of Nuclear Weapons," New York, 25 April 2000

36. See Col. Gen. Yevgeny Maslin remarks on U.S. and Russian Perspectives on the Cooperative Threat Reduction Program, made at the U.S. Defense Special Weapons Agency conference, "Walking the Walk: Controlling Arms in the 1990s," in Summary of the Fifth Annual International Conference on Controlling Arms, 3–6 June 1996, Norfolk, Virginia.

37. See Maslin remarks, "Walking the Walk: Controlling Arms in the 1990s."

38. See Col. Gen. Yevgeny Maslin, "Summary of the Proceedings of the U.S. Defense Nuclear Agency's 4th Annual International Conference on Controlling Arms," 19–22 June 1995, Philadelphia, Pennsylvania.

39. See Col. Gen. Yevgeny Maslin, "Cooperative Threat Reduction: The View from Russia," in Proceedings of the NATO Advanced Research Workshop on Dismantlement and Destruction of Chemical, Nuclear and Conventional Weapons, Bonn, Germany, 19–21 May 1996 (Dordrecht, The Netherlands: Kluwer Academic Publishers, 1997); Maslin, "Walking the Walk: Controlling Arms in the 1990s."

40. For an analysis of Russian nuclear weapons storage systems, see Joshua Handler, "Lifting the Lid on Russia's Nuclear Weapons Storage," *Jane's Intelligence Review* (August 1999).

41. See John Deutch, director, Central Intelligence, "Statement before the Senate Permanent Subcommittee on Investigations," hearing on "Global Proliferation of Weapons of Mass Destruction," Part II, 22 March 1996, S. Hrg. 104–422, Pt. 2; Gordon Oehler, director, Nonproliferation Center, CIA, testimony before the Senate Armed Services Committee, on "Intelligence Briefing on Smuggling of Nuclear Material and the Role of International Crime Organizations, and on the Proliferation of Cruise and Ballistic Missiles," 31 January 1995; Gloria Duffy, testimony before the House Foreign Affairs Committee, Subcommittee on Europe and the Middle East, Hearings on "FY 1995 Foreign Aid Requests for Russia and the Other New Independent States (NIS) of the Former Soviet Union," 24 March 1994; U.S. Department of Defense, *Proliferation: Threat and Response*, November 1997.

42. This image is derived from U.S. Declassified Corona Reconnaissance Satellite Image from Mission No. 1115–2, 18 September 1971 (U.S. National Archives and Joshua Handler).

43. U.S. Department of Defense, *Proliferation: Threat and Response*, January 2001.

44. See Robert Norris and William Arkin, Natural Resources Defense Council (NRDC) Nuclear Notebook, "U.S. Nuclear Weapons Stockpile," *Bulletin of the Atomic Scientists* (June 1991 and June 1992); "Nuclear Notebook: Estimated Soviet Nuclear Stockpile (July 1991)," *Bulletin of the Atomic Scientists* (July/August 1991); Alexei Arbatov, "Deep Cuts and De-Alerting: A Russian Perspective," in Harold Feivson, ed., *The Nuclear Turning Point: A Blueprint for Deep Cuts and De-Alerting of Nuclear Weapons* (Washington, D.C.: Brookings), 1999.

45. See Hans Kristensen and Joshua Handler, "Appendix 10A. World Nuclear Forces," *SIPRI Yearbook 2002.*

46. Of note, Ambassador Robert Grey informed the 2000 NPT review conference that "The US has reduced its non-strategic nuclear weapons by 80 percent since the fall of the Berlin Wall." U.S. Ambassador Robert Grey, statement to the Main Committee I, The 2000 Review Conference of the Treaty on Non-Proliferation of Nuclear Weapons, 27 April 2000.

In 2002, the United States added, "Following initiatives by former President Bush in 1991/1992, NATO has reduced its non-strategic nuclear weapons by more than 85 percent, most of which have been dismantled. All nuclear weapons were removed from ground forces and naval surface ships. Gravity bombs were reduced by more than 50 percent. Worldwide the United States has eliminated all nuclear weapons from surface ships, including terminating the nuclear role for its carrier-based dual capable aircraft. In sum, the Army, Marine Corps, and surface and air components of the Navy have been denuclearized." Information paper by the United States Concerning Article VI of the NPT, 2002 NPT Preparatory Committee (PrepCom), 11 April 2002, New York.

47. See Igor Ivanov, "Organizing the World to Fight Terror," *New York Times,* 27 January 2002.

48. See Robert Norris and William Arkin, "Beating Swords into Swords," *The Bulletin of the Atomic Scientists* (November 1990).

49. Despite the many concerns raised since 1989–90 about the security of Soviet tactical nuclear weapons, the Soviet and then Russian military has consistently denied reports that any nuclear weapons are missing and that nuclear weapons in storages are insecure. The only attempt to filch a Soviet tactical nuclear weapon about which any details are known was made by the environmental group Greenpeace. In the summer of 1991 Greenpeace tried to "borrow" a Soviet nuclear weapon from its storage site in East Germany in order to show it to the world's press for an antinuclear weapons protest in Berlin. The weapon was to be returned after the action. The plan fell apart when the remaining Soviet nuclear weapons were removed from East Germany in July–August 1991. See William Burrows and Robert Windrem, *Critical Mass: The Dangerous Race for Superweapons in a Fragmenting World* (New York: Simon and Schuster), 1994, 246–51.

50. See "Safety Rules for U.S. Strike Aircraft," U.S. Air Force Instruction 91–112, 1 June 2000.

51. Twice a year, the Navy selects an attack submarine for a "regeneration" exercise to evaluate the ability to redeploy nuclear-armed cruise missiles on submarines. The exercise tests the ability of the crew to reestablish nuclear capability in a "relatively short time." U.S. Office of the Secretary of Defense, *Nuclear Weapons Systems Sustainment Programs,* May 1997.

52. See Greg Mello, "New Bomb, No Mission," *The Bulletin of the Atomic Scientists* (May/June 1997).

53. See John Gordon, Undersecretary for Nuclear Security, and administrator, National Nuclear Security Administration, U.S. Energy Department, "Statement Before the House Armed Services Committee, Procurement Subcommittee," 12 June 2002.

54. See Pavel Felgengauer, "A Clean Nuclear Bomb," *Moscow News,* Number 12, 26 March–1 April 2002.

55. See interview with General Igor Valynkin, head of the 12th GUMO by Alexander Dolinin and Nikolai Poroskov, "The Nuclear Genie of Russia Sleeps," *Krasnaya Zvezda,* 31 August 1999.

56. Andrei Lyamkin, "Sharp Eyes and a Sharpshooting Shell," *Soldier of the Fatherland,* 22 March 2000; Andrei Lyamkin, "One Tenth Is Given for Artillery's Survival," *Soldier of the Fatherland,* 16 September 2000. The latter article describes an exercise in August 2000 of the 27th Motor-Rifle Division, where an "imitator" nuclear artillery shell was fired. When it exploded an orange cloud was released to simulate a nuclear explosion.

57. Bill Gertz, "Satellites Pinpoint Russian Nuclear Arms in Baltics," *Washington Times,* 15 February 2001.

58. "In addition to accelerating the acquisition of Tactical Tomahawk, the Navy also wants Raytheon to begin remanufacturing in 'large numbers' the nuclear-tipped TLAM-Ns, which have been in storage and out of the deployment arsenal since the

early 1990s." Hunter Keeter, "PGM Funding May Top List For Short-Term Military Spending Increase," *Defense Daily*, 20 September 2001.

59. See Capt. William Norris (Ret.), "What Is TLAM/N and Why Do We Need It?" Lt. Michael Kostiuk, "Removal of the Nuclear Strike Option from United States Attack Submarines," and LCDR David DiOrio, USSTRATCOM, "The Role of Nuclear Sea-Launched Cruise Missiles in the Post Cold War Strategy," all in *The Submarine Review* (January 1998); Capt. Howard Venezia (Ret.), "The Sub Launched Nuclear Cruise Missile Debate," letter in *The Submarine Review* (April 1998).

60. See Rear Admiral Albert H. Konetzni, U.S. Navy Commander, Submarine Force United States Pacific Fleet, Statement before the House Armed Services Committee Procurement Subcommittee Submarine Force Structure and Modernization Plans Hearing, 27 June 2000.

Safranchuk, Chapter 3

1. See Vladimir Belous, "Sredstvo politicheskogo I voennogo sdergivaniya" (Means of political and military deterrence), *Nezavisimoe voennoe obozreniye* (Independent Military Review), 26 September 1996.

2. See, for example, P. Bracken, *The Command and Control of Nuclear Forces* (New Haven, Conn.: Yale University Press, 1989), 132.

3. See George Lewis and Andrea Gabbitas, "What Should Be Done about Tactical Nuclear Weapons?" The Atlantic Council of the United States, occasional paper, 1–3 March 1999.

4. See SALT II, Art. II, paragraph 1, 2, 3c, 4.

5. See START I, Art. II, paragraph 1, Art. V, paragraph 18d, 18e.

6. See A. Carnesale, P. Doty, S. Hoffman, S. Huntington, J. Nye, and S. Sagan, *Living with Nuclear Weapons* (Cambridge, Mass.: Harvard University Press, 1983), 126.

7. See M. Mandelbaum, *The Nuclear Future* (Ithaca, N.Y.: Cornell University Press, 1983), 27.

8. See A. Kenny, *The Logic of Deterrence: A Philosopher Looks at the Arguments for and against Nuclear Disarmament* (London: Firethorn Press, 1985), 88.

9. To a large extent, the different definitions of strategic and INF nuclear weapons in Russia and the United States result from variances in their geostrategic situations. The classifications are determined by the types of combat missions performed and their impact on the balance of power in the times of peace.

10. See D. Schroder, *Science, Technology and Nuclear Age.* (New York: John Wiley and Sons, 1984), 10.

11. See Bracken, *Command and Control of Nuclear Forces*, 235.

12. For instance, some Western experts believed that INF are tactical nuclear weapons. See Shroder, *Science, Technology and Nuclear Age*, 277. At the same time, some agreed that the U.S. INF in Europe comprised strategic arms if targeted against the Soviet Union/Russia. The Russian specialists also rarely treated the INF as tactical nuclear weapons.

13. See *Presidential National Security Address to the Federal Assembly of the Russian Federation* (M., 1996), 24.

14. See Lord Zuckerman, *Star Wars in a Nuclear World* (London: William Kimber, 1986), 59.

15. See V. D. Sokolovsky, ed., *The Military Strategy* (Voyennaya Strategiya) 1st Edition, Moscow: Voyenizdat, 1962.

16. See Joseph D. Douglass, Jr., "The Theater Nuclear Threat," *Parameters* 12

(December 1982). See also Earl F. Ziemke, "Superweapons," *Parameters* 12 (December 1982).

17. See Harriet Fast Scott and William F. Scott, *Soviet Military Doctrine* (Boulder, London: Westview Press, 1988), 90.

18. See James R. Schlesinger, "The Theater Nuclear Forces Posture in Europe—A Report to the U.S. Congress," unclassified version, April 1975, 8.

19. Pure weapons are those with zero or minimally accepted correlate damage; dirty are those that can impose unintended or even unexpected damage. The conclusion that Russia and the United States continue work on new generation of pure weapons is based on the April 1999 Security Council meeting for Russia, and the January 2002 Nuclear Posture Review for the United States.

20. Military experts have often studied the deterring factors for various states and leaders. The difference in the political system, political culture, and traditions have an impact on the perception of threats and, therefore, on deterrence. This is why in the 1980s, some experts in the West proposed to contain the USSR by making strikes against the Soviet party elite and KGB units. See Keith Payne and Neil Pickett, "Vulnerability Is Not an Adequate Strategy," *Military Review* 61, No. 10 (October 1981): 67.

21. SMF have in their structure interceptors for missile defense located around Moscow. Traditionally they were part of Air Defense Forces. However in 1997 Air Defense Forces were terminated as an independent branch of the military forces: most of it was transmitted to Air Forces, but missile defense structures were attributed to SMF. The 2000 reform of SMF, when some of its functions (space forces) were taken away from SMF, did not touch on missile defense structure. From 1997 they remain in SMF.

22. See *RIA-Novosti*, 25 September 1997.

23. See *Literaturnaya Gazeta*, 1 June 1994. See Lockwood Dunbar, "Nuclear Weapon Developments," *SIPRI Yearbook 1996.*

24. See A. Vorobyev and B. Kvok, "Disarmament. Keep Patience!" *Mezhdunarodnaya zhizn* No. 2 (1996), 38.

25. See Norris Robert and Arkin William, "Nuclear Notebook: Estimated Soviet Nuclear Stockpile (July 1991)," *Bulletin of Atomic Scientists* (July/August 1991), 48.

26. See statement by Secretary of Defense William Perry, 22 September 1994, *Department of Defense News Release*, No. 546, 1994.

27. See Coll Steve and Ottaway David, "Rethinking the Bomb," *Washington Post*, 13 April 1995. The authors argue that after START II implementation, the parties will have 3,000–3,500 strategic nuclear warheads, or about 10,000 warheads in total, including tactical nuclear weapons.

28. See David Hoffman, "Kremlin to Bolster Nuclear Stockpile. NATO's Airstrikes Are Making Russia Worried, Sources Say," *Washington Post*, 30 April 1999.

29. See NRD, "Nuclear Notebook, Estimated Russian Stockpile, September 1996," *Bulletin of the Atomic Scientists* (September/October 1996): 63.

30. See Joshua Handler, "Progress in Nuclear Disarmament and Confidence Building Measures Related to Nuclear Weaponry," Fourth Pugwash Workshop: The Future of the Nuclear Weapon Complexes of Russia and the USA. Moscow and Snezhinsk/Chelyabinsk-70, 8–14 September 1997, 7.

31. This results from the official position that all Russian nuclear weapons are under the control of the president.

32. See statement by the President of the Soviet Union, Michail Gorbachev, 5 September 1991.

33. TV statement of the President of the Russian Federation, Boris Yeltsin, 29 January 1992.

34. See statement by U.S. President George H. W. Bush, from the White House, 27 September 1991.

35. See Handler, "Progress in Nuclear Disarmament and Confidence Building Measures Related to Nuclear Weaponry."

36. See *Interfax*, 26 September 1996.

37. See "Russia Honours Pledge to Destroy Some Kinds of Nuclear Arms," *RANSAC Nuclear News*, 12 October, 1998.

38. Harold A. Feiveson, ed., *Nuclear Turning Point* (Washington, D.C.: Brookings: 1999), 319

39. See *Presidential National Security Address to the Federal Assembly* (M., 1996).

40. See Robert McNamara, *Blundering into Disaster: Surviving the First Century of the Nuclear Age* (NY, 1986), 21–23.

41. Ibid., 23.

42. See *NAPSNet Daily Report*, Nautilus Institute, 17 March 1992.

43. See *Nezavisimoye voennoye obozreniye*, No. 22, 28 November 1996, 1.

44. See David Hoffman, "Kremlin to Bolster Nuclear Stockpile. NATO's Airstrikes Are Making Russia Worried, Sources Say," *Washington Post*, 30 April 1999.

45. See V. Vasilenko and G. Kuznetsov, "Russian Mission in Maintaining Nuclear Parity on the Eve of the New Age," *Strategicheskay Stabilnost (Strategic Stability Journal)* No. 1 (1998): 11.

Nelson, Chapter 4

1. The classified Nuclear Posture Review was delivered to Congress in January 2002. Its contents were eventually leaked to the press and summarized by William Arkin, "Nuclear Warfare; Secret Plan Outlines the Unthinkable," *Los Angeles Times*, 10 March 2002.

2. See Stephen M. Younger, "Nuclear Weapons in the Twenty-First Century," Los Alamos National Laboratory Report, LAUR-00-2850, 27 June 2000.

3. See Thomas W. Dowler and Joseph S. Howard II, "Countering the Threat of the Well-Armed Tyrant: A Modest Proposal for Small Nuclear Weapons," *Strategic Review* (Fall 1991).

4. See Walter Pincus, "Senate Bill Requires Study of New Nuclear Weapons," *Washington Post*, 12 June 2000.

5. There is no restriction on developing more advanced delivery systems, however, so some Pentagon plans involve using existing warheads in a modified or newly designed earth-penetrating bomb casing.

6. See Maj. Gen. G. L. Curtin and G. W. Ullrich, "The Threats Go Deep," *Air Force Magazine* (October 1997).

7. See R. W. Nelson, "Low-Yield Earth-Penetrating Nuclear Weapons," *Science and Global Security* 10, No. 1 (January 2002).

8. Ibid.

9. See Samuel Glasstone and Philip J. Dolan, *The Effects of Nuclear Weapons*, 3d ed., (Washington, D.C.: U.S. Department of Defense and Department of Energy, 1977).

10. Ibid.

11. See Dan Stober, "Two U.S. labs will compete to design H-bomb to pierce underground sites," *San Diego Union-Tribune*, 26 March 2002.

Millar, Chapter 5

1. "Osama bin Laden has been in contact with various sources, including Russian mafia groups, in an attempt to obtain radiological materials, perhaps tactical nuclear

weapons," Peter Barnes quotes former FBI investigator Oliver Revell in "Tiny Nukes Pose Big Threat: Could Terrorists Have Cold War Era Portable Nuclear Weapons?" ABCNews.com, Sci/Tech, 9 October 2001. See also Steven Erlanger, "Lax Nuclear Security in Russia Is Cited as Way for bin Laden to Get Arms" *New York Times*, 12 November 2001.

Citing "Arab security sources," the London-based Arabic newspaper *Al-Sharq al-Awsat* reported that "Chechen elements" loyal to Osama bin Laden are "searching for ready-made nuclear weapons . . . in former Soviet republics, which have such weapons." The article said that the intelligence service of "a European country" had thwarted an attempt to ship nuclear warheads to the Taliban in Afghanistan and to Osama bin Laden. The warheads were reportedly taken from nuclear arsenals in Ukraine, Kazakhstan, Turkmenistan, and Russia. (According to available open-source information, all former Soviet nuclear weapons have been returned to Russia from other former Soviet republics.) The article said that five nuclear experts from Turkmenistan had served as brokers in the deal, saying that one of these experts had worked in the Iraqi nuclear program in the 1980s. It also hinted that other former Soviet nuclear experts may have participated in the operation or been hired by bin Laden to assist in the acquisition of a nuclear capability. Arab sources were also cited as saying that these experts were now working on transforming the 20 nuclear warheads into smaller-sized weapons more suitable for terrorist use. Such nuclear smuggling operations, according to the article, were now taking on a new dimension as a result of cooperation between the Chechen mafia in the former Soviet Union and bin Laden's organization. The article argued that this case shows that Chechen and Russian organized crime groups are planning to work with the Taliban (the world's largest producer of opium) and bin Laden to build a trade in which nuclear weapons are exchanged for narcotics. The Russian Federal Security Service (FSB) responded to the article by issuing a statement saying that repeated investigations had produced no evidence supporting reports of sales of nuclear weapons, materials, and technologies to the Taliban from Russia. *Al-Sharq al-Awsat* (London), 25 December 2000.

2. Remarks by President Bush to Warsaw Conference on Combatting Terrorism, Warsaw, Poland, 6 Nov. 2001. See also Jeffrey Donovan "U.S.: Bush Concerned about Terrorists Seeking Nuclear Bomb," Radio Free Europe, *Radio Liberty*, 7 November 2001.

3. Donald Rumsfeld, Secretary of Defense, testimony before the Subcommittee of Senate Appropriations Committee, Washington, D.C., 21 May 2002.

4. NATO, "Statement on Combating Terrorism: Adapting the Alliance's Defense Capabilities," NATO Press Release (2001), 18 December 2001, 173.

5. Sam Nunn, William Perry, and Eugene Habiger, "Still Missing: A Nuclear Strategy," *Washington Post*, 21 May 2002.

6. According to the IAEA, since 1993 there have been 175 cases of *trafficking in nuclear material* and 201 cases of trafficking in other radioactive sources (medical, industrial, etc.). However, only 18 of these cases have actually involved small amounts of highly enriched uranium or plutonium, the material needed to produce a nuclear bomb. IAEA experts judge the quantities involved to be insufficient to construct a nuclear explosive device. "However, any such materials being in illicit commerce and conceivably accessible to terrorist groups is deeply troubling," says Mohamed El-Baradei. IAEA press release, "Calculating the New Global Nuclear Terrorism Threat" 1 November 2001. On the case of the two Lithuanian arms dealers, see Aleksey Agureyev, "Two Lithuanians Sentenced In Missile Plot in USA," ITAR-TASS, 20 August 1998.

7. See Gary Milhollin, "Can Terrorists Get the Bomb?" *Commentary Magazine* (February 2002), 45–49.

8. See Howard Baker and Lloyd Cutler, "Final Report: Task Force on DoE Nonproliferation Programs in Russia," January 2001.

9. "A few high-profile episodes point to a spreading ethos of corruption in the Russian nuclear establishment that could presage major covert exports of fissile material, weapons components, and even intact nuclear weapons." Rensselaer Lee, Foreign Policy Research Institute analyst, quoted in F. R. Duplantier "Who's Minding Russia's Nuclear Store? No one knows for sure what's become of the nuclear material stockpiled by the former Soviet Union," *Behind the Headlines,* 17 June 2001.

10. See Canadian Security Intelligence Service report, "Chemical, Biological, Radiological and Nuclear (CBRN) Terrorism," 2 December 1999.

11. Secretary of State Colin Powell, testimony before the Senate Foreign Relations Committee hearings on the Treaty on Strategic Offensive Reductions, 9 July 2002.

12. See Graham H. Turbiville, "Russian Officer Admits Concerns over Nuclear Theft," *Special Warfare,* January 1996.

13. Nuclear Intelligence Council, *Annual Report to Congress on the Safety and Security of Russian Nuclear Facilities and Military Forces,* February 2002.

14. Matthew Bunn, as quoted by Tony Wesolowsky in his article, "Russia: Nuclear Security Poses Challenges," Radio Free Europe, *Radio Liberty,* 8 November 2001.

15. See *CIA Annual Report to Congress on the Safety and Security of Russian Nuclear Facilities and Military Forces,* February 2002.

16. See remarks by Rep. Curt Weldon, House Committee on National Security, Military Research, and Development Subcommittee, 1 October 1997.

17. See statement by George J. Tenet, director of CIA, to the Senate Select Committee on Intelligence, 7 February 2001.

18. See National Intelligence Council report, "Unclassified Summary of a National Intelligence Estimate: Foreign Missile Developments and Ballistic Missile Threat through 2015," December 2001.

19. See "World Missile Chart," Carnegie Endowment for International Peace, 8 February 2002.

20. See National Air Intelligence Center, "Ballistic and Cruise Missile Threat," NAIC-1031-0985-98.

21. See "Missiles & the Devil's Brews," on the website of Centre for Defence and International Security Studies, University of Lancaster, U.K. http://www.cdiss.org/devils.htm (accessed 22 October 2002).

22. See LTC Ed Gjermundsen's presentation, "Low Cost Cruise Missile Defense (LCCMD) Program," Defense Advanced Research Projects Agency, DARPATech '99, June 1999.

23. See Christopher Bolkcom and John Pike, "Attack Aircraft Proliferation: Issues for Concern," chapter 5, Federation of American Scientists, d. unk.

24. For more information on the Chinese purchase of *Sovremenny*-class destroyers, see "DoD 101: Rest-of-World Ships," on the Federation of American Scientists' website at http://www.fas.org (accessed 15 June 2002).

25. See William M. Arkin, Robert S. Norris, and Joshua Handler, "Taking Stock: Worldwide Nuclear Deployments 1998," report by Natural Resources Defense Council, March 1998.

26. See Nikolai Sokov, "Russia's New National Security Concept: The Nuclear Angle," an assessment of the National Security Concept, Center for Nonproliferation Studies, 19 January 2000. He notes, "The hallmarks of the new defense policy are (1) the perception that NATO uses force freely and will not hesitate to use it against Russia over political disagreements, and (2) a realistic appreciation of how Russia's weakened conventional forces are unable to resist a large-scale conventional attack by NATO. Nuclear weapons are seen as the only reliable means to dissuade NATO from using force against Russia, and the harsh language of the recent official documents is clearly intended to ward off this perceived threat."

For an overview of factors motivating Rusia's possible increased reliance in tactical nuclear weapons, see David S. Yost, "Russia and Arms Control for Non-Strategic Nuclear Forces," in Jeff Larsen and Kurt Klingenberger, eds., *Controlling Non-Strategic Nuclear Weapons: Obstacles and Opportunities* (Colorado Springs: U.S. Air Force Institute for National Security Studies, 2001).

27. See Secretary of State Colin Powell's testimony before the Senate Foreign Relations Committee hearings on the Treaty on Strategic Offensive Reductions, 9 July 2002.

28. Statement by G-8 Leaders, "The G8 Global Partnership against the Spread of Weapons and Materials of Mass Destruction," Government of Canada Press Release, 27 June 2002.

29. See Michael R. Gordon, "Misunderstandings Still Hinder Russia-NATO Partnership," *New York Times*, 28 May 1998.

30. See statement by Ambassador Leif A. Ulland, Special Adviser on Disarmament for Norway, to the United Nations General Assembly 55th Session, First Committee, 10 October 2001.

31. For the text of the report, see NATO Press Release M-NAC-2(2000)121, "Report on Options for Confidence and Security Building Measures (CSBMs), Verification, Non-Proliferation, Arms Control and Disarmament," December 2000.

32. Ibid.

33. Ibid.

34. Final communiqué of the ministerial meeting of the North Atlantic Council held at NATO Headquarters, Brussels, 6 December 2001.

35. See Joshua Handler, "The September 1991 PNIs and the Elimination, Storing and Security Aspects of TNWs," presentation for "Time to Control Tactical Nuclear Weapons," hosted by UNIDIR et al., United Nations, 24 September 2001. See also Martin Butcher, Otfried Nassauer, and Stephen Young, "Nuclear Futures: Western European Options for Nuclear Risk Reduction," *BASIC/BITS Research Report* 98, 6 December 1998.

36. See NATO Press Communiqué M-Nac-2(2000)121, "Report on Options for Confidence and Security Building Measures (CSBMs), Verification, Non-Proliferation, Arms Control and Disarmament," 14 December 2000.

37. See Jeffrey Kluger, "The Nuke Pipeline—The Trade in Nuclear Contraband Is Approaching Critical Mass. Can We Turn Off the Spigot?" *Time*, 17 December 2001.

38. See Amy F. Wolf, "Nuclear Weapons in Russia, Safety, Security and Control Issues," CRS Issue Brief for Congress IB98038, updated 5 December 2001.

39. See statement by President George H. W. Bush, "Address to the Nation on Reducing United States and Soviet Nuclear Weapons," 27 September 1991. Available in the Appendix in this book.

40. See NATO's 1999 Strategic Concept.

41. See Kanti Bajpai, "The Military Utility of Nuclear Weapons and the Case for Disarmament," paper presented at Pugwash Conference, School of International Studies Jawaharlal Nehru University, New Delhi, India, 25–27 March 2001.

42. For example, during the post–Cold War round of NATO enlargement, Anatoli Diakov, Timur Kadyshev, Eugene Miasnikov, and Pavel Podvig made this case in the paper: "NATO Expansion and the Nuclear Reductions Process" presented at a conference titled NATO Movement to the East–Security Problems for Russia and the C.I.S. States (St. Petersburg, Russia: 28–29 April 1999).

Also, according to Russia's Representative at NATO Headquarters in Brussels, General Leontiy Chevtsov, "any Russia-NATO political accord concerning the enlargement of the Alliance would have to rule out the deployment in new NATO States of nuclear weapons capable of striking Russia." Describing such deployment as "completely unacceptable. . . . The presence of tactical nuclear weapons in the potential new NATO countries would bring about appropriate action on our part." What this "appropriate" action might be was not mentioned in reports of Chevtsov's remarks. However, U.S. Defense Secretary Perry has recently been expressing concern about the number of tactical nuclear weapons still possessed, though not currently deployed, by Russia. From report by Agence France-Presse, "NATO Makes Fresh Attempt to Break Deadlock with Russia," *International News*, 24 October 1999.

43. See James Schlesinger's testimony before the Senate Subcommittee on International Security, Proliferation, and Federal Services, Senate Committee Governmental Affairs, 27 October 1997. "If, for example, NATO is expanded to include the Baltic states, no conventional defense would be possible. Under such circumstances, if we were to fulfill a commitment to provide protection, we would be driven back to threatening a nuclear response to a conventional attack—a commitment from which we have only escaped recently. Given the nature of our foreign policy agenda and given the unique geopolitical role of the United States, a decline in the confidence in U.S. nuclear weapons cannot therefore be viewed with equanimity."

44. See remarks by Under Secretary of Defense for Policy Douglas J. Feith at DoD news briefing, "Breakfast Meeting in Washington, D.C. with the Defense Writers Group," 20 February 2002.

45. See NATO press release "NATO-RUSSIA Permanent Joint Council Meeting at the Foreign Minister Level," in Brussels, 7 December 2001.

46. See interview with John Bolton in *Arms Control Today*, 20 February 2002.

47. Sam Nunn, cochairman, Nuclear Threat Initiative Testimony before the U.S. Senate Committee on Foreign Relations on the Treaty between the United States of America and the Russian Federation on Strategic Offensive Reductions, 23 July 2002.

48. See "Debt Reduction for Nonproliferation Act of 2001."

49. Final Communiqué ministerial meeting of the Defence Planning Committee and the Nuclear Planning Group held in Brussels, 6 June 2002.

Hoyt, Chapter 6

1. Timothy D. Hoyt is an Associate Professor of Strategy and Policy at the United States Naval War College. The views expressed in this chapter are those of the author, and do not reflect the policy or position of the Department of Defense or any other official body of the United States.

2. The best single volume on this issue is Scott D. Sagan and Kenneth N. Waltz, *The Spread of Nuclear Weapons: A Debate* (New York: W. W. Norton, 1995).

3. See Kenneth Waltz, *The Spread of Nuclear Weapons: More May Be Better*, Adelphi Paper no. 171 (London: International Institute of Strategic Studies, Autumn 1981); Kenneth N. Waltz, "Nuclear Myths and Realities," *American Political Science Review* 84:3 (September 1990): 73745; and John J. Mersheimer, "The Case for a Ukrainian Nuclear Deterrent," *Foreign Affairs* 72:3 (Summer 1993): 50–66. One of the earliest works in this vein is Pierre Gallois, *The Balance of Terror: Strategy for the Nuclear Age* (Boston: Houghton Mifflin, 1961).

4. See Scott D. Sagan, "The Perils of Proliferation: Organization Theory, Deterrence Theory, and the Spread of Nuclear Weapons," *International Security* 18:4 (Spring 1994): 66–107. See also Peter D. Feaver, "Neooptimists and the Enduring Problem of Nuclear Proliferation," *Security Studies* 6:4 (Summer 1997): 93–125.

5. An excellent study of U.S.-Soviet nuclear strategy is Lawrence Freedman, *The*

Evolution of Nuclear Strategy, 2d ed. (London: International Institute for Strategic Studies, 1981, 1989).

6. For discussions of emerging nuclear arsenals, see Jordan Seng, "Less Is More: Command and Control Advantages of Minor Nuclear States," *Security Studies* 6:4 (Summer 1997): 50–92; and David J. Karl, "Proliferation Pessimism and Emerging Nuclear Powers," *International Security* 21:3 (Winter 1996/97): 87–119.

7. See, for example, Rodney W. Jones, *Minimum Nuclear Deterrence Postures in South Asia: An Overview*, Defense Threat Reduction Agency Advanced Systems and Concepts Office, Washington, D.C., 1 October 2001.

8. See George Perkovich, *India's Nuclear Bomb* (Berkeley: University of California Press, 1999), 182.

9. See "The Prime Minister's Announcement of India's Three Underground Nuclear Tests on May 11, 1998," and "Press Conference, Dr. R. Chidambaram (RC), Chairman, AEC & Secretary, DAE; Dr. A. P. J. Abdul Kalam (K), scientific adviser to Raksha Mantri and secretary, Department of Defence Research and Development; Dr. Anil Kakodkar, director, BARC; Dr. K. Santhanam, chief adviser (Technologies), DRDO, 17 May 1998."

10. See "Press Release on India's Nuclear Tests, May 11 and 13, 1998," Federation of American Scientists.

11. For a discussion, see Hilary Synnott, *The Causes and Consequences of South Asia's Nuclear Tests*, Adelphi Paper 332 (London: International Institute for Strategic Studies, 1999), 54–56; and Ashley J. Tellis, *India's Emerging Nuclear Posture: Between Recessed Deterrent and Ready Arsenal* (Santa Monica, Calif.: RAND, 2001), 519–22.

12. Reactor grade plutonium is typically 65 to 70 percent Pu-239 and has other isotopes that lower the explosive yield of the nuclear reaction. However, weapons using reactor-grade plutonium have been successfully tested by the United States, and Perkovich believes one of India's "low-yield" tests used non-weapons-grade plutonium. Perkovich, *India's Nuclear Bomb*, 428–29.

13. See David Albright, "India's and Pakistan's Fissile Material and Nuclear Weapons Inventories, end of 1999," Institute for Science and International Security (ISIS), 11 October 2000.

14. See "Pakistan's Nuclear Arsenal Understimated, Reports Say," *Washington Times*, 9 June 2000.

15. See "Pakistan completes the current series of nuclear tests . . . Foreign Secretary, Mr. Shamshad Ahmed's statement at the Press Conference in Islamabad on 30 May 1998." Many analysts speculate that the rationale for six tests resolves around matching India's cumulative total of five (1998) plus one (1974).

16. See "Pak Conducted One, Not 5 Tests on May 28," *Hindustan Times*, 31 May 1998.

17. See "Pakistan Started Preparing for N-Tests Six Days after Pokhran II," Rediff. com, 30 June 1998.

18. See the analysis by the Federation of American Scientists in "Pakistan Nuclear Weapons." See also Perkovich, *India's Nuclear Bomb*, 435.

19. See Albright, "India's and Pakistan's Fissile Material."

20. See "U.S. Labs at Odds on Whether Pakistani Blast Used Platonium," *Washington Post*, 17 January 1999.

21. The best single volume history of India's nuclear weapons program is Perkovich, *India's Nuclear Bomb*.

22. Ibid., 296.

23. See Maj. General Som Dutt, *India and the Bomb*, Adelphi Paper 30 (London: International Institute for Strategic Studies, 1966).

24. Regarding India's unusual civil-military relationship and strategic culture, see

Lorne J. Kavic, *India's Quest for Security: Defence Policies 1947–1965* (Berkeley: University of California Press, 1967); and George Tanham, *Indian Strategic Thought: An Interpretive Essay* (Santa Monica, Calif.: RAND, 1992).

25. This is the focus of Perkovich, *India's Nuclear Bomb.*

26. Even hawkish analysts have difficulty defining a credible Chinese threat to India. While India attempted to use the Chinese threat to justify its 1998 tests, it quickly backed away from this contention. A chapter in an edited volume by one of India's leading hawks fails to present a compelling vision of a Chinese threat. See Ravi Rikhye and Pushpindar Singh, "External Threats and India's Conventional Capabilities: Perspectives till 2010," in *Future Imperilled: India's Security in the 1990s and Beyond,* ed. Bharat Karnad (New Delhi: Viking Books, 1994), 85–98.

27. The stability-instability paradox was first identified in by Glenn Snyder in the 1960s, and is discussed in Robert Jervis, *The Meaning of the Nuclear Revolution* (Ithaca, N.Y.: Cornell University Press, 1989), 19–22. See also Michael Krepon and Chris Gagne, eds., *The Stability-Instability Paradox: Nuclear Weapons and Brinkmanship in South Asia* (Washington, D.C.: Henry L. Stimson Center, June 2001).

28. See the Indian Draft Nuclear Doctrine, 17 August 1999.

29. See "Fernandes Unveils 'limited war' doctrine," *Hindu,* 25 January 2000; "When Words Hurt: No Limits on a 'Limited War,'" *Asiaweek* 26:12 (31 March 2000).

30. See "Military Option If Diplomacy Fails," *Hindu,* 4 January 2002.

31. See "Army Ready for War, Says Chief," *Statesman* (India), 12 January 2002.

32. See "India Tests Missile, Stirring a Region Already on Edge," *New York Times,* 25 January 2002.

33. For an overview, see Timothy D. Hoyt, "Pakistani Nuclear Doctrine and the Dangers of Strategic Myopia," *Asian Survey* 41:6 (November/December 2001): 956–77; and Zafar Iqbal Cheema, "Pakistan's Nuclear Use Doctrine and Command and Control," in *Planning the Unthinkable: How New Powers Will Use Nuclear, Biological, and Chemical Weapons,* ed. Peter R. Lavoy, Scott D. Sagan, and James J. Wirtz (Ithaca, N.Y.: Cornell University Press, 2000), 158–81.

34. See Zulfikar Ali Bhutto, *The Myth of Independence* (London: Oxford University Press, 1969). Bhutto, the foreign minister under President Ayub Khan in the mid-1960s, became the president of Pakistan from 1971 to 1977 (and prime minister 1973–77) after the independence of Bangladesh.

35. The Pressler Amendment, Section 620E(e) of the foreign Assistance Act of 1961, became law in 1985. It required the U.S. president to certify that Pakistan did not possess a nuclear weapon in order for foreign aid to be distributed. President Reagan so certified during each of his years in office, but with the waning of the Soviet war in Afghanistan and the increased evidence of Pakistan's nuclear weaponization, President Bush was unable to certify Pakistan in 1990, and economic and military assistance was suspended.

36. See Perkovich, *India's Nuclear Bomb,* 252–59.

37. For details, see Devin T. Hagerty, *The Consequences of Nuclear Proliferation* (Cambridge, Mass.: MIT Press, 1998); Kanti P. Bajpai, P. R. Chari, Pervaiz Iqbal Cheema, Stephen P. Cohen, and Sumit Ganguly, *Brasstacks and Beyond: Perception and Management of Crisis in South Asia* (Urbana-Champaign, Ill.: ACDIS, June 1995). A very interesting work is Ravi Rikhye's *The War That Never Was: The Story of India's Strategic Failures* (New Delhi: Chanakya Publications, 1988), which points out the serious flaws in Indian military planning while simultaneously rejecting the possibility of a Pakistani nuclear capability.

38. The nuclear deployment report comes from Seymour Hersh, "On the Nuclear Edge," *New Yorker,* 29 March 1993: 55–73, and is repeated in William E. Burrows and

Robert Windrem, *Critical Mass* (New York: Simon & Schuster, 1994): 60–90. According to the U.S. ambassadors in New Delhi and Islamabad at the time, however, the U.S. government was unaware of any nuclear deployment, or even of the evacuation of nuclear materials from Kahuta. See Michael Krepon and Mishi Faruqee, eds. *Conflict Prevention and Confidence-Building Measures in South Asia: The 1990 Crisis*, Occasional Paper no. 17 (Washington, D.C.: The Henry L. Stimson Center, April 1994).

39. See Hersh, "On the Nuclear Edge," 68–73.

40. See "Pakistan Can Build One Nuclear Device, Official Says," *Washington Post*, 7 February 1992.

41. See Cheema, "Pakistan's Nuclear Use Doctrine and Command and Control," 159.

42. Ibid., 158.

43. See statement by General Musharraf, 12 April 1999, cited in *From Surprise to Reckoning: The Kargil Review Committee Report* (New Delhi: SAGE, 15 December 1999), 242.

44. See "Nuclear Safety, Nuclear Stability and Nuclear Strategy in Pakistan," *A Concise Report of a Visit by Landau Network—Centro Volta* (January 2002). The lead investigators on this project were Professor Paolo Cotta-Ramusion and Professor Maurizio Martellini.

45. See "Pakistan clarifies threat to use nukes," Rediff.com, 10 April 2002.

46. An excellent sense of the proximity problem, and of the history of the nuclear programs in both states, can be found in Rodney W. Jones and Mark G. McDonough, *Tracking Nuclear Proliferation: A Guide in Maps and Charts, 1998*, with Toby F. Dalton and Gregory D. Koblenz (Washington, D.C.: Carnegie Endowment for International Peace, 1998), 111–46.

47. See *Military Applications of Nuclear Technology*, Part I, Hearings, Joint Committee on Atomic Energy, Congress of the United States, 93d Congress (22 May, 29 June 1973), 15–17, cited in M. Leitenberg, "Background Information on Tactical Nuclear Weapons (Primarily in the European Context)," in *Tactical Nuclear Weapons: European Perspectives* (London: Taylor & Francis Ltd., 1978), 5.

48. Artillery shells are particularly problematic because of the limited heavy artillery fielded by both sides. The United States first fielded an unwieldly 280 mm howitzer, and then later developed nuclear shells for the M-110 8-in and M-109 155 mm self-propelled howitzers. The Soviets also deployed artillery weapons for a 203 mm (8-in) howitzer and 152 mm guns and howitzers. India currently deploys both 155 mm Bofors and 152 mm howtizers of Soviet origin, while Pakistan uses the M-109. Given the fact that nuclear rounds for these smaller weapons were developed *at least* 11 years after the first tactical nuclear (large-bore) shells were developed, it seems unlikely that either India or Pakistan has fully mastered these capabilities. See *Tactical Nuclear Weapons*, 110–14; David Miller, *The Cold War: A Military History* (New York: St. Martin's Press, 1998), 438–40.

49. See "Small Is Scary," *Outlook*, 10 June 2002. According to this report, an unnamed Indian general said, "We know that Pakistan will use a tactical nuclear weapon if it finds itself cornered." A Pakistani report stated that the two countries have deployed tactical weapons. " 'Tactical' N-Warheads Moved Along Borders," *News International* (Pakistan), 28 May 2002.

50. Dr. P. K. Iyengar, former chief of the Indian Atomic Energy Commission, has argued for enhanced radiation tests in "India Should Test Neutron Bomb, Says AEC Ex-Chief," *Times of India*, 1 May 2000.

51. See, for example, Morton H. Halperin, *Limited War in the Nuclear Age* (New York: John Wiley & Sons, 1963), 58.

52. This analysis assumes that India is the most likely state to be threatening a significant conventional victory and that Pakistan is relatively more likely to be forced to first use of nuclear weapons, based on the imbalance of conventional forces and the proximity of crucial Pakistani infrastructure to the international border and Line of Control. However, this analysis could equally apply in the case of a potentially decisive penetration of Indian territory by either Pakistan or China.

53. These disadvantages, obviously, are not necessarily a major weakness. The delay between request for use and delivery allows for the possibility of intercession by higher military or political authorities that might avert nuclear use. The difference in accuracy can be overcome by substitution of a higher-yield warhead with greater destructive radius.

54. For an Indian perspective, see Gurmeet Kanwal, *Nuclear Defence: Shaping the Arsenal* (New Delhi: Knowledge World and the Institute for Defence Studies and Analysis, April 2001), 57–70, 97–102.

55. General K. Sundarji discusses some of this issues in his novel *Blind Men of Hindoostan: Indo-Pak Nuclear War* (New Delhi: UBS Publishers, 1993), 131–40. Curiously, however, he chooses to have Pakistan "mix-and-match" countervalue and military targets in their nuclear strike, with little explanation.

56. See Raj Chengappa, *Weapons of Peace* (New Delhi: HarperCollins Publishers India Pvt Ltd, 2000), 437.

57. See, for example, K. Sundarji, *Effects of Nuclear Asymmetry on Conventional Deterrence*, Combat Paper No. 1 (Mhow, India: College of Combat, 1981).

58. See Stephen P. Cohen, "Why Did India 'Go Nuclear,'" in *India's Nuclear Security*, ed. Raju G. C. Thomas and Amit Gupta (Boulder, Colo.: Lynne Rienner, 2000), 22.

59. See Brahma Chellaney, "Tactical Nukes," *Hindustan Times*, 26 January 1999; Gurmeet Kanwal, "Does India Need Tactical Weapons," *Strategic Analysis*. http://www.idsa-india.org/an-may-03.htl (accessed 1 April 2002).

60. Rear Admiral Raja Menon, *A Nuclear Strategy for India* (New Delhi: SAGE, 2000); Kanwal, *Nuclear Defence: Shaping the Arsenal*, particularly 90–107; Brigadier Vijai K Nair, *Nuclear India* (New Delhi, Lancer International, 1992).

61. See Ashley J. Tellis, *India's Emerging Nuclear Posture: Between Recessed Deterrent and Ready Arsenal* (Santa Monica, Calif.: RAND, 2001).

62. A discussion of these options can be found in Waheguru Pal Singh Sidhu, "India's Nuclear Use Doctrine," in *Planning the Unthinkable*, 150–152.

63. See "A Unique Army Exercise," *Hindu*, 30 December 2001. An earlier exercise in May 2001 had tested similar capabilities. See "Heat and Dust: Exercise Poorna Vijay," *Strategic Affairs* (1 September 2001). For a powerful critique of some of the more exaggerated claims, see Tellis, *India's Emerging Nuclear Posture*, 42–44, especially n. 78.

64. See, for example, Dr. Shireen Mazari, "Formulating a Rational Strategic Doctrine," Pakistan Institute for Air Defence Studies.

65. See Hoyt, "Pakistani Nuclear Doctrine."

66. See Colonel Muhammad Azam Khan, "Military Strategy—The Next Step," *Defence Journal* (April 2002).

67. Peter Feaver refers to the "always/never" problem—the tension between assuring that weapons *always* work when necessary and that they *never* be used without appropriate authorization. Peter Douglas Feaver, *Guarding the Guardians: Civilian Control of Nuclear Weapons in the U.S.* (Ithaca, N.Y.: Cornell University Press, 1992), 12.

68. At the time this was written, the two states had maintained an unprecedented mobilization of conventional forces in place on the border and Line of Control for over five months.

Ferguson, Medeiros, and Saunders, Chapter 7

1. See *Zhongguo Junshi Baike Quanshu (Chinese Military Encyclopedia)* (Beijing, China: Academy of Military Science Publishers, July 1997), 1107.

2. This is one of the central arguments of John Wilson Lewis and Xue Litai, *China Builds the Bomb* (Stanford, Calif.: Stanford University Press, 1988.)

3. The major studies addressing Chinese TNWs include Robert S. Norris, Andrew S. Burrows, and Richard W. Fieldhouse, *Nuclear Weapons Databook, Volume V: British, French, and Chinese Nuclear Weapons* (Boulder, Colo.: Westview Press, 1994); Chong-pin Lin, *China's Nuclear Weapons Strategy: Tradition within Evolution* (Lexington, Mass.: Lexington Books, 1988); Ken Allen, "China's Perspective on Non-Strategic Nuclear Weapons and Arms Control," in *Controlling Non-Strategic Nuclear Weapons: Obstacles and Opportunities,* ed. Jeffrey A. Larsen and Kurt J. Klingenberger (Washington, D.C.: Institute for National Security Studies, United States Air Force, 2001); Gregory B. Owens, *Chinese Tactical Nuclear Weapons,* Naval Postgraduate School, Monterey, Calif., June 1996.

4. See Robert Manning, Ronald Montaperto, and Brad Roberts, *China, Nuclear Weapons, and Arms Control: A Preliminary Assessment* (New York: Council on Foreign Relations, 2000.)

5. See Norris et al., *Nuclear Weapons Databook,* 324.

6. See Robert S. Norris and William M. Arkin, "Chinese Nuclear Forces, 2000," *The Bulletin of the Atomic Scientists,* November 2000, 78.

7. See *People's Republic of China Nuclear Weapons Employment Policy and Strategy,* Defense Intelligence Agency, March 1972.

8. See *People's Republic of China Nuclear Weapons Employment Policy and Strategy,* table 5.

9. See *Nuclear Weapons Systems in China,* Defense Estimative Brief, Defense Intelligence Agency, 24 April 1984. Declassified version from the National Security Archive.

10. See *People's Republic of China Nuclear Weapons Employment Policy and Strategy,* Annex D; Lewis and Xue, *China Builds the Bomb,* Appendix B.

11. See Chong-pin Lin, *China's Nuclear Weapons Strategy,* 89.

12. See Yin Chun, "Zongzidian: Jiqun Tanke de Kexin" (*Neutron Bomb: The Killer of Tank Formations) Jiefangjun Bao,* 30 August 1981, 2.

13. See *Facts Speak Louder Than Words and Lies Will Collapse by Themselves—Further Refutation of the Cox Report,* Information Office of the State Council, Beijing, China, 15 July 1999.

14. To be sure, such reporting by the Chinese could have been part of a denial and deception campaign to cloak the shortcomings of the PLA's actual nuclear capabilities. For example, in the early 1980s Chinese articles began to discuss the virtues of neutron bombs; yet it was not until 1988 that China conducted nuclear tests believed to have been used for the specific development of such a weapon.

15. See Chong-pin Lin, *China's Nuclear Weapons Strategy,* 89.

16. See Xu Baoshan, "We Must Be Prepared to Fight Nuclear War in the First Stages of Any Future War," *Jiefangjun Bao,* 16 September 1979. "The Might of Helan Shan Shakes," *Ningxia Ribao,* 29 June 1982, FBIS-China, 3 August 1982. The *Ningxia Daily* reported the exercise and published a photograph of a mushroom cloud with the caption, "An 'atomic bomb' exploding deep in the ranks of the 'enemy.'" "China Simulates Atomic Blast in War Games Aimed at Soviet," *New York Times,* 14 July 1982. The *New York Times* article cited Western military sources as saying the exercise was held in the remote Ningxia region, 435 miles south of the border of Soviet-allied Mongolia,

and involved several hundred thousand men. The authors are grateful to Ken Allen for this data.

17. See Chong-pin Lin, *China's Nuclear Weapons Strategy,* 92–93.

18. See Footnote 111 in Alastair Iain Johnston, "China's New 'Old Thinking': The Concept of Limited Deterrence," *International Security* 20, No. 3 (Winter 1995/96): 5–42. Johnston cites (1) an NRDC estimate (a July 1995 interview with an NRDC analyst) that "China may have enough fissile material to expand its current forces 2 or 3 times (from 300 up to 600–900) warheads; (2) a Union of Concerned Scientists lower-bound estimate is that China has stockpiled enough highly enriched uranium (HEU) and separated plutonium (Pu) for about 200 more warheads. Lisbeth Gronlund, David Wright, and Yong Liu, 'China and a Fissile Material Production Cut-Off,' *Survival* (Winter 1995–96); and (3) David Albright puts the stockpile of HEU around 20 tons (± 25 percent) and Pu at 3.5 tons (± 50 percent) or enough for 700 more warheads (± 50 percent)."

19. See *Selected Military Capabilities of the People's Republic of China,* Report to Congress Pursuant to Section 1305 of the Fiscal Year 1997 National Defense Authorization Act, Office of the Secretary of Defense, U.S. Department of Defense, April 1997; *Report on the Current and Future Military Strategy of the People's Republic of China,* Report to Congress Pursuant to the FY2000 National Defense Authorization Act, Office of the Secretary of Defense, U.S. Department of Defense, 23 June 2000.

20. See *The Military Balance 1999–2000,* International Institute for Strategic Studies, (Oxford, U.K.: Oxford University Press, 1999), 178.

21. See Lewis and Xue, *China Builds the Bomb.*

22. See "Statement of the Government of the People's Republic of China," 16 October 1964.

23. See Alastair Iain Johnston, "Prospects for Chinese Nuclear Force Modernization: Limited Deterrence versus Multilateral Arms Control," *The China Quarterly* 146 (June 1996): 552.

24. See John Wilson Lewis and Hua Di, "China's Ballistic Missile Programs: Technologies, Strategies, Goals," *International Security* 17, No. 2 (Fall 1992): 5–40.

25. However, there were suggestions in the 1970s and 1980s that China's NFU commitment might not apply to the use of nuclear weapons on its own territory to defend against an invasion. See "No-First-Use (NFU)," *China Profiles Database,* East Asia Nonproliferation Program, Center for Nonproliferation Studies.

26. On China's civil defense efforts, see Johnston, "China's New 'Old Thinking,'" 29–31. On the "third front," see Barry Naughton, "The Third Front: Defense Industrialization in the Chinese Interior," *China Quarterly* 115 (September 1991): 351–86.

27. See Jiang Siyi, "Guofang Jianshe He Jundui Jinashe Zhidao Zixiang Zhanluexing Zhuanbian" (The Strategic Transition of the Guiding Thought Concerning Defense Building and Army Building) in *Zhongguo Renmin Jiefangjun Dashidian, Xiace,* ed. Jiang Siyi et al. (The Dictionary of the Major Events of the Chinese People's Liberation Army, Vol. II) (Tianjin: Tianjin renmin chibanshe, 1992), 1948. Cited in Nan Li, "The PLA's Evolving Warfighting Doctrine, Strategy, and Tactics, 1985–95: A Chinese Perspective," *China Quarterly,* 146 (June 1996): 445–46.

28. See Harlan W. Jencks, "Chinese Evaluations of 'Desert Storm': Implications for PRC Security," *Journal of East Asian Affairs* 6, No. 2 (Summer–Fall 1992): 447–77, and David Shambaugh, "China's Military: Real or Paper Tiger?" *Washington Quarterly* 19, No. 2 (Spring 1996): 25–29.

29. See Johnston, "China's New 'Old Thinking'" and Johnston, "Prospects for Chinese Nuclear Force Modernization," 548–76.

30. See Johnston, "China's New 'Old Thinking,'" 26–29.

31. See John Wilson Lewis and Xue Litai, *China's Strategic Seapower: The Politics of Force Modernization in the Nuclear Age* (Stanford, Calif.: Stanford University Press, 1994); Bates Gill and James Mulvenon, "The Chinese Strategic Rocket Forces: Transition to Credible Deterrence," China and Weapons of Mass Destruction, Federal Research Division, Library of Congress, 11–58, http://www.cia.gov/nic/pubs/conference_reports/weapons_mass_destruction.html (accessed 5 June 2002); and Phillip C. Saunders and Jing-don Yuan, "China's Strategic Force Modernization: Issues and Implications for the United States," in *Proliferation Challenges and Nonproliferation Opportunities for New Administrations*, ed. Michael Barletta, Center for Nonproliferation Studies Occasional Paper No. 4. (Monterey, Calif.: Center for Nonproliferation Studies, 2000), 40–46.

32. A conventional Western or Russian analysis of China's strategic situation in the 1970s and 1980s would have concluded that TNWs would have considerable value for a PLA facing a powerful Soviet army equipped with vastly superior weapons. During much of the Cold War, the United States and NATO relied on TNW to compensate for NATO's conventional military inferiority relative to the Warsaw Pact. In the post–Cold War era, Russia's conventional military weakness has prompted a revision in nuclear doctrine that increases the Russian military's reliance on TNW. This analysis would suggest that China had strong incentives to develop an operational TNW capability. However, the meager evidence available suggests that Chinese strategists did not focus on the potential military value of TNWs in confronting a Soviet invasion until the late 1970s and early 1980s. One possible explanation is that the Chinese expectation of a major nuclear war reinforced the belief that strategic nuclear weapons could and would be used in the event of war, reducing the need to develop and deploy TNWs. An alternative explanation is that concerns about the international political costs of violating China's NFU commitment either caused China to forego the potential military advantages of TNW or to develop and deploy TNWs covertly (and forego some of the potential advantages of a more credible deterrence posture). Concerns about the increased risk of inadvertent or unauthorized use of TNWs might have stopped China from deploying TNWs to PLA field units. Technological limitations on China's ability to miniaturize its nuclear warheads may also have placed some TNW options (such as nuclear artillery shells) off limits. Finally, it is possible that China *did* deploy TNWs in the 1970s, but was able to conceal this deployment from U.S. intelligence.

33. This includes the infamous exchange between Chas. W. Freeman and a Chinese official reported in the *New York Times*. See Patrick E. Tyler, "As China Threatens Taiwan, It Makes Sure U.S. Listens," *New York Times*, 24 January 1996, p. A3. Chas. W. Freeman, the former Defense Department official to whom the statements were made, has commented that the Chinese official's statement "came out in garbled form in the *New York Times*." Freeman added that "the statement is in a deterrent context and it is consistent with no first use. It is not a threat to bomb Los Angeles." Carnegie Endowment for International Peace, *Proliferation Brief* 2, No. 10 (11 May 1999).

34. The 1996 pledge came in response to a previous statement by a Chinese official suggesting the NFU might not apply to Taiwan because it was Chinese territory.

35. See Chuck DeVore, "Taiwan Is Standing in China's Way," *Taipei Times*, 29 August 2001.

36. A ground burst could create EMPs that would damage unprotected electrical and electronic equipment over an area of 10 to 20 kilometers in radius from ground zero. This type of explosion would not destroy or disable most of Taiwan's communications systems and would likely cause significant casualties. A nuclear weapon exploded high in the atmosphere could knock out many of Taiwan's communications systems. However, if the explosion is too powerful (megaton range) and too high up

(a few hundred kilometers or higher), Chinese communications could also suffer tremendously. For example, a 1-megaton bomb exploded at an altitude of 300 km would result in an EMP that could spread over 1,700 km. In comparison, the distance across the Taiwan Strait is on the order of 100 km. See Kosa Tsipis, *Arsenal: Understanding Weapons in the Nuclear Age* (New York: Simon & Schuster, 1985), 59.

37. See "Taipei Ready to Buy U.S. Missile Defense," *South China Morning Post* 22 April 1999; and John Raedler, "Security Expert: China Can Take Taiwan without Firing a Shot," 29 July 1999, CNN.com (accessed 10 October 2002). Protective measures against EMP employ either metallic shielding or tailored hardening. While both methods are expensive, hardening only the most critical components costs the least amount, but can still be expensive. The major caveats are that the effects of EMP are hard to predict and protective measures provide no guarantees that they will work perfectly.

38. China is making a significant investment to develop improved cruise missile capabilities, but there is no indication that its cruise missiles will carry nuclear weapons.

39. A classic case is the 1922 Washington Naval Reduction Treaty, which focused on capital ships, such as battleships, and left out relatively weak powers, such as Germany. Some parties to the treaty maneuvered around the provisions by increasing the rate of production of other warships, while some nonparties like Germany were not limited by this treaty. One party, Japan, renounced the treaty in 1934 and launched an unrestricted naval arms buildup. Therefore, leading up to World War II, some nations engaged in a highly competitive naval arms race regardless of this treaty.

40. See, for example, the discussions in the "Purpose of Arms Control" section in Lawrence Scheinman, "Nuclear Weapons and Peace in the Middle East," chapter 2 in *The Dynamics of Middle East Nuclear Proliferation*, ed. Steven L. Speigel, Jennifer D. Kibbe, and Elizabeth G. Matthews (Lewiston: The Edwin Mellen Press, 2001).

Cortright and Gabbitas, Chapter 8

1. The United States has about 1,120 TNWs, 320 of which are in storage in the United States. The rest are tactical nuclear bombs deployed at NATO air bases across Europe. See "U.S. Nuclear Forces, 2001," *The Bulletin of the Atomic Scientists* (March/April 2001): 77–79.

2. For detailed assessments of these cases and recent UN sanctions experience, see David Cortright and George A. Lopez, *The Sanctions Decade: Assessing UN Policy in the 1990s* (Boulder, Colo.: Lynne Rienner, 2000); and David Cortright and George A. Lopez, *Sanctions and the Search for Security: Challenges to UN Action* (Boulder, Colo.: Lynne Rienner Publishers, 2002).

3. See Kimberly Ann Elliott and Gary Clyde Hufbauer, "Same Song, Same Refrain? Economic Sanctions in the 1990s," *American Economic Review* 80, no. 2 (May 1999): 403–408.

4. These studies and an analysis of the role of incentives are contained in David Cortright, ed., *The Price of Peace: Incentives and International Conflict Prevention* (Lanham, Md.: Rowman and Littlefield, 1997).

5. See Nicole Bell, Jordana D. Friedman, and Caleb S. Rossiter, "The Role of International Financial Institutions in Preventing and Resolving Conflict," in Cortright, *The Price of Peace*, 246–52; James K. Boyce and Manuel Pastor, "Aid for Peace: Can International Financial Institutions Help Prevent Conflict?" *World Policy Journal* 15, No. 2. (Summer 1998).

6. See Alexander L. George and Richard Smoke, *Deterrence in American Foreign Pol-*

icy: Theory and Practice (New York: Columbia University Press, 1974), 2 and 33. For a thorough discussion of inducement strategies in the context of differing theories of international relations, see Tuomas Forsberg, "The Efficacy of Rewarding Conflict Strategies: Positive Sanctions as Face-Savers, Payments, and Signals," paper prepared for the annual meeting of the International Studies Association, San Diego, California, April 1996, 16–20.

7. See Roger Fisher, *International Conflict for Beginners* (New York: Harper and Row, 1969), 106.

8. See George and Smoke, *Deterrence*, 606–607.

9. See David A. Baldwin, *Economic Statecraft* (Princeton, N.J.: Princeton University Press, 1985), 42.

10. See George and Smoke, *Deterrence*, 608–609.

11. See Gitty M. Amini, "A Larger Role for Positive Sanctions in Cases of Compellance?" Working Paper No. 12, Center for International Relations, University of California, Los Angeles, May 1997.

12. See Amini, "A Larger Role for Positive Sanctions," 27–28. In their study of 116 sanctions cases, Han Dorussen and Jongryn Mo also find that "incentives increase the effectiveness of sanctions." Han Dorussen and Jongryn Mo, "Sanctions and Incentives," paper delivered at the 1999 annual meeting of the American Political Science Association, Atlanta, Georgia, 2–5 September 1999, 2.

13. See Dorussen and Mo, "Sanctions and Incentives," 2.

14. See Paul Gordon Lauren, "Coercive Diplomacy and Ultimata: Theory and Practice in History," in *The Limits of Coercive Diplomacy*, 2d ed., ed. Alexander L. George and William E. Simons (Boulder, Colo.: Westview Press, 1994), 28.

15. See Martin Patchen, *Resolving Disputes between Nations: Coercion or Conciliation?* (Durham, N.C.: Duke University Press, 1998), 271. This idea was echoed by several other scholars. Stephen Rock noted that "concessions are most likely to be effective when coupled with a resolute deterrence posture," a policy that has been termed "generosity from strength." See Stephen R. Rock, *Appeasement in International Politics* (Lexington: The University Press of Kentucky, 2000), 19. Russell Lang has observed that offers "are more likely to be effective when the influencer has the requisites for the effective use of negative inducements as well." See Russell Lang, "Influence Techniques among Nations," in *Behavior, Society, and International Conflict*, vol. 3, ed. Philip E. Tetlock et al. (Oxford, U.K.: Oxford University Press, 1993), 115.

16. See Robert Axelrod, *The Evolution of Cooperation* (New York: Basic Books, 1984).

17. See Lloyd Jensen, "Negotiating Strategic Arms Control, 1969–1979," *Journal of Conflict Resolution* 28 (1984): 535–59.

18. See William Gamson and André Modigliani, *Untangling the Cold War* (Boston: Little, Brown & Company, 1971).

19. See Patchen, *Resolving Disputes*, 262.

20. See "An Assault on Nuclear Arms," *U.S. News & World Report*, 7 October 1991, 24–28.

21. See Charles E. Osgood, *An Alternative to War or Surrender* (Urbana: University of Illinois Press, 1962).

22. See Alexander George's analysis in Alexander L. George, Philip J. Farley, and Alexander Dallin, eds., *U.S.-Soviet Security Cooperation: Achievements, Failures, Lessons* (New York: Oxford University Press, 1988), 705–707.

23. See Alexander Wendt, "The Anarchy Is What States Make of It: The Social Construction of Power Politics," *International Organization* 46, No. 2 (Spring 1992): 420–22.

24. See Deborah Welch Larson, "Crisis Prevention in the Austrian State Treaty," *International Organization* 41, No. 1 (Winter 1987): 27–60.

25. See P. Terrence Hopmann, "Bargaining in Arms Control Negotiations: The Seabeds Denuclearization Treaty," *International Organization*, 28, No. 3 (Summer 1974), 318.

26. See Arnold Wolfers, "Power and Influence: The Means of Foreign Policy," in *Discord and Collaboration: Essays on International Politics*, ed. Arnold Wolfers (Baltimore, Md.: Johns Hopkins University Press, 1962), 107–108.

27. See Rock, *Appeasement*, 159.

28. Ibid., 161–62.

29. Ibid., 160–62.

30. See Fisher, *International Conflict for Beginners*, 119–23.

31. See Axelrod, *The Evolution of Cooperation*, 185.

32. See Denis Goulet, *Incentives for Development: The Key to Equity* (New York: Horizons Press, 1989), 11.

33. See Rock, *Appeasement*, 163.

34. See Virginia I. Foran and Leonard Spector, "The Application of Incentives to Nuclear Proliferation," in Cortright, *The Price of Peace*, 21–53.

35. See Foran and Spector, "The Application of Incentives to Nuclear Proliferation," 28–29.

36. Ibid., 33.

37. Ibid., 32.

38. Ibid., 34.

39. Ibid., 39.

40. See "Trilateral Statement by the Presidents of the United States, Russia, and Ukraine," *Arms Control Today* 24, No. 1 (January/February 1994): 21.

41. The best single account of this episode is Leon V. Sigal, *Disarming Strangers: Nuclear Diplomacy with North Korea* (Princeton, N.J.: Princeton University Press, 1998).

42. See Leon V. Sigal, "Averting a Train Wreck with North Korea," *Arms Control Today* 28, No. 8 (November/December 1998): 12.

43. See David Wright, "Cut North Korea Some Slack," *The Bulletin of the Atomic Scientists* 55, No. 2 (March/April 1999): 54–55.

44. These negotiations were suspended in 1993 during the crisis over Pyongyang's threatened withdrawal from the NPT.

45. Quoted in Sigal, "Averting a Train Wreck with North Korea," 14.

46. See David E. Sanger, "U.S. Aide Due in North Korea with Deal to Lift Sanctions," *New York Times*, 21 May 1999.

47. For a complete description of the threat posed by tactical nuclear weapons, see the introduction in this volume.

48. On the role of U.S. TNWs in Europe, see Maynard W. Glitman, "U.S. Sub-Strategic Nuclear Forces and NATO," in *Controlling Non-Strategic Nuclear Weapons: Obstacles and Opportunities*, ed. Jeffrey A. Larsen and Kurt J. Kingenberger (Washington, D.C.: U.S. Air Force Institute for National Security Studies, 2001), 63–76.

49. See Michael R. Gordon, "Nuclear Arms: For Deterrence or Fighting?" *New York Times*, 11 March 2002. See also Paul Richter, "U.S. Works Up Plan for Using Nuclear Arms Military: Administration, in a Secret Report, Calls for a Strategy against at Least Seven Nations: China, Russia, Iraq, Iran, North Korea, Libya and Syria," *Los Angeles Ties*, 9 March 2002.

50. See Jensen, "Negotiating Strategic Arms Control," 535–59.

51. For a list of the different opposition groups and their concerns, see Michael McFaul, "Hearing on U.S.-Russian Relations: An Assessment," testimony before the U.S. House of Representatives, Committee on International Relations, Subcommittee on Europe, 27 February 2002.

52. See "Joint Statement on Counterterrorism by the President of the United States and the President of Russia," *Shanghai*, 21 October 2001.

53. See Foran and Spector, "The Application of Incentives to Nuclear Proliferation," 33.

54. This list is not meant to be exhaustive, but it does address many of the most compelling inducements that could be offered to Russia. Although other inducements would be attractive to Moscow, this article cannot possibly address all the options. For instance, although the withdrawal of U.S. impediments to Russian cooperation with Iran would be attractive, alone it would be unlikely to persuade Russia to dismantle its TNWs, thus it was not addressed in this article.

55. In November 2001 Presidents Bush and Putin declared that their respective countries would reduce their strategic arsenals to between 1,500 and 2,200 warheads, though President Bush refused to sign a treaty to that effect as Putin desired. The United States later clarified this number to mean "strategically deployed" warheads, noting that it planned to store approximately 2,400 of the weapons slated for eduction instead of dismantling them. This seemingly abrupt change in U.S. policy has made it even more important to Russia that a signed document confirms the slated reductions. See Jonathan Wright, "USA: Update 1-U.S. Will Hold 2,400 Warheads in Short-term Reserve," *Reuters English News Service*, 22 March 2002; Alexander G. Higgins, "Top Russian, U.S. Negotiators Plan Warhead Cuts to Take 10 Years," *Associated Press Newswires*, 12 March 2002.

56. In fact, after the series of unreciprocated concessions that Russia has made following 11 September, unilateral concessions are even more unlikely. Speaking in the context of strategic reductions, Russian Defense Minister Sergei Ivanov has declared publicly that "there will be no unilateral concessions on issues affecting Russia's national interests." Higgins, "Top Russian, U.S. Negotiators Plan Warhead Cuts to Take 10 Years."

57. See William C. Potter, "Practical Steps for Addressing the Problem of Non-Strategic Nuclear Weapons," in *Controlling Non-Strategic Nuclear Weapons: Obstacles and Opportunities*, ed. Jeffrey A. Larsen and Kurt J. Kingenberger (Washington, D.C.: U.S. Air Force Institute for National Security Studies, 2001), 219.

58. See, for instance, Peter Baker, "Moscow Chides U.S. on Plan to Store Warheads; Decision Defies Bush-Putin Commitments to Cut Nuclear Arsenals, Russians Say," *Washington Post*, 12 January 2002, A16.

59. On estimated lifespan of Russian nuclear weapons, see Dean A. Wilkening, "The Evolution of Russia's Strategic Nuclear Force," Center for International Security and Arms Control, Stanford (California) University, July 1998.

60. See, for instance, Pamela Hess, "U.S., Russia Preparing New Relationship," *CDI Russia Weekly*, No. 178, Center for Defense Information, 31 October 2001.

61. This is a distinction that the United States has drawn since it announced that it would store some of the warheads that it pledged in November 2001 to eliminate. U.S. officials have called weapons that will be stored a U.S. "responsive force" to be held in reserve in case of major strategic changes that would necessitate their redeployment.

62. See "Russia Defense Min Hopeful over Nuclear Arms Deal with U.S.," *Dow Jones International*, 26 March 2002.

63. See Todd S. Purdum, "Powell Says U.S. Plans to Work Out Binding Arms Pact," *New York Times*, 6 February 2002.

64. See Michael Wines, "NATO and Russia Shake Hands, but Will They Come Out Sparring?" *New York Times*, 29 May 2002, 12.

65. On Blair's endorsement of a Russia-NATO relationship, see Rosemary Bennett and David Buchan, "Blair Pledge on Greater Russian Role With NATO," *Financial Times*, 22 December 2001.

66. See Jeremy Brantsen, "Russia: Economist Discusses Pros and Cons of WTO Membership," Radio Free Europe/Radio Liberty, 27 April 2001.

67. See Alexander R. Vershbow, "A New Economic Relationship between Russia and the United States," *Kommersant*, 26 November 2001. This would likely mean accession by the end of 2003 or early 2004. See Peter Goldstein, "Russia Will Realize WTO Dreams by '04," *Kiplinger Forecasts*, 8 January 2002.

68. For an examination of the debate over Russian membership in the WTO see "Russia in the WTO: Myths and Reality," Center for Economic and Financial Research, July 2001.

69. On China's negotiations with the WTO, see Greg Mastel, "China, Taiwan, and the World Trade Organization," *Washington Quarterly* 24, No. 3. (2001): 45–56.

70. See James Fuller, "Debt for Nonproliferation: The Next Step in Threat Reduction," *Arms Control Today* (January/February 2002).

71. See "Russia's Arms for Iran," *Jane's Intelligence Digest*, 8 December 2000. See also Susan B. Glasser, "Russia, Iran Renew Alliance Meant to Boost Arms Trade; Tehran Seeking Advanced Technology; U.S. Is Concerned," *Washington Post*, 13 March 2001, A14.

72. Russia said that it was able to pay its 2001 obligation of $14 billion (which amounts to 37 percent of its foreign reserves), largely as a result of strong oil prices in 2001. However, a drop in oil prices has made it difficult to finance its 2002 debt. "Russia: External Accounts on Good Footing," *Emerging Europe Monitor*, December 2001; "Russia to Pay $14.05 billion in foreign debt in 2002," *Tri City Herald*, 12 December 2001. Cited in Fuller, "Debt for Nonproliferation: The Next Step in Threat Reduction."

73. Much of the debt owed by Russia is held by commercial creditors, while some of Russia's debt is left over from the Soviet era. Of the Paris Club debt of $71.5 billion (held by 18 creditor nations), Germany holds $26.3 billion and Italy holds $6.4 billion. See Paolo Cotta Ramusino et. al., "A Comprehensive European Cooperation Effort towards the Russian Nuclear Cities: The European Nuclear Cities Initiative (ENCI), the International Working Group and the Debt-for-Security Swap Concept," presentation to the Carnegie International Non-Proliferation Conference, 2001.

74. See Mary Beth Warner, "Russia Would Swap Debt for Nuclear Non-proliferation under Senate Bill," *National Journal News Service*, 14 November 2001.

Dean, Chapter 9

1. Details of this proposal can be found in Harold Feiveson, ed., *The Nuclear Turning Point* (Washington, D.C.: The Brookings Institution Press, 1999), especially chapters 8 and 10.

2. See Appendix in this volume for text of statements. The START I Treaty contains a "declaration" by the United States limiting deployment of U.S. long-range (over 600 km) nuclear-tipped sea-launched cruise missiles to 880 (far more than the United States now has). Russia wanted this limitation to be a formal part of the treaty and has raised this issue subsequently.

3. See Joshua Handler's chapter in this volume.

4. See Alexei Arbatov, "Deep Cuts and De-Alerting: A Russian Perspective," *The Nuclear Turning Point* (Washington, D.C.: Brookings Institution Press, 1999), 320.

5. Personal communication to author.

6. Specific estimates are available for Russian nuclear-tipped surface-to-air missiles—1,200; gravity bombs (including naval aircraft)—480. See "Nuclear Notebook,"

Bulletin of the Atomic Scientists (May/June 2001). Russia is also credited with five types of nuclear warhead cruise missiles and two types of torpedoes.

7. See Joshua Handler's chapter in this volume.

8. See text of Helsinki Agreement, START III, "Joint Statements on Parameters on Future Reductions on Nuclear Reductions," Helsinki, Finland, 21 March 1997.

9. Many arms control solutions to tactical nuclear weapons have been proposed. A useful collection of works containing these proposals is included in the Appendix to this book.

10. See Linton Brooks, "Diplomatic Solutions to the 'Problem' of NSNW," in *Controlling Non-Strategic Nuclear Weapons: Obstacles and Opportunities,* ed. Jeffrey A. Larsen and Kurt J. Klingenberger (Washington, D.C.: U.S. Air Force Institute for National Security Studies, 2001) 197–210.

11. See Arbatov, "Deep Cuts and De-Alerting."

Appendixes

1. President George H. W. Bush's 27 September 1991 "Address to the Nation on Reducing United States and Soviet Nuclear Weapons," found on http:bushlibrary.tamu.edu (accessed 15 May 2002).

2. Soviet President Mikhail Gorbachev's 5 October 1991 "Address to the Nation on Reducing and Eliminating Soviet and United States Nuclear Weapons," found on http://www.bits.de/NRANEV/START/documents/gorbachev91.htm (accessed 20 October 2002).

3. Statement by President Boris Yeltsin, "On Russia's Policy in the Field of Limiting and Reducing Armaments," 29 January 1992. ITAR-TASS.

Glossary of Acronyms

AAA	Air-to-air missile
ABM	Anti-ballistic missile
ACM	Advanced cruise missile
ADM	Atomic demolition munitions
AFAP	Artillery-fired atomic projectile
ALCM	Air-launched cruise missile
ASM	Air-to-surface missile
ASW	Anti-submarine warfare
CDI	Center for Defense Information
CEP	Circular error probable
CFE	Conventional Forces in Europe (Treaty)
CIA	Central Intelligence Agency
CSBMs	Confidence building and security measures
CTBT	Comprehensive Test Ban Treaty
CTR	Cooperative Threat Reduction efforts
DIA	U.S. Defense Intelligence Agency
DoD	U.S. Department of Defense
DPRK	Democratic People's Republic of Korea
EMP	Electromagnetic pulse
EPW	Earth-penetrating weapon
EU	European Union
FAS	Federation of American Scientists
FROG	Free rocket over ground
GLCM	Ground-launched cruise missile
GRIT	Graduated and reciprocated initiatives
GUMO	(Glavnoye Upravleniye Ministerstvo Oborony) 12th GUMO Russian military organization responsible for nuclear munitions
HEU	Highly enriched uranium
HWT	Heavy-weight torpedoes
IAEA	International Atomic Energy Agency
ICBM	Intercontinental ballistic missile

INF	Intermediate-Range Nuclear Forces (Treaty)
KT	Kiloton
MRS	Multiple-rocket system
MT	Megaton
MTCR	Missile Technology Control Regime
NATO	North Atlantic Treaty Organization
NFU	No first use
NMD	National Missile Defense
NNSA	National Nuclear Security Administration
NNWS	Nonnuclear weapons state
NPR	Nuclear Posture Review
NRDC	Natural Resources Defense Council
NPG	Nuclear Planning Group
NPT	Non-Proliferation Treaty
NSNW	Nonstrategic Nuclear Weapons
NTS	Nevada Test Site
NWFZ	Nuclear weapon-free zone
NWS	Nuclear Weapon Site
PALs	Permissive action links
PLA	People's Liberation Army (China)
PNIs	Presidential nuclear initiatives
PRC	People's Republic of China
PJC	Permanent Joint Council (NATO-Russia)
PrepCom	Preparatory Commission
RNEP	Robust Nuclear Earth Penetrator
SALT	Strategic Arms Limitation Treaty
SLBM	Submarine-launched ballistic missile
SLCM	Submarine-launched cruise missile
SNF	Strategic nuclear force
SMF	Strategic Missile Force (Russia)
SNW	Strategic nuclear weapon
SRAM	Short-range attack missile
SRBM	Short-range ballistic missile
SSBN	Class of nuclear-fueled ballistic missile (*Ed note:* ship submersible ballistic nuclear)
SSN	nuclear submarine
START	Strategic Arms Reduction Treaty
TEL	Transporter erector launcher
TNT	Trinitrotoluene, trotyl, trilite, triton
TNW	Tactical nuclear weapon
UCS	Union of Concerned Scientists
USAF	United States Air Force
WMD	Weapons of mass destruction
WTO	World Trade Organization

Index

Page numbers in *italics* indicate photographs

About the Authors

Brian Alexander has written on Cuba, international policy, missile defense, and intelligence issues. Recent publications include a coauthored article on intelligence reform in the Summer 2001 edition of the *International Journal of Intelligence and Counter-Intelligence* and an analysis on the Cuban economy for *Cuba Today*. From 2001 to 2002 he was research analyst at the Fourth Freedom Forum's Washington, D.C., office, and he currently works on U.S.-Cuba political and trade relations in Washington, D.C.

David Cortright is president of the Fourth Freedom Forum and a visiting faculty fellow at the Joan B. Kroc Institute for International Peace Studies at the University of Notre Dame. Dr. Cortright was executive director of SANE, the largest U.S. peace organization, from 1977 to 1987, and was the recipient of a research and writing award for peace and international cooperation from the John D. and Catherine T. MacArthur Foundation. He has authored several books and numerous articles about peace issues.

Ambassador Jonathan Dean works on issues related to national and European security, arms control, and international peacekeeping at the Union of Concerned Scientists (UCS). Before joining UCS in 1984, Dean served as the U.S. representative and deputy representative to the NATO-Warsaw Pact force reduction negotiations in Vienna between 1973 and 1981. Dean began his foreign service work in 1950 in Bonn as liaison officer between the U.S. High Commission and the Federal German government. Later he served as desk officer for East Germany in the Department of State and as first secretary at the American Embassy in Prague. In the early 1960s he was principal officer in Elisabethville, Katanga, during the Tshombe secession and the subsequent UN peacekeeping intervention, and deputy director of the Office of United Nations Political Affairs, Department of State, where he worked on peacekeeping and economic sanctions. In 1968 he returned to the American embassy in Bonn as deputy U.S. negotiator for the 1971 quadripartite agreement on Berlin.

Charles D. Ferguson is Scientist-in-Residence in the Washington, D.C., office of the Center for Nonproliferation Studies (CNS). He joined CNS from the U.S. Department of State, where he was a foreign affairs officer in the Office of the Senior Coordinator for Nuclear Safety in the Bureau of Nonproliferation. At the State Department, he helped coordinate U.S. government interagency nuclear safety policy on decommissioned Russian marine nuclear reactors, the Korean Peninsula Energy Development Organization (KEDO) light water reactor project in the DPRK, Indian and Pakistani commercial nuclear power plants, and Russian plutonium production reactors. He has also served as a nuclear arms control and nonproliferation analyst at the Federation of American Scientists (FAS), where he directed the Nuclear Policy Project. His opinions and commentary have appeared in a wide range of publications, including *The Bulletin of the Atomic Scientists, Defense News, Physics Today* and the *Washington Post*. A United States Naval Academy alumnus, achieving a B.S. degree with distinction in physics and a commission as an officer in the U.S. Navy, Dr. Ferguson graduated from the Naval Nuclear Power School and the Submarine Officers School. Upon leaving the Navy, he earned an M.A. and a Ph.D. in physics from Boston University.

Andrea Gabbitas is a Ph.D. candidate in the Security Studies Program at the Massachusetts Institute of Technology. She specializes in European Security, South Asian nuclear stability, and nuclear nonproliferation. Ms. Gabbitas has also worked as a consultant to the RAND Corporation concerning South Asian nuclear issues and U.S. compellence strategies. She has taught courses on international relations, the causes of war, and U.S. foreign policy.

Joshua Handler is an American Political Science Association Congressional Fellow. He has worked extensively on nuclear weapons issues in Russia and other former Soviet states, and is published widely on the topic. Mr. Handler is the recipient of the CIS/MacArthur Predoctoral Fellow for 2000–2001, and holds a Ph.D. from Princeton University, Woodrow Wilson School of Public and International Affairs.

Timothy D. Hoyt is Visiting Assistant Professor in the M.A. in Security Studies Program at Georgetown University. He is also Professor of Strategy and Policy for the U.S. Naval War College, College of Continuing Education in Washington, D.C., and a guest lecturer for the Naval War College in Newport, Rhode Island. Dr. Hoyt has designed and coordinated political-military simulations for universities, the U.S. Department of Defense, and the Emirates Center for Strategic Studies and Research in Abu Dhabi, United Arab Emirates. He has worked for the U.S. Army, the U.S. Department of State, and as a researcher on defense issues for the Library of Congress. He has written on a variety of subjects, including the diffusion of military technologies and practices, the proliferation of conventional and unconventional weapons, regional security in the Middle East and South Asia, and the evolution of strategy and arms production in the developing world.

Evan S. Medeiros recently joined the RAND Corporation's National Security Research Division to work on Asian security issues. Previously, he conducted research on Chinese foreign and national security issues as a senior research associate at the Monterey Institute's Center for Nonproliferation Studies. He holds an M.Phil in international relations from the University of Cambridge, an M.A. in China Studies from the University of London's School of Oriental and African Studies, and a Ph.D. from the London School of Economics.

Robert W. Nelson is a theoretical physicist who is on the research staff of Princeton University. He is a consultant to the Federation of American Scientists and an authority on low-yield nuclear weapons.

Alistair Millar is Vice President of the Fourth Freedom Forum and Director of its Washington, D.C., office. Mr. Millar was a senior analyst at the British American Security Information Council. He has written on a wide range of issues, including the foundation of NATO, Soviet foreign policy, and NATO expansion. His opinion, editorials, and articles have appeared in several publications, including the *Los Angeles Times*, *The Nation*, *Defense News*, and the *Journal of International Affairs*.

Ivan Safranchuk is head of the Moscow branch of the Center for Defense Information (CDI). A well-known nuclear analyst in Russia, he spent four years at the PIR Center in Moscow before joining CDI—including as director of the center's "Nuclear Weapons and Their Future" project. He has written extensively on nuclear weapons and arms control issues in both Russian and English, and is a frequent contributor to *Yaderny Kontrol* and *Arms Control Letters*.

Phillip C. Saunders is Director of the East Asia Nonproliferation Program at the Monterey Institute of International Studies. He has worked or consulted on Asian security issues for the United States Air Force, the Council on Foreign Relations, and RAND. His articles on China and Asian security have been published in journals, including *International Security*, *China Quarterly*, *The China Journal*, *Pacific Review*, and *Orbis*. A graduate of Harvard College, he holds two master's degrees and a doctorate from Princeton University's Woodrow Wilson School of Public and International Affairs. His doctoral dissertation examines priorities in U.S.-China policy from 1989 to 1998. Dr. Saunder's research interests include Sino-U.S. relations, Chinese foreign policy, and East Asian security and proliferation issues. He speaks Mandarin Chinese and has studied, taught, and conducted research in China.